ASK A
NORTH
KOREAN

ASK A NORTH KOREAN

DEFECTORS TALK ABOUT THEIR LIVES INSIDE THE WORLD'S MOST SECRETIVE NATION

Daniel Tudor
Foreword by **Andrei Lankov**

Translations by
Elizabeth Jae, Nara Han, Ashley Cho and **Daniel Tudor**

TUTTLE Publishing
Tokyo | Rutland, Vermont | Singapore

ABOUT TUTTLE
"Books to Span the East and West"

Our core mission at Tuttle Publishing is to create books which bring people together one page at a time. Tuttle was founded in 1832 in the small New England town of Rutland, Vermont (USA). Our fundamental values remain as strong today as they were then—to publish best-in-class books informing the English-speaking world about the countries and peoples of Asia. The world has become a smaller place today and Asia's economic, cultural and political influence has expanded, yet the need for meaningful dialogue and information about this diverse region has never been greater. Since 1948, Tuttle has been a leader in publishing books on the cultures, arts, cuisines, languages and literatures of Asia. Our authors and photographers have won numerous awards and Tuttle has published thousands of books on subjects ranging from martial arts to paper crafts. We welcome you to explore the wealth of information available on Asia at www.tuttlepublishing.com.

Published by Tuttle Publishing, an imprint of Periplus Editions (HK) Ltd.

www.tuttlepublishing.com

Copyright © 2017 by Daniel Tudor & NK Consulting, Inc.

B&W photos © Marcel Pedro

Library of Congress CIP data in progress

ISBN 978-0-8048-4933-3

20 19 18 17   5 4 3 2 1
1710HX

Printed in China

TUTTLE PUBLISHING® is a registered trademark of Tuttle Publishing, a division of Periplus Editions (HK) Ltd.

Distributed by:

North America, Latin America & Europe
Tuttle Publishing
364 Innovation Drive
North Clarendon
VT 05759-9436, USA
Tel: 1 (802) 773 8930
Fax: 1 (802) 773 6993
info@tuttlepublishing.com
www.tuttlepublishing.com

Japan
Tuttle Publishing
Yaekari Building 3rd Floor
5-4-12 Osaki Shinagawa-ku
Tokyo 1410032, Japan
Tel: (81) 3 5437 0171
Fax: (81) 3 5437 0755
sales@tuttle.co.jp
www.tuttle.co.jp

Asia Pacific
Berkeley Books Pte Ltd
61 Tai Seng Avenue #02-12
Singapore 534167
Tel: (65) 6280 1330
Fax: (65) 6280 6290
inquiries@periplus.com.sg
www.periplus.com

Contents

Foreword

I f one has a look at a publication list, it becomes obvious that North Korea punches well above its weight when it comes to attracting the attention of foreign academics and journalists. Though its economic power and population are roughly similar to those of Mozambique, North Korea is well represented in English language articles and books.

However, a closer look uncovers a major problem. Most of these publications belong to one of only two major groups. First, there are numerous studies related to North Korean politics—above all, the nuclear program and associated problems of international diplomacy. Second, there are testimony-style books, written by defectors who tell horror stories about a country that is, indeed, run by a highly repressive regime.

However, the existing literature has a number of serious gaps. First, the real daily experiences of the vast majority of the North Koreans is overlooked—and these people are not in prison camps, and generally live normal, if often impoverished and regimented, existences. They tend to have the same feelings and concerns that dominate the lives of people in New York City or London, even if their environment appears to be very different.

Second, there is a remarkable shortage of North Korean voices. Studies of the former Soviet Union and Eastern Bloc countries were once much influenced and even, sometimes, dominated by exiles from those countries; but there are very few journalists, writers and academics of North Korean origin who are prominent in the field.

There are reasons for the absence of authentic North Korean voices. Unlike the Cold War era émigré community, most North Korean refugees come from the underprivileged and poorly-educated strata of North Korean society. They have no command of English (the world's major international language), and are seldom used to expressing themselves in it.

NK News, a website I have been working with for years, has initiated a program whose task is not merely to introduce the daily lives of common North Koreans to world readers, but also to do it using the authentic voices of North Korean contributors. This is how the "Ask a North Korean" column came into being.

The columns concentrate on issues people seldom can read about elsewhere. When dealing with food, for instance, contributors talk about ways of cooking, tastes and table manners—not about grain production and rice distribution policy. When they talk about the hereditary *songbun* caste system, they do not see it as a factor in the country's political surveillance network, but rather as something to pay attention to while seeking a marriage partner.

This might appear trivializing to those who expect righteous invectives unmasking the human rights abuses of the regime. However, there is a simple truth: as many people who lived under authoritarian governments (including the present author) will testify, even under the most repressive of regimes life does not necessarily consist of suffering, torture and fear. Actually, and fortunately, most people live normal lives, even in bad times and bad places, and we will not be able to understand them if we do not know how their lives are.

Fortunately, the *NK News*' "Ask a North Korean" project gives us a glimpse into those lives.

Introduction

I t should go without saying that although North Koreans live under a very unusual and often deeply cruel and incompetent system of rule, they are above all human beings with more or less the same desires, worries, and aims that you and I have. But it is customary to dismiss of North Koreans as brainwashed automatons or victims, whilst making little attempt to try and understand what their daily lives might be like, or what they think about the society they live in.

This is in spite of the fact that there are a huge variety of books about North Korea. In the past decade or so there has been a never-ending flow of books about the geopolitical situation; the ruling Kim dynasty; and, the dramatic escapes of defectors from North Korea.

It is difficult, however, to think of many that were written by North Koreans themselves. Even popular defector memoirs tend to be ghostwritten. The purpose of this book, then, is to allow North Koreans to speak for themselves, and give you, the reader, a true picture of North Korea straight from the horse's mouth.

There is one caveat, though. The people who submitted the essays contained in this book are all defectors from North Korea. Defectors are those who were unhappy or disadvantaged enough to take the great risk of crossing the border and then making their way to South Korea from China, a country whose government often sends defectors back to the North. Their views may not always be representative of the general North Korean population.

That said, we have put together a range of writers hailing from different parts of North Korea, both female and male, young and old. Some are from elite backgrounds, and others extremely poor.

This means that by reading this book, you'll be exposed to quite a diverse range of opinions. If you asked a wealthy Manhattanite and a rural Arkansan to describe life in the United States, you'd likely get divergent answers. The same is true of North Korea, so we thought it important to ask a wide range of people to contribute, rather than just telling you about life in North Korea through the eyes of one particular defector.

Most of this book concentrates on how ordinary people live, work, love, study, and so on. Unless you already know North Korea very well, you'll be in for surprises on each page. You'll hear how young North Koreans drink moonshine and dance to South Korean K-pop in abandoned buildings; you'll hear about what it is like to be rich in the country labelled as the last genuine Communist/Stalinist place on earth; you'll hear about North Korean fashion and beauty, and even plastic surgery; you'll learn some new slang; and you'll learn about the difficulties of holding a funeral in North Korea, among many other things.

We do touch upon the repressiveness of the state, which is an unavoidable fact of life in North Korea. But while reading this book you may notice that our focus is quite different to other books on North Korea. You may find it jarring or strange at first, to read about (for instance) skinny jeans and gambling in the context of such a country. But skinny jeans may mean a kind of liberation for a young North Korean woman, and a wager on a card game may provide a temporary thrill and escape from the daily pressures of life for others. We don't want to "whitewash" the behavior of the regime. Our point is simply that North Koreans are human, and have more in common with the rest of us than typical media portrayals would have you believe.

A note on the material in "Ask a North Korean"

Most of the material in this book originally comes from the "Ask a North Korean" section of *NK News*. It has however been re-edited and tidied up, and organized into relevant sections. Many new essays were also commissioned, to take into account recent developments and any previously untouched subjects we felt needed attention.

The essays are presented in question-and-answer form, and most were translated into English from Korean by Elizabeth Jae, Nara Han, and Ashley Cho. A small number were translated by Daniel Tudor. Editing was handled by Rob York and Daniel Tudor.

Thanks

We would like to thank "TK" of the "Ask a Korean" blog, for inspiring us to start the "Ask a North Korean" column.

Thanks are also due to Sokeel Park, for making valuable introductions.

Contributors

Cho Ui-seong
Cho Ui-seong dropped out during the final year of his electronic engineering degree to come to South Korea. He originally wanted to be a journalist in Seoul but is now training to be an elementary school teacher. He is 28 years old.

Mina Yoon
Mina Yoon is a former soldier who left the northeast of North Korea in 2010. She is now a student in Seoul.

Ji-min Kang
Ji-min Kang is in his late twenties, and left North Korea in 2005. He first went to South Korea, but now lives in London, England.

Kim Cheol
Cheol is from Hamheung, in the province of South Hamgyeong. After escaping North Korea he became a university student in Seoul. He is now in his second year.

Jinhyok Park
Jinhyok Park joined *NK News*' "Ask a North Korean" as a contributor in spring 2016, and has worked and studied in Pyongyang, North Korea and Washington, D.C. He is in his late thirties and married to a fellow North Korean defector. He came to the United States in 2011 and is studying at a U.S. college.

Kim Yoo-sung

Kim Yoo-sung is an "Ask a North Korean" contributor who left Giljoo County, Hamkyungbuk-do, in 2005.

Je Son Lee

Je Son is an "Ask a North Korean" contributor. She is in her late twenties and left the Mt. Paektu area in 2011.

There are several other contributors who appear in the round table discussion sections. If you wish to know more about these individuals, please see the "Ask a North Korean" section of the *NK News* website.

Economic Life

[Introduction]

T he Democratic People's Republic of Korea (DPRK), better known around the world as North Korea, is considered a byword for communist, collectivist economic control. But how accurate a depiction is this?

Not very, is the answer. When state founder Kim Il Sung was alive, citizens received rations, free education, housing and healthcare from the state—though admittedly, the standard of these was not necessarily great. But following the collapse of the Soviet Union, and more importantly, a devastating nationwide famine in the mid-1990s, this system broke down. Today, the average North Korean receives almost nothing from their government.

As a result of the state's virtual bankruptcy, almost all North Koreans today are dependent upon private trade, otherwise known as "capitalism." Those with connections and border access can bring in goods from China; middlemen can transport those goods across the country; middle-aged ladies can sell them in street markets; and officials can collect bribes for looking the other way. Senior officials in Pyongyang can collect much larger bribes from members of a newly-emerging financial elite, who engage in industries as diverse as apartment construction, department stores, and craft beer pubs. None of this is technically legal. But it is a culture that has grown to the point where the state cannot truly control it.

In the past, all but the elite lived in the same way. Today, though, there are North Koreans with money, and who want to show it. Those who can afford it may take regular vacations, and drive fancy cars, have plastic surgery, and use imported cosmetics (see below for more on these).

Sadly, extreme poverty still exists in North Korea. Particularly in rural areas and smaller cities away from either Pyongyang or the Chinese border, life is tough for the majority.

Is it true that there is no tax system in North Korea?

DT: Under a communist system, there is no tax—because everything is already owned by the state. It is no surprise, then, that the DPRK doesn't have a formal tax system. But in reality, North Korea is not communist any more. People make their own money, and the state must find ways to claim a piece of it, as is the case anywhere else.

Kim Yoo-sung:

Yes, you're right—there's no tax system in North Korea, officially. On March 21, 1974, the Supreme People's Assembly declared the abolition of all forms of taxation. To this day, North Korea celebrates "The Day of the Abolition of the Tax System" on April 1, the day the law went into effect that same year.

Yet North Korea still collects taxes from people, just calling it something else. True, people don't pay money directly to the government, but the government does extort most of the goods and labor people produce. In short, North Korea collects more taxes from its people than any other country.

North Koreans are no longer obligated to give some portion of their income to the government, but they are forced to offer labor free of charge, and if North Koreans had a choice, they would rather pay taxes like in other countries than have to give their labor and receive nothing in return for it.

Last year, the North Korean government announced that they would extort only 70 percent of the crops people produce and the citizenry would be allowed to consume 30 percent of what they produced for themselves. They added that the amount they take would be reduced to 50 percent of the harvest once the country's economy improves.

No one believes them, of course. Why would they, when North Koreans work so hard every day but the government says they're entitled to only 30 percent of what they produce through their labor?

It's ridiculous for Kim Jong Un to make such statements, as if he's offering a huge favor by letting people keep 30 percent of their own harvests. The real reason they take such a large portion of the crops is to stop the black market from growing any bigger.

When North Korea "officially" abolished the tax system in 1974, the government boastfully called the move "a huge leap forward from the old system and a historical change towards making the dreams of Koreans come true." Furthermore, they even said they didn't have to revive the tax system during the Great Famine thanks to the "benevolent" politics and leadership of Kim Jong Il. However, since 2000, North Korea has been collecting taxes from its people— only they have a different name for it.

To make matters worse, the North Korean economy has suffered even more following a series of natural disasters and the sanctions imposed by the United States. Under such hopeless conditions, both central and regional governments in North Korea were faced with serious debt and financial difficulty. They had no choice but to begin taking money from the people. Hence, they began to charge people for using electricity and water, and renting out property and land. They made everyone pay the same amount of money, no matter how much they used.

This is not very different from the tax system in capitalist states, yet differences do exist. First, it's true that the North Korean government began to collect money from its people for using electricity, water, etc. Still, the amount of tax revenue collected is far smaller than in capitalist states. Second, in most capitalist countries such as South Korea, rich people pay greater amounts of tax than those who make less. But in North Korea, everyone pays an equal amount of tax. These are the two big differences in how the tax system works between North Korea and other countries.

Since officially ending the tax system in 1974, the government has been claiming that there are no taxes in North Korea. But when you actually look closely, North Korea collects tax in its own special way.

How can we describe the lives of the poorest socioeconomic class in North Korea?

DT: It would surely not surprise you to know that the poorest people in North Korea live in truly dire material circumstances. Though grassroots capitalism is enabling many to make a better living these days, malnutrition is still a problem. If you spend time anywhere in North Korea outside Pyongyang, you will definitely see evidence of this.

Cho Ui-seong:

If we were to divide people into a social hierarchy, the criterion for the lowest strata would be economic. The great famine of the 1990s (referred to as the "Arduous March") divided people into those who had to worry about their next meal and those who didn't, and in accordance with this many people were reclassified as part of the lowest social class. The media tends to focus on the horrible lives of North Koreans, and many people have already testified about that awful time. It pains me to even think of it, so I would rather try to show the persistence of life overcoming death, the North Koreans pioneering a new way of life, and the wellspring of compassion that rises up from the bottom of society.

First of all, you misunderstand if you imagine that those in the bottom level of North Korean society are ignorant and frivolous people. There are many cultured, intellectual people among them. This is because those hit hardest by the famine were the intellectual and literary class who were working for society and trusted in the rationing system. Their kind of knowledge did not help them understand and respond quickly to the danger. In fact, it did the opposite. Those who fell into famine included many intellectuals. But those who survived have had a considerable impact on so-called "lowest class" culture. They have played a leading role in the creation and spread of common culture in areas such as the education of children, economic activity, simple humor and jokes amid a rapidly changing environment.

I sense that the poorest people are the most filled with *jeong* [human warmth and mutual sacrifice]. Sometimes it seems like the most desirable kind of life. I hope you do not think me too objective or "literary" for saying that, because I have experienced life at the bottom of the bottom. It isn't as terrible as you may imagine. There is a kind of humor allowing people to laugh at their difficulties, and there is *jeong*, which fills the void of poverty. It is a bare place, but one where children run wild to their heart's content. If happiness is subjective, the children of North Korea must be ten times happier than those in South Korea, who are locked in constant competition over grades at schools and private academies.

The most memorable treat from my childhood was "Speed Battle Rice Cake." You add water to the powder that comes when you modify corn, and after stirring it for five minutes you get rice cake [of course it isn't literally "rice" cake]. It is a specialty that men, women, and children like. It is sticky and just a few can fill your belly for the whole day. But we couldn't have it often.

Anyone who has ever seen how important speed is to a hungry person will agree. It is also a favorite food for college students, who are always hungry. One day a guest came, and my mother made some of that "Speed Battle Rice Cake." She'd saved the ingredients for special occasions. There was no happier day than that one, because we got to eat the rice cake.

In North Korea, we emphasize hospitality to the extent that there is an expression, "eating well thanks to a guest" [i.e., all the good food comes out when a guest arrives]. In any house, the best blanket is the guest blanket.

People laugh and cry because of *jeong*, and through this feeling, those at the very bottom overcome difficulties and survive.

The good news is that things are much better now. People have gradually learned to live with a market system, and no longer will people die in huge numbers for putting their trust in the state. Now the idea that people are responsible for their own lives has taken hold.

But maybe people don't have as much *jeong* as before, as the markets are growing and people are becoming interested in money. In the countryside, though, things are unchanged. Rural people, who are still not completely free from hunger themselves, will still feed passing travelers.

While there isn't enough space to go into detail about the various aspects of life that I have seen, heard and felt as I traveled around North Korea, I hope this article goes some small way to adding brightness and warmth to the image of desolation and darkness of the poorest in North Korean society.

How do you get a job in North Korea? And can you change jobs easily?

DT: The famine of the 1990s changed everything. Prior to this catastrophic event, the government assigned you a job, and you did it—for the rest of your life. Today though, you'll probably bribe your way out of that useless job, and do something else.

Mina Yoon:

Traditionally, people in North Korea did not have the freedom to choose their occupation. You were assigned a job by the government, and it became your lifelong job. The reason for this is very simple: As part of maintaining strict control over all kinds of resources under its collectivist system, the government researches how many people are needed in each industry and location, and assigns people accordingly.

But things changed after the rationing system broke down in the 1990s. Your official job is now nothing more than a meaningless title you can mention when asked, "Where do you work?" The factories stopped manufacturing long ago, and factory workers cannot expect compensation for their labor. Even though you have a job from the government, you have to find your own ways of earning a living. That's why many parents in North Korea have started bribing government officers even before their kids graduate high school. They want their kids to get decent jobs that still pay salaries and provide rations.

Among the most popular workplaces in North Korea are organizations earning foreign currency. Those organizations, launched in the early 2000s, have now spread everywhere in North Korea. What they are doing is basically exporting North Korean resources abroad and creating funds for the government. People working in those organizations still receive rations, and on top of that, they also have a chance for additional income, depending on their performance. People working in these organizations are admired, much like those in big companies such as Samsung in South Korea.

Foreign currency-earning organizations are very powerful because most of them are under the umbrella of the party, the armed forces or other powerful government agencies. Competition to get into those organizations is severe, and you need to have either a very strong family background or a lot of money to be employed there. Actually, most of the people working in those organizations are children of party officers or executives of wealthy foreign currency-earning organizations.

Some factories have been very popular among job seekers, due to their being under the direct supervision of Kim Jong Il or Kim Jong Un. Direct supervision from the Kim family means exceptionally good conditions. It means raw materials will be provided by the government so that actual production can take place. Workers will therefore receive rations. Also, some workers will have access to products that they can steal and sell elsewhere.

Due to increasing demand for more rewarding jobs, bribery is becoming more common in North Korea. There are certain steps to follow to get the desired job: First, you have to bribe government officers and steal your personnel record from the local administrative agency. Then you have to bribe the factory manager or local party secretary so that they will issue a letter of confirmation that they would like to hire you. Finally, you have to submit that letter to the administrative agency in charge of assigning jobs. Everyone involved knows about the other parties' bribery, but they overlook it.

These days, parents try to think of any possible way to get their kids good jobs through bribery or using their family background. People who cannot afford to bribe officers just send their kids wherever they are assigned. Instead, they bribe managers in the factory so that their kids do not have to go to work; they then go and work in the market instead, but they have to give part of their income to the factory. A majority of the younger women work as vendors in the market with their names registered in their formally assigned workplaces. What is important is that they are registered; in North Korea, not having a job is illegal and can result in punishment.

Veterans who served in the military for more than 10 years are also assigned new jobs when they are discharged. Most of them go back to their hometown and work where the local government tells them to. However, some unlucky soldiers are not allowed to return to where they came from. The government assigns thousands of recently discharged veterans onto national projects or businesses that need large-scale manpower. Those subject to these assignments have no choice but to go.

For example, when Kim Jong Il was alive, he supervised Taehong-dan-gun in Ryanggang province, which is rich with potatoes but has few people living in it. Kim Jong Il started supervising the region and soon he figured out there were not enough people to grow the potatoes. So thousands of veterans had to move to Ryanggang and become lifelong potato farmers.

They had to build houses to live in with their own hands. They were also concerned about their children's future, because the children of farmers might also be assigned to work in the farms when they grew up. Despite these concerns, there was nothing they could do. It was a policy set by Kim Jong Il and they did not want to rebel.

There was also a lack of women for them to marry. Many of the veterans in Ryanggang still have not found spouses. Taehong-dan-gun is just one example; this kind of forcible placement is happening all over the country with many different national businesses, making soldiers nearing their date of discharge worry about their future.

However, as I described so far, strict regulations on occupations now exist in name only, since the collapse of the social system in North Korea. Bribery has become so widespread that it is now uncontrollable. I think these changes are clearly another symptom of the failed system of socialism.

What is life like for a "one-percenter" in North Korea?

DT: "Rich" and "North Korean" might seem mutually exclusive terms. These days, though, that's not always the case. The emerging North Korean capitalism means that most people have more than before, but also that a small handful are becoming very wealthy indeed.

Kim Yoo-sung:

My wife's father is known as the richest man in her hometown. I had no knowledge of this until another North Korean from the same province told me. He said that he would even call my wife's father "Lee Kun-hee" (Samsung Electronics chairman), or even the Donald Trump of that province. According to him, everyone in that region would immediately recognize my father-in-law by his name. That's how rich he was.

My father-in-law was in charge of a company that made a net profit of $6–7 million per month. When his business was doing really well, the company would earn much more than that.

What did they normally eat on a daily basis? The kinds of food on their table included lamb, seal, sea urchin roe, pollock eggs and chicken eggs. These were always on the table for every single meal, simply because my father-in-law enjoyed them. Despite the widespread image of a poverty-stricken North Korea, rich families can easily afford to eat luxuriously like this in North Korea. The dishes specified above were in addition to a bigger set of dishes my wife ate every day. My wife would go into more detail, but thinks North Korean authorities could use additional details about his diet to track him down.

Car owners are the most admired people in North Korea. It isn't easy to own a car there, even if you have the money to buy one. My wife tells me that her dad owned a couple of the most luxurious, expensive cars in North Korea. He had one for commuting to work and another for business trips. In addition to owning two expensive cars, he also had a servant who wiped and washed his car every morning.

My wife says her father was a successful businessman but loved to laugh and enjoy his leisure time. On New Year's, North Koreans have a blast and grownups don't forget to give pocket money to children. But she says her dad would frequently take $500—in American dollars—out of his wallet and give it to her. Even in the U.S. or South Korea, I don't think they would just take $500 out their wallets and give to their children on the spot just because they feel like it—unless, of course, they were rich too.

I myself come from a town far from Pyongyang, and my family was never rich. During holidays, I always stayed at home and celebrated with my family and relatives. But my wife says she traveled to Pyongyang, where her father showered her and her mom with expensive gifts of clothing and gourmet dishes on New Year and Chuseok. My wife went to the Moranbong entertainment facilities and the family had delicious noodles at Pyongyang's famous Okryukwan.

They would go to sauna at the end of the day. My wife says the sauna charged $100 per person. Even in the U.S. and South Korea, it has to be an expensive sauna if you have to pay $100 to get in, right? In North Korea most ordinary people make less than $100 a month. I can't even begin to imagine how luxurious it must be inside if it costs $100 to take one bath there.

And her weekend fun didn't end there. My wife would go bowling with her parents and to sporting events. North Korea has beautiful places where people like to go sightseeing, but not everyone can afford to go. But thanks to her dad, who enjoyed sightseeing and had money, my wife went to see all those famous mountains and holiday destinations, including Baekdu, Chilbo, Kumgang and Yongmun-daegul.

Want to hear another big perk of having a rich dad? Lo and behold, famous actors were invited to her birthday parties. There was an actor who was often dubbed the nation's biggest heartthrob. My wife's dad knew that she was a huge fan, so he personally invited this actor to his daughter's birthday party. I know how teenage girls rave about actors and singers. In the U.S., when *Twilight* was popular, teenage girls were crazy about Robert Pattinson, weren't they? Can you imagine your dad inviting Robert Pattinson to your home for your birthday party?

Undoubtedly, my wife was one lucky child throughout her school years. She took on the leader's role and responsibilities in her class every year. She was at the forefront of every duty at school. Her maids prepared a home-cooked lunchbox, which she took to school for her homeroom teacher. Thanks to this, her teacher never had to worry about lunch. If something troublesome happened at school, she would have her dad take care of it, since he had money and power.

Of course, my wife had a personal computer at home. So, whenever her friends had homework requiring the use of a computer, they would come by her house. Her dad always sent two sacks of rice worth half a million North Korean won. Other teachers were always jealous of her homeroom teacher. They would often tell my wife, "You should be in my class. Why don't you just come to my class?" When the winter approached, her family hired servants to make special kimchi for them. They made sure that the servants make three or four kinds of kimchi.

When her dad was in his car on the road, cops would come and say, "Dear comrade, please help us." That was one of the usual things my wife would hear when she was in the car with her dad. Her dad was not just making money but he was contributing a handsome amount of money to the regime. So, people treated him differently and they always favored him. Her dad was always dealing with governors of provinces. He wouldn't spend time having small talk with officials of lower rank, such as mayors. He thought it was a waste of time.

On Chuseok, a national holiday, North Koreans walk to the graves of their ancestors to pay respects. But my wife's family was chauffeured to the graves, of course. My wife says they had over-flowing boxes of apples, pears and South Korean snacks, such as Choco-Pies and *chaltteok* pie in storage. Everyone in the family would help themselves to these foods.

Her dad traveled to other countries such as Mongolia and China. Every time he went to China, he would always bring a variety of nice clothes for my wife. In winter, he would bring mink coats for his baby girl.

My wife came to South Korea two years ago and her father still lives in North Korea. Therefore, I choose not to reveal his name, nor his company's name, for the sake of his safety. If I were to reveal any of his personal information, the North Korean authorities could track him down. I'm sure you can imagine what would happen to him.

I have not met him, since he is still in North Korea and I met my wife here [in South Korea]. But he's still my father-in-law, and he brought my wife into this world, so I worry about his well-being and pray for his safety every day. Even if he weren't related to me, I wouldn't want to do anything to put him in immediate danger.

My wife has been at my side as I've been telling this story. She says talking about her dad brought back many memories and she misses her dad terribly. My wife has one message for her dad:

"Dear Dad, I'm doing well in the South. I pray for your health and happiness every day. I will never cease to do so. You're always in my thoughts and prayers. Oh, and you have a granddaughter now! Until unification, please be well, be safe, be happy. I pray for you here in the South."

How did North Koreans turn towards capitalism?

DT: "Profit" used to be a dirty word in North Korea—until it became a necessity. Back in the 1990s, it was said that the only way to survive was by defying the state's orders and going out to make money for oneself. North Koreans have remembered that lesson, and are not looking back. Despite the rise of marketization, North Korea still lacks the capability to produce goods that can compete with imports. Anything foreign is prized over a local equivalent, even a toothbrush.

Jimin Kang:
It is often said that the North Korean economy is a catastrophe and that as long as the Kims are in power, things will never improve. But if that's true, why has the North Korean regime never collapsed, despite periods like the Great Famine, when hundreds of thousands of people died?

While North Koreans once relied on the government for all food, consumer goods, appliances, and housing, you might be surprised to learn that it was actually the famine that would ultimately improve our livelihood and choices.

I remember North Koreans who survived the Great Famine of the 1990s would often say things like: "The idiots have already gone. Only the survivors are left, the most strong-willed of all North Koreans who are capable of surviving famines again and again."

You see, it was the innocent people who were obedient to the government and did not try and figure things out for themselves who starved to death first during the Great Famine. Without a ready supply of food, the government was unable to protect common people, and as abject poverty built up, people started turning against even their cousins and relatives. Essentially, North Korean society became a cold, ruthless place, with no sympathy or compassion.

During these difficult times, people had to figure out ways to survive by themselves. As a result, people naturally became attracted to capitalist ideas—values that they had never been taught about, but which could mean survival.

Prior to the famine, North Korean markets were tiny places where farmers who worked on their collectively-owned farms sold vegetables, small animals, and seafood that they caught in rivers and ponds. People used to really view these places as basic farmers' markets, primitive places with few goods available. But when the government cut off the public distribution system during the famine and people had to start fending for themselves, everyone rushed to the markets and began to trade their valuables to get food.

At that time, I remember a North Korean TV broadcast showing old members of communist parties from Eastern Europe selling their party membership documents and medals in markets. The aim was to make enthusiastic North Korean party members angry or disgusted. But during that time the situation in North Korea was not very different from Eastern Europe, and as long as customers existed, people sold anything and everything they owned.

Back then people were even happy to sell gifts given to them by people as senior as Kim Jong Il. As a result, even my father—a zealous party member—sold his television without hesitation, despite it being a direct gift from the government. Even watches and televisions with founding President Kim Il Sung's name inscribed into them appeared in the markets, something that would have been unthinkable during the good times.

It was in these circumstances that the capitalist market was truly born in North Korea, and quickly spread all over the country. As the markets grew, products and goods from China and Japan became dominant, as North Korean factories shut down as the economic situation progressively worsened.

At one time it was easy to find toothpaste and brushes made in North Korea, but following the famine these items were hardly seen in the markets any more. And if they could be found, they were no longer much in demand by people, as they were now seen to be of low quality.

In the past, people received goods on a ration basis. So, for example, when they were out of soap, toothpaste or toothbrushes, there was absolutely no way for them to find replacements until they were given. And if they received vegetables that had already gone bad, they had no way or right to put in a complaint about the problem. But when the markets came, North Korea dramatically changed: suddenly we had more choices with the little money we had.

Surprisingly, life in North Korea was still difficult, but the quality of life got better and better following the famine. Electrical appliances, furniture and consumer goods were all increasingly available. Moreover, even in the center of Pyongyang—which was dubbed the heart of Socialist Chosun—a big market emerged and became a popular place for people to visit. And while the government later tried to shut down the market several times, it was so popular they failed each time. In the end, the government found its own way of making money from the market, by renting spots for vendors. I heard the revenue they earned was substantial.

Looking back, it seems the influence and existence of markets was a lot more powerful than the government ever expected, directly helping to keep an increasingly large number of people alive. Thanks to the existence of such markets, a petit bourgeoisie began to emerge in Pyongyang. And as time went by, I remember the market becoming one of the most important places for people to go, regardless of whether they were rich or poor.

While I admit that a ruthless, uncompassionate capitalist economy has its own problems and negative side effects, I truly hope that North Korea will become a country where people can make a living by freely competing with each other.

How do North Korean women buy cosmetics?

DT: Where there is even the slightest amount of disposable income in an economy, a beauty industry will spring up. The way it has developed in North Korea can tell us quite a lot about the informal nature of capitalism there, as well as social attitudes and women's role in society.

Je Son Lee:
Women in South Korea and some other countries make sure they have perfect makeup on before they step out of their houses. Many times it seems to me that wearing perfect makeup is the top priority of many South Korean women.

North Korean women do not put on makeup to that extent, but they do enjoy taking care of themselves, including putting on makeup to enhance their appearance, just like in other countries.

Basically, there are two reasons why North Korean women would ever wear makeup. First, they may just want to look prettier, like most other women. Second, as it is a patriarchal society, it is thought by many that women should wear makeup out of consideration for others. Most women in North Korea start wearing makeup when they graduate from high school. However, during the time you're in school, you're never allowed to wear makeup.

I remember when I was about 15 or 16, I put on makeup with my friends and went to school with it on. As we were going through the tumultuous time of adolescence, we feared almost nothing. We proudly strode into our classroom. But we were soon caught by our teacher, and as punishment we had to stay behind to clean up the classroom and were only allowed to go home after writing a letter of apology.

I still remember very vividly what our teacher told us as we were on our way home: "After you graduate from high school, I will never care whether you put on makeup or not."

After that incident, we never wore makeup to school ever again. Well, of course I had my eyebrows waxed and put on some powder, but I never used eyeliner or mascara because I would've been caught right away.

In South Korea, there are tons of cosmetics stores and almost every street has one. But in North Korea, street vendors sell cosmetics at the market. I don't know how women bought them in the 1990s. But since the beginning of the 2000s, the market was the place where women got cosmetics—since markets in North Korea have almost everything that you can find in any other country. Without a doubt, cosmetics from South Korea were the most popular and expensive of all.

In South Korea, people seem to buy anything imported and always want to buy things that are more expensive. It was exactly the same in North Korea. Some cosmetics were not of distinctively better quality than Chinese products, but they were still sold at a higher price, just because they were made in South Korea. They were so popular that I still remember the exact brand names. It was called "Man with Flowers" from VOV. When I came to South Korea, I was shocked to find out that it was the cheapest kind, because if you used this product in North Korea it meant that you were wealthy. Everyone wanted to have it.

Because these South Korean cosmetics were smuggled through China, heavy government restrictions existed. Therefore, people hid them from the authorities and sold them on the black market and the price went through the roof. Though they were very expensive, they sold out immediately, because every woman wanted to have them. At first, it was usually foundation and powders that were seen at the market. But with the increase in demand, eye shadow, eyeliner, mascara and lipstick could easily be found in North Korean markets. Because they were so expensive, only a few people could afford to own one of every kind.

Still, even if you owned only one of these, people would still envy you for that. My mom almost always used VOV and I tried it for myself when Mom wasn't home and was always pleased with the quality. When you put on Chinese or North Korean powder, it darkens your skin tone. But I liked VOV because it made my skin shine and look natural, as if I hadn't put any makeup on. As long as you have money, you can get any kind of cosmetics you want.

Most North Koreans traditionally used skin toner and lotion only. But from 2000 North Korea began to produce its own cosmetics line called "You and I" in its Hamhung factory. This cosmetics line was created to be supplied to high-ranking government officials, as well as to be exported. They added a line of nutrition cream to skin toner and lotion. As they were cosmetics made mostly of natural ingredients with hardly any chemicals, they were very expensive. At a time when you could buy other cosmetics for $5–10, these cost $250–300.

But they were still so popular. Since my mom knew someone at the factory and could acquire the products quickly, I was lucky enough to try this popular line of cosmetics for myself. I was satisfied with the quality of these cosmetics and I loved using them. Now that I think about it, it isn't surprising that my skin got better after using them. I used to only apply skin toner and lotion before then.

But most people thought it was too much work to wear eyeliner, so many resorted to getting their eyeliner tattooed. It greatly reduced the time we would spend on getting our makeup done. In North Korea, everyone wanted to get everything done faster than everyone else. These days, though, getting your eyelids tattooed is considered out of fashion. So, more and more people have begun to remove the tattoos along their eyelids.

In my case, I wear makeup exactly the same way I did in North Korea. From time to time, South Korean students tell me that they like my makeup. After all, I think people are pretty much the same wherever you are in the world.

Who gets to drive a car in North Korea?
DT: A car is a definite status symbol in North Korea. Only those with political power or money—like Kim Yoo-sung's father-in-law—can have one. Even those who work as drivers for others are considered lucky by the rest of society. But there's a price to pay: You might have to wait years to take your test and get on the road.

Mina Yoon:
This question immediately reminded me of a person that I have never stopped missing since I left North Korea—my younger brother, who is still there. When he was six years old, he said he wanted to be an aide to General Kim and drive his car when he grew up. My sister and I encouraged his dream, thinking there would be no bigger honor. When I think about it now, I say to myself, "In how many countries would children desperately dream to be a driver?" Aren't dreams supposed to be a little bit too big and unrealistic to achieve? Actually, the dream of being a driver may be just unrealistic enough in North Korea, considering that my brother has not yet realized his dream.

Other than in a city like Pyongyang, you rarely see more than two or three cars a day on the road. In the countryside, people are more familiar with tractors than cars. Except on special occasions when officials from the central government come to visit, rural people really don't have many chances to see cars.

When I was young, I lived in Kangwon province, a region that is surrounded by mountains. I still remember how excited I got whenever I saw a car on the street. I bragged about it to my friends all day saying, "You know what I've just seen? A car! A black one. It just passed by on the new road." Then my friends joined me fussing about it, saying, "Seriously? Do you think it will pass by again? Should we go out and wait?" Then, we actually went out and waited for the car.

Now I live in Seoul, a city that suffers from too many cars and chronic traffic congestion. Whenever I see cars out of my window I smile, thinking about my old days in North Korea, where a car was the object of such great wonder. Nowadays, they make me feel the opposite way. The great admiration and excitement about cars that I once held in my mind has now turned into frustration and exhaustion on the congested roads of Seoul.

Driving conditions in North Korea are also very bad. Roads are rarely paved, except in certain parts of the city. Usually, roads are simply bare ground covered with pebbles or sand. And because they are not separated from the sidewalks, people have to step aside when they hear a car approaching behind them. They stand there covering their mouths and noses to prevent inhaling all the dust the cars kick up, then they wait until the cloud is gone and they can see again.

When it rains, the sandy roads soak up the water. So, it's not too bad for drivers. However, if the road is covered with moist soil, the rain turns it into a huge swamp. Another challenge comes from the North Korean landscape, a huge part of which is hilly and mountainous. Without tunnels, you have to drive over them to get to the other side. From a distance, these roads look like thin white lines swirling around the mountains. These are actually very dangerous to drive on. Worse still, the roads are very sharply angled and there are no guardrails, so any small mistake means your car ends up off the road.

Despite all these dangers and difficulties, being a driver is still a coveted job among the younger generation. In North Korea, individuals are not permitted to own cars, but the government assigns cars to high-level officials. The drivers are assigned along with the cars, so drivers serve the highest level of North Korean elites. Interestingly, once you're assigned a car, that doesn't change, even if the officer you work for changes. Therefore, when you become a driver, the car becomes an important part of your life, even though you're not allowed to drive the car for personal use.

Working as a driver also guarantees a decent quality of life. Most government officials in North Korea are involved in bribery, and naturally, the drivers see everything that goes on. If a driver opens his mouth, all the misdeeds of his boss will easily be uncovered. Moreover, because the drivers are not directly hired by the officers but assigned by the government, the officers do not have strong control over their drivers. North Korean people do not use bank accounts or credit cards, so the only way to deliver bribes is to hand money over directly, which makes it extremely hard to hide. So, officials make concerted efforts to maintain good relationships with their drivers. Otherwise, a driver could easily turn into an informant. Because of all these benefits—and the job security that comes with the job—becoming a driver is quite competitive. The positions are pretty much limited to children from wealthy families or those of high-level executive officers.

Even getting a driver's license to begin with in North Korea takes a lot of time; there are only two driving academies nationwide. When you enter the academy, you're required to take a two-year-long training course. It is difficult to get in, and it is even more difficult to graduate, as the academies cannot afford enough gasoline to run the street-driving test, which is a requirement for graduation. Hundreds of students are waiting for their turn to take the test and graduate; some people wait for more than a year. Isn't it ridiculous that a South Korean driver's license can be issued in three days, but it takes more than three years in North Korea?

Because of this, bribing officials to get an illegal driver's license has become commonplace in North Korea. Even if you have an illegal license, you can at least work as a truck driver. My brother did this—he learned how to drive a truck by shadowing one of his neighbors, a truck driver, all day for a couple of months. However, after I left North Korea, I heard the unfortunate news that he broke his arm in an accident with the truck. I felt really bad that I could not do anything for my injured baby brother.

I sometimes daydream about what I could do for my brother when we one day meet again. I think it would be great if I could help him open up a driving school. I believe he would make a great driving instructor, with his love and passion for cars and driving. Now, my question is: When will that day finally come?

Can you buy plastic surgery in North Korea, like you can in the South?

DT: Barely a month goes by without a major international newspaper "revealing" South Korea's obsession with plastic surgery. Lesser known is North Korea's growing demand for double-eyelid procedures, reflecting the growing influence of South Korean TV shows (smuggled in on USB sticks), increased disposable income, changing social attitudes towards "standing out," and the abandonment of socialism.

Kim Yoo-sung:

Yes, there is plastic surgery in North Korea. People in North Korea do get plastic surgery to improve their appearance. But plastic surgery really only exists in North Korea to the extent of double eyelid surgery and nose jobs. The kinds of plastic surgery you can get in North Korea are not as diverse as in South Korea, which even offers double jaw (bimaxillary) surgery and breast implants.

Some media reports say that Kim Jong Un has had plastic surgery in order to look like his late grandfather, Kim Il Sung. It is thought that top elites in North Korea can get high-quality plastic surgery. But still, for most of us, the most common plastic surgeries are still nose jobs, double-eyelid surgery and the removal of skin wrinkles. Other types of plastic surgery, which require high-quality equipment or medical skills, are not common in North Korea yet.

In South Korea, certified surgeons who graduated from medical schools perform plastic surgery on their patients. But in North Korea, when it comes to double eyelid surgery, ordinary people who aren't qualified surgeons perform surgery on other people. Still, as far as I know, doctors at the hospitals perform nose jobs and remove skin wrinkles.

When plastic surgery was introduced in North Korea, it was for the purpose of removing scars from the face or body. To the best of my knowledge, people gradually began to get plastic surgery with the aim of improving their appearance and looking prettier.

I asked my wife about how plastic surgery is done in North Korea. It costs around 120,000 won in North Korean currency, or about 100 Chinese renminbi. Please bear in mind that there could have been a change in the price since my wife left North Korea. Also, a nose job costs around $100 in U.S. currency.

It's very hard to find a plastic surgeon in North Korea. One has to find someone who can perform the surgery through people they know. I heard that people usually get double-eyelid surgery at someone's house. In North Korea, one does not get anesthetized when getting double-eyelids (ouch!). This is because people believe that your eyes will look more natural and won't become puffy if you don't have an anesthetic. But regardless, I heard that some North Koreans who had double eyelid surgery were unable to open their eyes for a whole week due to side effects of the surgery.

I assume that a North Korean woman with money would at least get double eyelids done. I also assume that there will be some North Korean men who have gotten plastic surgery, like in South Korea. But plastic surgery for men is not as popular in the North as it is in the South.

The price for plastic surgery ranges from 100 yuan to 1,000 yuan in Chinese renminbi. Actually, if you get plastic surgery at a proper hospital, you don't need to pay—but some people give a bundle of cigarettes to their doctor as a present so that they will take more effort and caution when performing surgery on them.

So, plastic surgery does exist in North Korea. If medical technology improves in the North, I'm sure people will get a wide range of plastic surgeries, not just limited to nose jobs or double eyelids—just like in South Korea.

Would North Koreans be able to adapt to a market economy? And what about free speech?

DT: Although North Korea doesn't have an "open" economy, there have been huge economic changes from the ground up in the past 20 years. Politically, though, things are no different to before. This author doesn't see much prospect for positive political change, but one can hope.

If the DPRK state collapsed tomorrow, the North Korean people would see great long-term benefits, but also go through a degree of shock and confusion in the short term. We asked a group of North Korean defectors if they thought their compatriots would adapt well.

Joo Sung-ha:

It should not be difficult for North Koreans to understand and adapt to these concepts. I think North Koreans are ready for them now. It has already been 20 years since North Korea discontinued socialism. North Koreans are actually dependent on the black market economy, known locally as *Jangmadang*.

Recent defectors understand you cannot earn money without working harder than previous generations. The economic crisis in North Korea forced people to learn about the market economy independently. As such, the pursuit of material wealth is actually stronger in the North than in the South.

Of course, understanding and experiencing are two very different things—it will be more difficult for North Koreans to put these ideas into practice than to simply understand them.

However, while it will not be that difficult for people to accept society opening up and ensure freedom of speech, it will be difficult to curb fraud, trickery, and corruption.

Jihyun Park:

These things might have been difficult up until the 1990s, but in reality North Korea today operates as a market economy. Therefore, it will not be too difficult to accept a capitalist economic system. Opening up and freedom of speech will not be very difficult either.

People already feel differently than before, since they have heard a lot of news from the outside and there are open cities like Rajin or Sonbong [where the "free economic zone" is located].

One challenge would be to set up a way to share the positive aspects of each system so they can be implemented. But as of now, there seems to be no way of accomplishing this.

In my opinion, South Korean capitalism is a failure. The world may look at it as an advanced country, but there have been many negative side effects, such as the widening rich-poor gap and the highest suicide rate among developed nations.

If North Korea were to adopt this system, it would hurt the defector community even more. It might seem like there is an easy solution to the problem, but that could make things even more difficult.

Choi Sung-guk:

As long as Kim Jong Un's regime exists, it will not be easy for North Koreans to properly understand the concept of liberation, freedom of speech, or a free economy. But once Kim's control over the country collapses, it will be a lot easier than many people speculate.

Although North Koreans might not have a deep understanding of the free market, they are already familiar with it. Also, the many defectors successfully living in South Korea will be able to positively influence North Koreans' view of the capitalist system.

Most of all, since both Koreas speak the same language, and the South is economically superior to the North, there will not be many obstacles to overcome.

Ji-min Kang:

I think it would be natural for the North Korean people to transition to a capitalist market economy. If you look at North Korea today, the system is already being sustained through market activities. People's opinions have also changed quite a bit, which will help make the transition even smoother.

Of course there will be some things that will be hard for the North Korean people to understand.

Most North Koreans have never been exposed to a competitive environment, except in the political realm. For them, the fiercely competitive nature of capitalism will be difficult to grasp at first. North Korea is a planned economic system where market competition does not exist. Essentially, it's a society devoid of competition, that failed to progress.

With no sense of ownership, no one in North Korea was motivated to work hard, and it became commonplace for people to cut corners in their work. This mindset will gradually change as people learn to survive in a competitive system. This transition will not be difficult to implement, since North Korea's modern economy is already a de facto capitalist system.

A change in public opinion will also serve to change North Korea. The introduction of advanced culture through reform will change the people of North Korea, and a free press would further increase people's awareness. Freedom of the press is the most urgent problem that needs to be addressed in North Korea. It is not an overstatement to say that the current situation in North Korea is largely a result of press censorship.

Oh Se-hyok:

Perhaps it would not be as difficult as we think because markets have already become an important part of daily life in North Korea. I think people would not have any problems understanding the fundamentals of a market economy.

One challenge would be building trust and maintaining long-term relationships. It will also be difficult for North Koreans to understand long-term growth. For example, they might make a profit one day and then not make a profit for a long time. I think that peoples living in former socialist countries might have shared this experience. And this could affect business transactions with North Koreans because they would not be planning for the long-term. People might start to rely on illegal transaction methods more and avoid official business channels.

I think it will take a while for North Koreans to understand freedom of the press under the current circumstances. First, I think it is essential for people to understand what press freedom is and how it contributes to social growth. Achieving that will take time. For example, if I tried to explain this to North Koreans who fled to China or are visiting China, I think it would be a difficult concept for them to understand.

Ham Jin-woo:

All North Koreans are well aware that capitalism is superior. They are also asking for openness and reform. But, they stop short of openly expressing these opinions due to fear of negative political repercussions.

North Koreans already know that neighboring countries such as China, Russia, and Vietnam are better off than North Korea because they implemented economic reforms. It is only a matter of time before they reform too.

If one person—Kim Jong Un—is removed from power, North Korea would easily adjust to economic reforms.

PART 2

The Powers That Be

[Introduction]

Government is a factor in all of our lives. It provides us with services and protection, in return for our taxes and our compliance with certain rules. As we have already learned, this social contract has been gravely undermined in North Korea.

In other ways though, the relationship between people and state is extremely close in North Korea—whether the people like that or not. Though the policing of "ordinary" crimes is considered quite ineffectual, The DPRK's secret police agency is said to be able to know everything about you, right down to how many spoons you have in your kitchen. This is not necessarily a great exaggeration, given that one in every five households is a family of informers.

Those who fall foul of the authorities—having been accused of holding critical views of Kim Jong Un, or watching foreign TV shows, for instance—may find themselves subject to brutal interrogations, and labor camp sentences if found guilty. As may be expected, guilt and innocence are rather arbitrary notions, depending upon the whims (and corruptibility) of officials. A woman wearing revealing clothes, or a man with long hair, may also be judged to be committing a crime against public morals.

Times are changing though, as North Koreans are now far less cooperative with the authorities than they used to be. People are less likely to inform on each other, and officials themselves are much more open to taking a bribe to look the other way. However, the idea of open resistance to authority is still more or less unthinkable.

For men, the state imposes another burden: Military service, usually for a period of ten years. This brings special challenges of its own, as you will see below.

Do people criticize the Kims behind closed doors?

DT: Do North Koreans genuinely love their leader, or is it more the case that they simply "have" to love him? These days, it is more likely to be the latter. But the power of propaganda still works on many people.

Jae Young Kim:

My parents used to repeat an old North Korean proverb, "The bird listens during the day and the mouse does at night."

In my fatherland, the meaning of this was clear. You're always being watched. From a young age, I learnt to think of the potential consequences of everything I might say, before I said it. One wrong word could have potentially severe implications for our whole family. A visit from the Ministry of State Security (MSS) was something to be feared.

Criticism of the leaders is something that can lead to someone being sent from their city to the countryside, to a prison camp, or even worse. Because of the potential for punishment, it is risky for people to criticize the leaders, even behind closed doors.

This is why so few of us complained, even if we wanted to.

But not all of us wanted to. From a young age we are submerged in an intensive ideological curriculum that teaches us to refer to the leader using terms like "Dear General" or "Dear Leader." We learn that their real names—Kim Jong Il, Kim Il Sung—are to be held with reverence, and to never say them in vain. There is a genuine myth and intrigue surrounding North Korea's leaders. A lot of people simply believe in their greatness. For many, they are simply too far away to criticize.

When I was living in North Korea, I rarely called the Kims by their real names and I never dreamt of questioning their leadership. In a country where we grow up thinking about our leaders as gods, for many of us it would just never make any sense to even think about criticizing them.

However, not everyone is like me. I've got one friend, who also defected, who told me that she used to criticize the leaders quite regularly at home with her family. They used to blame the regime for the extreme poverty faced by the country.

Many people still think the poverty in North Korea is because of sanctions from the outside world, rather than the corruption and inefficiency of the leadership. Even if people do have doubts, it is hard for them to talk to each other about this. I didn't find out the truth until I left North Korea and spent time in China and South Korea.

Things are changing, though. With the increasing levels of information coming into North Korea through foreign videos and radio, people are starting to realize that North Korea is much poorer than the outside world. When I watched foreign DVDs in North Korea, I used to get so jealous of Chinese and South Koreans living in huge houses, wearing nice clothes, driving amazing cars, and having freedom. But for me, I kept this jealousy in my head.

Having grown up in the system I've just described, you can't understand how surprised and amazed I was when I came to South Korea and heard people even casually saying the name of the president, let alone even criticizing him. For North Koreans, we simply don't have the right to express anything publicly that isn't positive. Even though things are slowly changing, I can't imagine people publicly criticizing the leader for some time yet.

Is there a state secret service with a network of informants, like the KGB in the old Soviet Union?
DT: North Korea's secret police organization is arguably the most ruthlessly efficient of its kind in the world. Without it, the DPRK state would surely have disappeared long ago. Referred to as *Bowibu*, this agency has arbitrary powers to torture, imprison and kill.

Ji-min Kang:
Yes, a network of concealed informants similar to the Soviet Union's

KGB or East Germany's Stasi exists in North Korea. It is called the Ministry of State Security (MSS), and is known to everyone.

To this day, secret informants who work for the MSS monitor and spy on many ordinary North Koreans. Their purpose is to prevent and suppress any opposition to the government and identify those who are not cooperative with the state. And to do its job, the Ministry has an extended network that spreads out far from the party center, much like a spider's web.

Unfortunately, it is very difficult to tell secret service agents apart from other ordinary North Koreans. They look just like normal citizens and obviously don't wear a uniform or anything that would indicate their role to anyone. That said, I have heard that they do supposedly wear military uniforms when working inside the office buildings of the MSS.

So how does the MSS work?

You might be surprised, but the MSS has offices in nearly every neighborhood throughout the country, with some informants required to reside in these buildings during working hours. From here their job is to collect information about the local population through a network of people they get to know in the neighborhood.

The MSS system is a lot harsher than you'd think. In North Korea it's always possible that your friend, neighbor or co-worker could be working for the network of people who help the MSS. In other words, your own friends and co-workers could be giving away information about your activities to these informants any time they want to. And unfortunately, this often keeps people from building trust with one another. As a result, some North Koreans are unable to trust even lifelong friends, neighbors or co-workers.

Also, you should know that North Korea has a policy of inspection known as the "one in five households" system. Essentially, one in five households in North Korea works on behalf of the MSS as a local spy cell. Sometimes these informants catch people for real crimes, but unfortunately some individuals abuse the system by taking revenge against those who they hold grudges against. From time to time, innocent victims are arrested due to the "one in five" system.

What's worse is that some of the agents working directly for the MSS weren't much different than the household inspectors when I lived in North Korea. For example, they sometimes used their power to report innocent people just so they might stand a better chance of getting a promotion. And some were so powerful that local people would do all they could to avoid getting on their nerves. In extreme cases, some of the MSS agents could even cause trouble for members of the Workers' Party of Korea—and if charges were strong enough, these people could even face being sent to prison camp or worse.

Yet, things are changing now.

These MSS agents were once invincible. But today they're not as powerful as they used to be. Compared to the past, it seems many North Koreans are not as cooperative as they once were, and are less willing to report their close acquaintances to the secret police.

If, for example, it was revealed to your neighborhood that you had been working as an informant for the MSS, people would turn their back on you. You'd be given the cold shoulder by the local community. On top of this it seems that informants aren't as loyal as they used to be, especially since private enterprise—and corruption— have become so widespread in North Korea.

What is an *Inminban*, and how does it operate? How has its role changed over time?
DT: An *Inminban* is something like a cross between Neighborhood Watch, a community voluntary organization, and a spying operation. It is one of the cornerstones of North Korean state control of the people. However, as Kim Cheol explains, its role has changed somewhat over the years.

Kim Cheol:
Inminban (Neighbourhood Units) can be considered the peripheral nerves of the North Korean regime. Each consists of around 20–50 or more households, and is under the direct control of the local city or district committee. The role of the *Inminban* is to disseminate the ideas of Kim Il Sung and Kim Jong Il and the position of the Work-

ers' Party to residents, control residents' thoughts and lives, and give various administrative directives.

An *Inminban* is led by a captain, a head of household, and head of hygiene. The captain and head of household are housewives, and the head of hygiene someone from among the community who can help with various *Inminban* duties. The head of household is in charge of cleaning, but in practice is a deputy to the captain.

The captain earns a salary, but only a nominal one. However, because it is a job that helps with networking and can thus be useful in business, it is a relatively favorable position among housewives. A woman engaged in any particularly specialized business would consider it time-consuming and wouldn't want it, but it is considered a good job for general housewives.

Connecting the *Inminban* to local government are *Eup*, *Myeon*, and *Dong* offices (nb. these are administrative divisions based on population sizes, highest first). Because there are hundreds of *Inminban* in a city, the local people's committee will not be able to control the leaders of all of them. To make things run smoothly, an office is set up for their smooth governance.

Also, around 5–10 *Inminban* will collectively form a *jigu* (zone), with a zone captain.

This person's role is to take orders from the office and transmit them to the *Inminban* captains. But in the case of important decisions, the office may gather the *Inminban* heads and tell them directly. Usually the zone captain also serves as an *Inminban* captain.

The North Korean government stipulates that "by cooperating with the maintenance of social order and by strengthening the revolutionary institutions and order to prevent the counterrevolutionaries from taking steps, it will contribute to the maintenance of our national social system." Thus a managing officer (from the police) will identify ideological trends, whether there are any outside visitors or long-term sojourners, and unemployed people with the help of the *Inminban* captain.

Because of this role, community members cannot ignore the captain's status and consider them a minor power. Almost all economic activity in North Korea is part of the underground economy and is illegal, whether big or small. Therefore, it is essential to maintain a good relationship with the *Inminban* captain.

Lately, North Korea has been using *Inminban* as means of mobilizing labor and gaining foreign currency. Construction, disaster recovery, cleaning, and so on, are supposed to be taken care of by relevant public organizations, but their service provision is suspended as the efficiency and willingness of these organizations has been greatly reduced (nb. this is because the state has very little money). The *Inminban* are filling this vaccum.

Recently it has been emphasized that *Inminban* should gain foreign currency or collect "loyalty funds." Collecting loyalty funds through schools and workplaces has limitations, because there are no legal penalties for bosses failing to collect anything. They won't have their wages or rations frozen or be arrested if they don't collect any money.

When collecting loyalty funds through the *Inminban* though, people would feel socially embarrassed to not give money to people they live cheek by jowl with. For this reason, the paradigm of loyalty fund collection is gradually changing.

One can also find cases of *Inminban* captains accumulating large slush funds. Unemployment is illegal in North Korea, and those who do not work for six months may be sent to labor camps. The police investigate such people through the *Inminban* captains. The Inminban captain may receive a payment each month in return for protection. (Nb. The "unemployed" are not usually unemployed in practice; they are avoiding working at state organizations to engage in private business.)

Inminban captains can use these slush funds to help local people, but in big-city cases where there is a lot of money and the captain doesn't get on well with the members of the *Inminban*, the captain might steal the money. This can lead to friction in the community and there are cases where such captains have been arrested.

What does the average person know about political prison camps?
DT: There may be people who do not know exactly what goes on in a political prison camp, but everyone in North Korea knows they exist, and that they are a fate worse than death.

Ji-min Kang:
I doubt there is anyone who has lived in North Korea for a certain period of time that does not know the basics about political prison camps. And there will be no one who does not know what kind of person gets taken there, and what happens to them after that.

It was not too long ago that North Korea's political prison camps became known to the world as symbols of human rights abuses. Probably the true nature of these places wouldn't have become widely known without mass defections from North Korea caused by economic hardship.

North Korean political prison camps date back to the late 1950s.

Since that time, several political prison camps have been created around North Korea that can accommodate tens of thousands of people. The detainees are those who are hostile to the so-called authorities. They have diverse backgrounds, all the way from top cadres down to country farmers.

There are countless victims, including those who did not even do anything themselves but rather have been unfairly punished according to *yeonjwaje* [meaning "guilty by association"], the rule under which one can be punished for the crimes of one's father or other direct family members.

There are also those who had previously escaped abroad and became Christians, and those who had planned to defect to South Korea. In the eyes of the authorities, Christianity is the worse crime in that it denies loyalty to the Kims; the blocking of the continuing wave of defectors wanting to escape to the South is the authorities' desperate move to maintain a system that cannot compete [with that of the South].

Even North Korean children know that North Koreans can be taken to political detention camps and that if they are taken to one, they will not be able to return to the outside world again. Of course, there is no legal process, such as a trial. They are simply taken away by a truck in the night and nobody knows where they have gone.

They do not notify their family members or relatives, and if family members go and protest, the authorities threaten them and don't reveal anything about the whereabouts of their loved one.

Anyway, the most important thing is that they are guilty. This is a horrendous contravention of the constitutional values of North Korea. Both South and North have freedom of expression. But North Korea has no freedom *after* expression.

A complaint against the top leaders of North Korea is treated as a great sin that will not be forgiven until three generations has passed. This is a crueler and more merciless punishment than the kind meted out during the days of the Joseon Dynasty. Because of this, there are even people who are dragged off to prison camps due to the "crimes" of relatives they have never even met.

Within the political prison camps, disease and torture are rampant, and officials of the North Korean National Security Agency and the Ministry of Defense that run the camps also have the authority to execute captives. Ultimately, captives must live in the camps all their lives, and endure illness, hunger and torture until they die.

As the political prison camps are such closed environments, they have existed behind a veil for many years, and even now their true nature cannot be fully seen.

My two uncles were also taken to political prison camps because of my grandfather. Because of my grandfather's sins, they were detained along with their families. We don't even know if they are alive or dead.

Through the construction of the cruelest and most inhumane prison camps in history, [the North Korean authorities] have obliterated even the most basic human rights in their quest to maintain power. And in perpetuating the politics of fear, they have made all North Koreans into their compliant slaves.

I do wonder though: Are they not afraid of the coming judgment?

What are "elections" like in North Korea?
DT: It may surprise you to know that a country like North Korea bothers having elections. But actually, it works to the state's advantage to hold them. And besides, as Je Son Lee explains, there is no genuine choice anyway.

Je Son Lee:
In North Korea, elections are nothing more than ceremonies. On election day, North Korean people go to the voting booth. But they don't really get to choose who they want to represent them. Though they may cast a ballot, North Korean voters aren't able to influence public officials and lawmakers.

Among the variety of slogans widely found in North Korea, one prominent one reads: "Once the Workers' Party Makes Up Its Mind, It Has to Be Done." Since the Workers' Party has decided to hold elections in the country, they are held regularly.

The "Dear Leader" is the "Sun of the Communist Future" and father figure for all people in North Korea. He is flawless and makes no errors. To say a divine figure like our Dear Leader made a mistake is like saying Jesus Christ murdered someone. In North Korea, the Workers' Party is practically equal to Dear Leader Kim Jong Un, since its decisions reflect the wishes of the Dear Leader. There is no way to ever oppose its will.

Even if it becomes obvious later that the policies of the leadership are detrimental to the people of North Korea, such harm is regarded as the lesser evil. As a consequence, people don't feel disappointed or resentful. Instead, they become moved and touched by the depth of the affection the Dear Leader has for his people. Hence, voters in North Korean show high approval for the Workers' Party and its decisions. Of course, the ordinary people cannot afford to criticize policies implemented by the Workers' Party. Rather, they seek ways to win the favor of the Workers' Party, as this is a way for them to live a more comfortable life.

Also, people dream of becoming members of the Workers' Party. You should be qualified and possess the abilities desired by the party. Of course, you must be loyal. Then, you may have a chance to become a member of the party some day. Kim Jong Un alone cannot judge the qualifications of every candidate within the country. Such decisions are therefore left in the hands of local officials.

While I was living in the North, elections took place on public holidays. On election day, people wear their Sunday best to the voting booth. After casting their ballot, people come home to dance and sing together in their yards. That's the first thing that comes to mind when I think of election day in North Korea. At first I thought: Is it just me, or do other North Koreans have the same memories of election day? So, I asked my friends what they remembered about elections in North Korea. They all had the same memories. They all responded by saying: "We wore suits, *hanbok* and skirts and walked very elegantly all the way to the voting booth. On the way home, we would join a group of people dancing in the street. We all had a great time together, dancing and drinking." Election day in North Korea was always a festival day. Their memories and experiences were not the slightest bit different from mine.

What is an election? Officials in the party nominate one candidate for each district and voters decide whether they approve or disapprove of that candidate. Why do we vote for candidates? The party has already picked its own candidate. Why do we need to vote for that person? I'm sure that I'm not the only North Korean who wondered about this. There is only one name written on the ballot, only one candidate you can vote for. Therefore, every candidate is elected in North Korea. The nomination process is not open to the public. It's not transparent.

The voting process is too simplistic and undemocratic. Ordinary people are entitled to vote for representatives in local offices, but not for members of the Supreme People's Assembly. Voters receive a premade ballot and follow three or four steps and slide it into the ballot box. That's how you cast a ballot in North Korea.

The voting age is 18 or above and elections are public holidays. Except in case of imminent death, all people of voting age are expected to cast a ballot at the designated voting booth. Remember how I said it is inconceivable for ordinary North Koreans to oppose to any decisions made by the party? The moment you choose to do anything other than approve, you become a traitor.

Around election time, people are banned from traveling to other towns. People who secretly and illegally crossed over into China return to the North in time to participate in the election, or else authorities might notice they had been away.

People who don't show up to cast a ballot are considered to have expressed opposition to the decisions of the party. Simply put, if you skip an election day you become a traitor.

What is military service like in North Korea, and how long does it last?

DT: With over a million soldiers among a total population of only 25 million, North Korea is arguably the most militarized society in the world. The government says it all with its policy of *songun*, meaning "military first." If you want to understand North Korea, you'll definitely need to know a few things about how a Korean People's Army soldier lives. You may be surprised: Most are too poorly fed to be as fearsome as you'd expect, and spend as much time working as free laborers as they do on the parade ground.

Kim Yoo-sung:

In North Korea, most soldiers serve in the military for ten years, but female soldiers serve for seven. Those in Kim Jong Un's special bodyguard unit do 13 years.

As military service is compulsory in North Korea, most men enlist in the military after their high school graduation, with the disabled being exempt. People accepted into universities will enlist after they graduate from college. In this case, a man with a BA will serve for five years. Men who studied engineering or science will serve for three. It is well-known that the reason why men with science degrees serve for only three years is because Kim Jong Il wanted to encourage people to study science to contribute to the development of the country. Kim wanted to encourage people to study science by providing a big incentive—less time in the military!

The first difficulty men have to endure in the military is hunger. Soldiers in the special units won't have to worry about this, but most soldiers in the bases outside Pyongyang are given two or three potatoes per meal, or raw corn kernels or corn rice.

Military training is not all they are expected to do on such meager amounts of food. They're also told to help farmers in the rice paddies in summer. That's why so many North Korean soldiers become skinny and malnourished. They're made to provide this extra labor. Due to the threat of starvation, they turn to eating salted radish. As a result of devouring salted radish, some soldiers become plump. Some people may see them and think they're well-fed by the North Korean military, but that's not true: After eating nothing but salted radish, they may look fat on the outside but they're actually severely malnourished.

Many soldiers flee the military to escape malnourishment. Military police will be out in search of soldiers who escaped to look for food. Those soldiers who escape from their barracks will rob civilians of their food. They will rob civilians and the stockrooms in farming communities because they're so hungry. If it's edible, they will steal it. Some officers will even go as far as forcing soldiers to rob civilians. If the soldier fails to steal food, they will suffer retaliation and starvation in the barracks.

In my graduating class in high school, there were 25 guys. Five of them went to college and the remaining 20 went to enlist. Out of those 20, 10 of them returned home suffering from malnourishment. When recruits become malnourished, they're allowed to go home to recover. Most parents travel to the military barracks to pick up their sons. When they return home, their parents feed them. When their health improves, they're sent back to the military. Since they're severely malnourished, most of them are too weak to even walk by themselves. That's why parents travel all the way to military bases to pick up their sons and bring them home. Some of them even die from malnourishment before their parents arrive. North Korea may be the worst place in the world to do military service.

Those five of my classmates who didn't suffer malnourishment were lucky to serve in either a special unit or under good officers who took care of their soldiers. One of my friends went to serve on the North Korean side of Panmunjom at the 38th parallel. After I came to South Korea, I wanted to go to Panmunjom to see my friend's face from the South Korean side. But he had been discharged and so now I can't go to Panmunjom to see him.

All of this may sound unbelievable to soldiers in South Korea and America. The only thing North Korean parents pray for is the safe return of their sons from the military.

What is law and order like in North Korea?
DT: North Korea's prison camps are well-known, but what about the general system of law and order? As with any poor country where the rule of law is weak, there's often one set of rules for the poor and another for the rich.

Ji-min Kang:
The constitution represents the national identity and national law of a country, and no one, even the ruler, is above the constitution and the rule of law. At least, that's how a normal country works. The

North Korean constitution, on the other hand, is a nominal set of rules and there are people who have the power to revise the constitution to feed their appetites.

So how do people live day by day in a country where the rule of law does not apply to everyone equally?

North Korea is a country where human rights abuses are prevalent and those who face even execution are not given the right to an attorney or a fair trial. Crimes such as robbery, fraud and murder take place in North Korea as they do in other countries, but very few prisoners face justice for these offences—the police and justice system have other worries: political prisoners.

Of course, there are an abundant number of people charged with criminal offenses. But most of them cannot hire an attorney for themselves. Even worse, most North Koreans don't even know of the existence of lawyers, or what they do. Even if one hires an attorney, they have less chance of proving their innocence than of getting struck by lightning.

In North Korea, cops were always domineering, incessantly asking for bribes, and generally abusing their power in return for a reduction in a citizen's sentence. For this reason, while the ruling ideology states that everyone is created equal in North Korea, the poor face disproportionate punishment for petty crimes, while the rich can quite literally get away with murder.

For example, someone I knew killed five people in a car accident while driving drunk, but was sentenced to only three years in prison because his father was a high-ranking police officer. He was released after serving a year in prison, free to walk the streets again.

In contrast, a group of poverty-stricken people broke into a state-owned factory to steal food, probably the most common crime in North Korea. They were caught and faced public execution. Even though they should have been charged with just robbery, they were indicted on charges of plotting a rebellion against the North Korean government. Of course, they weren't allowed to hire an attorney, or even to appeal. Following their execution, their remaining family members were forced to move to rural towns.

This happens all over the country and all over the world: People who are starving steal food. But, since most North Korean cops are incompetent (and there's a shortage of cops in the DPRK), most of these crimes remain unsolved. Even if they become victims of robbery, people do not report it to the police—they don't expect the police to catch those responsible.

Most people found guilty of economic crimes receive three to ten years of prison time. But a sentence of more than five years is essentially a death sentence: Most prisoners do not survive more than three years of harsh forced labor and prison conditions.

Without family support, most prisoners would probably die in prison after one or two years. There are a number of so-called "Labor Training Centers" in North Korea. Thugs, illegal street vendors and people who travel without permission are sent to these places, where they are subject to forced labor for months. During this time, they disappear—their families aren't notified of their whereabouts.

At times when large numberzs of refugees are deported back to North Korea, the authorities can't imprison or execute all of them as political prisoners. Consequently, in towns near the border, many people have at least one neighbor who has previously escaped from North Korea.

This was why these Labor Training Centers were created. North Korean refugees who were sent back had to suffer forced labor at Labor Training Centers, without even knowing what they had been charged with. They only vaguely knew that it was a crime for them to escape from the North for economic reasons.

In North Korea, the law exists to protect those in power and to eliminate those opposed to them. The law is only a device to uphold the dictatorship of the Kim family. No one is entitled to protection under the law.

The deification of Kim Il Sung is more important than the constitution, and the will of the Kims superior to any law in North Korea.

Is it true that there is a real-life "fashion police" in North Korea?
DT: The state involves itself in virtually every aspect of people's lives, so it is hardly surprising to hear that North Koreans can be subject to crackdowns on how they dress. Women shouldn't wear "sexy" attire, or even long pants—though these days, this is slowly changing. Hair styles are also regulated. Stories in the international press about men having to wear compulsory Kim Jong Un haircuts are nonsense, though.

Je Son Lee:
Until 2010, North Korean women couldn't imagine wearing sleeveless shirts or miniskirts. Women were not allowed to wear pants, let alone short skirts. Tops were more loosely controlled, however: A friend who left North Korea this year said the authorities are now cracking down on women clad in short skirts and sleeveless tops. In North Korea, skirts should cover women's knees. They are allowed to wear half-sleeve shirts but not sleeveless tops. Also, women shouldn't reveal cleavage.

Women shouldn't wear pants at all, and aren't allowed to ride bicycles or motorcycles, either. Government rules apply to hairstyles, as well. Women should always wear either bobbed hair or pigtails. Women in college are required to wear a uniform (yes, college students in North Korea wear uniforms, as if still in high school!). It is considered inappropriate for students to wear anything else in public. You should never wear jeans, bell-bottoms or short skirts. But when you're told not to wear certain types of clothes, you're more tempted to wear them. Or is it just me who feels that way?

However, the authorities don't crack down all year round on women wearing short skirts, or those who have forgotten to wear their Kim Il Sung and Kim Jong Il badges. They only crack down at certain times in the year. During inspection season, officials are stationed on streets at intervals of 20 meters, checking the way passersby dress. Unless you're dressed in accordance with government guidelines, you will not get any further than 20 meters. It is easier for men to get past these inspectors, unless they have weird hairstyles.

However, a woman can never get past an inspector if she is not wearing a skirt. It doesn't matter how old you are. The same rule applies to grannies. Grannies heading out to the mountains to pick vegetables must wear skirts. You cannot complain or voice your opinion about what the government does in North Korea. Once I ran into an old lady I knew in my neighborhood and she was pulling her pants up as high as she could.

"What are you doing?" I asked her.

"I'm just trying to put my skirt on before I run into an inspector on the street," she said.

Then, she pulled some cloth from her pocket and draped it around her waist above her pants. It could definitely pass for a skirt. I thought it was ludicrous that a woman had to wear a skirt to go up a mountain, when it is already difficult enough to climb in pants. Most of these women aren't just out for a stroll. They're the breadwinners and they work hard every day to feed their families. Yet they're required to move about in uncomfortable skirts. They don't even have freedom to wear pants.

Also, when you take a look at everyone passing by on the street, almost no one is empty-handed. They're always carrying at least 5kg of goods, and it's not easy moving about in long skirts while carrying such heavy goods for work. Once, I wore pants to school and got caught by school inspectors. A male teacher looked at me as if he couldn't fathom why I would prefer pants over a skirt.

"Je Son, isn't a skirt much cooler? Skirts are good for circulating air. Why would you wear pants instead of a skirt? Why would you not wear a skirt? I cannot understand you."

A female who happened to pass by overheard the conversation and she snapped at him in defense of me.

"Sir, have you ever worn a skirt before?" she said. "How would you know without having worn one once in your life? Try on a skirt tomorrow and you'll change your mind."

I felt grateful for her brilliant response!

Whether you're still a student enrolled at school or already working in your unit, you'll be called upon by the *nyeomaeng*, an organization consisting of housewives, to work on assignments such as pulling out weeds, carrying stones, digging up sand, and so on. It would drive you nuts to do those assignments in skirts. Men have no idea how uncomfortable it is having to crouch down and stand up in skirts.

If you get caught wearing pants instead of a skirt, you're called on by the Workers' Party to write letters of self-reflection. Once I got caught wearing pants in public by a member of the local party office. As a punishment, I had to run around the playground 10 times singing a song entitled "Let us Sustain Socialism." After that, I had to pull out weeds on the playground for over an hour and write three pages of self-reflection letters before I was allowed to return home. On my way back home, I was so upset that I thought to myself, I will continue to wear pants and it will be okay as long as I don't get caught.

But I soon changed my mind. It wasn't worth getting into trouble and dealing with such people. Before that incident, whenever I saw women obediently wearing skirts in public, I thought they were being too submissive and timid. But I changed my view. I think they were actually being smart by avoiding trouble. Yes, most of these government rules in North Korea are utter nonsense! But the smartest way to protect yourself in such a country is to abide by them.

Have you ever seen any anti-government dissent?
DT: North Korea is arguably the most controlled state in the world. While gradual economic liberalization is taking place, political control is still total, and any transgression is handled with severity. The prospect of any "uprising" is remote then, and one would not want to imagine the outcome if such an event did take place.

Kim Yoo-sung:
Foreigners wonder why there is no anti-government movement to topple the dictatorship. Sometimes they think it's because we North Koreans are too stupid to carry out such an uprising. But ordinary North Koreans are simply too afraid to become part of an anti-gov-

ernment movement, because they know the truth: they cannot bring about change by themselves.

The reality is that North Korea cannot change unless the government itself decides to change. In countries such as South Korea and the United States, people can criticize their presidents or even go to the extent of protesting in the streets, and as long as such protests and demonstrations are legal, the government or police won't intervene. And even if the protesters happen to break the law, they are often only subject to minor legal consequences as a result.

But North Korea doesn't work like that. If people went out into the streets and said something negative about Kim Jong Un or the government's policies, they would be executed the moment they opened their mouths. Either that, or they'd be labeled as traitors to the entire Korean race and sent to political prison camps—a prospect that terrifies all North Koreans.

If other countries controlled their people in this way, no one in the world would be able to criticize their presidents or governments publicly.

In other words, it is simply not possible for ordinary North Koreans to topple the leadership by organizing an anti-government movement. So if you'd like to really help North Koreans, rather than sending leaflets, please help by sending donations such as medical products, medicine, and formula milk for North Korean children.

Another reason there are no anti-government protests in North Korea is the brainwashing that occurs in public schools. From kindergarten, North Koreans grow up being told about the superiority of North Korea's leaders. It makes people acquiesce to the leadership without questioning its decisions. As such, people struggle to have any anti-regime thoughts. There is an old Korean saying: "If you tell a lie 100 times, it becomes a truth." Since North Koreans are constantly brainwashed from birth to death, often they cannot bring themselves to think that anything the regime does could be wrong. That's another reason why it is not easy to start an anti-regime movement within North Korea.

I sometimes heard about limited forms of opposition when I was still living in North Korea—things like graffiti on walls or in toilets protesting the government. I even heard rumors in my hometown that someone once put up a *Taegukgi* (the national flag of South Korea) on the school grounds at night, something that would have been pretty shocking. However, I never saw any of this with my own eyes.

Occasionally, you hear negative rumors spreading about the government. However, as I said already, there is always a serious risk that people talking ill of the government may just disappear at night. Because of this, such rumors usually die out pretty quickly.

To give you an example, when I was in college, a classmate of mine was a son of a manager at the State Security Department. He once told me that someone had written an anti-government message on a toilet wall and somehow the State Security Department had successfully tracked them down. So while limited forms of dissent can pop up from time to time, it never gets big enough to cause the large-scale political unrest some might hope for. The State Security Department ruthlessly cracks down on this sort of behavior, and those involved are executed in underground prisons without any chance of a trial.

Overall, I think that if and when dissent does occur in North Korea, incidents are likely to be very minor, and suppressed quickly without any trace left. As such, whoever organizes anti-government activities would have to be a very brave person, and if he or she got caught, they wouldn't have much time left on this earth.

In short, the State Security Department is very good at making sure that any dissident or protest movement disappears long before it has a chance to spread to other regions, let alone ever grow to the point that it strikes a blow against the regime. I guess the State Security Department's surveillance gathering network is even more efficient than that of the NSA [the United States National Security Agency]. Indeed, the SSD can keep track of its people to the extent of keeping tabs on their whereabouts, what they're up to, and "even how many spoons and bowls they possess" (as one saying puts it).

How much longer can the DPRK system last?

DT: Pundits and the press love to speculate on "when" the North Korean state will collapse. But the DPRK has so far outlasted famine, war, the collapse of the Soviet Union, and a transformation from socialism to a sort of feudal monarchy.

When things unravel though, they tend to catch everyone by surprise—just look at the once-mighty Soviet Union itself. We asked a group of North Korean defectors their opinion on regime change, and how long it might take.

Choi Sung-guk:
At a minimum five years, and at a maximum, ten. Why do I think this way? Because as the years pass, North Korea's society is tending towards market economics above all else.

Back in the 1980s, the basic idea of buying and selling was limited mainly to older women who went out to markets. During the 1990s there were a few smart people involved, but their presence was not much welcomed by North Korean society. However, during the Arduous March (the economic crisis in North Korea from 1994 to 1998) people were forced to look for their own income sources. Today, it is clear that commerce has become the principal income source for smart people. This means that more than ever before, North Koreans are prioritizing their own wealth over national duty.

Why is this happening? The reason is simple: The market economy rewards people according to the amount of effort they put in. This tells us that the North Korean government's socially planned economy is already on thin ice.

Hyun-moo Jung:
When I left North Korea, it seemed that the Kim Jong Il regime was likely to collapse at any moment. But when I came to South Korea I learned about how it was able to survive so long. Nevertheless, after I witnessed the third stage of the Kim family succession I returned to thinking that the North Korean regime would collapse any time soon.

Unlike his father, Kim Jong Un is naive and inexperienced. There's no consistency in his policies—which is very obvious. His only goal in life is to retain power as the Supreme Leader. He tries to create fear in order to suppress the top elites. While this strategy may seem successful at first, it won't last long.

Nayoung Koh:
It is premature to predict the collapse of the North Korean regime—because China continues to play a huge role in propping it up.

A principal reason why the North Korean regime has survived so long is due to the socialist states that once existed and supported it. But although most socialist states have now collapsed, China still backs up North Korea.

This support is critical. When North Korea experienced the Great Famine—caused by natural disasters and isolation from the international community following the death of Kim Il Sung—the North Korean regime managed to survive thanks to the humanitarian aid offered from China. I wonder if the regime would have been able to survive if all that food and clothing aid had not come from China during the famine? As such, I believe that as long as China doesn't give up on North Korea, the regime will continue to survive.

Jinwoo Ham:

Kim Jong Il was able to rule the country for 40 years, from the 1970s until 2011, due to the fact he was seen as a divine successor, the son of Kim Il Sung. However, Kim Jong Il lost the trust of ordinary people during his time in power. There were many assassination attempts (the Ryongchon bombing), an attempted coup (the 6th Brigade Incident) and to me it seemed that approximately 70–80 percent of people were simply waiting for him to die.

Kim Jong Un's rise to power came amid a backdrop of strong public frustration with Kim Jong Il. To make things worse, Kim Jong Un is lacking a strong platform and is seen as a naive, young and inexperienced brat by the majority of people in North Korea. Things will be worse for him now that Jang Song Thaek [the uncle he executed] has gone.

I believe Kim Jong Un will be assassinated within the next three years due to a power struggle, and that this will lead to the collapse of the regime.

Se-hyok Oh:

Today it is clear that the North Korean system is not only being propped up by a crawling bureaucracy, but because the leaders in Pyongyang know the vulnerabilities of their system better than anyone else. The people have not come to realize this yet—and despite an urge to see their government reform, they don't yet have the strength to oppose the system.

Jang Seong Thaek was the only person who would have been able to simultaneously push through reforms in North Korea while also unifying the regime's bureaucracy. And now, while it's said that there are still those in the government who would like to see the country reform, if they can't unite with each other, they won't be able to show their strength. This is a shameful state of affairs.

Jihyun Park:
Although the current regime is under UN sanctions for last year's nuclear weapons and missile tests, it is still receiving economic aid from China—especially with the opening up of Rajin and Sonbong. Also, the DPRK continues to receive aid from South Korea through the Kaesong Industrial Complex [note: Kaesong has been closed since the author wrote this]. I therefore believe that as long as the outside world continues to provide it with aid, the regime will not collapse.

North Korea is like no other country in the world. It has 1 million soldiers out of a 25 million population. Most industrial facilities in North Korea are military factories, while the factories and businesses that could have improved the lives of the people have all closed. Under these circumstances, the collapse of North Korea will be difficult: The regime will preserve total power unless there are major disagreements within the government itself, or a rebellion that sees the people overthrow the regime.

Prof. Inae Hyun:
North Korea does not allow any outside information to be distributed within the country, instead preserving the exclusive right of promoting only official ideology over the people. Because its system controls every aspect of people's lives, it is impossible in the current environment to imagine any civil movement or revolution emerging. As such, we can only expect a military coup caused by instability among the top elites to create a major change.

Following the execution of Jang Song Thaek, it is apparent that there was a power struggle within the top elite. This struggle was caused primarily by economic factors. In addition, it seems that people have doubts about Kim Jong Un's abilities as a leader: I'm personally doubtful that he possesses the characteristics needed to lead such a poor and difficult country. Above all, I actually don't think he's clever enough.

Sung-ha Joo:

I believe it will last for at least five more years. Above all, it is difficult to imagine a coup d'etat occurring in North Korea. It is also clear that neighboring countries like South Korea do not wish a collapse to happen. As such, I believe the North Korean regime will only collapse when Kim Jong Un dies—but I can't see any factors threatening his life in the foreseeable future.

But what could cause a collapse of Kim Jong Un's regime? For me, only an assassination—or central government losing control due to a rapid expansion of market activity.

However, considering some experts said the unification of Germany would have been a lot more difficult to achieve than that of the Koreas, you can see how difficult it is to predict history. After all, who could have predicted the timing of the collapse of the Soviet Union?

PART 3

Media and Information

[Introduction]

Control of media and information is one of the main pillars of any dictatorship. And according to think tank Freedom House, North Korea has the least free press of any country in the world. You will simply never hear anything critical of the state from the small number of permitted sources of news and information in North Korea.

But that doesn't mean that North Koreans are completely unaware of what is going on. There are many who listen to shortwave radio broadcasts from abroad. There are those living near the China-DPRK border who secretly tune in to South Korean dramas broadcast on Chinese TV. There are many more—probably a majority of the population—who have watched South Korean TV shows brought in through China on DVD or USB drives.

South Korean drama shows are more important than foreign news, as they are entertaining. Just like back home, soap operas are more popular than serious news. But defectors often report that they were heavily affected by the sight of rich and relatively free-living South Koreans, in contrast with what they had been told by the state.

Though these developments are undermining the state's control over how people think, we should be careful not to jump to the tempting conclusion that major political change will result. From my own experience of discussions with North Koreans, it seems there are still relatively few who can even imagine the downfall of the regime; rather, future hopes are often expressed in terms of "I hope the government will undertake reform X." This is the product of a combination of residual respect for Kim Il Sung; fear; decades of propaganda; and the seductive power of monarchy, which North Korea now definitely is.

Nevertheless, growing consumption of foreign media—along with growing marketization—means a loosening of attitudes, even from those in power. There seems to be a new attitude of allowing more and more low-level freedoms (e.g., in how people dress), while continuing to crack down aggressively on anything that challenges real government control.

What do North Koreans think about South Korean and Western music and movies?

DT: This is not a trivial question, as one of the main drivers of social change in North Korea is the illicit importation of South Korean and Western TV shows, movies, and music. It is a phenomenon that influences the way people think, speak, and dress.

Ji-min Kang:

In North Korea, "Western culture" is often referred to as the "Yellow Wind." You probably won't be surprised to know, but at the time I left North Korea (2005) officials were labeling foreign movies and music an "imperialist cultural invasion" and ruthlessly banning them. Consequently, those caught watching Western movies would often have to face either public execution or jail time in the political prison camps. Still, no matter how hard the authorities tried to keep foreign culture out of North Korea, they obviously couldn't control everyone.

When I look back, it's clear that I indulged myself with Western and South Korean culture at great risk to my life and that of my family. But of course, my desire to access that new culture is also probably the reason why I'm in the UK today.

You see, the foreign cultures and lifestyles visible in the DVDs and TV shows in the 2000s were especially appealing to the younger generation in North Korea, the contents of which all had a dreamlike quality to us. So, just like in other countries around the world, the DVDs and films we watched had an affect on us—often leading to new trends in our sheltered North Korean culture, too.

At first, it was Western culture that initially swept across Pyongyang and other big cities in North Korea. After that, Chinese and Hong Kong culture was the next to reach the big cities. Then South Korean dramas and music started to arrive. This had a serious effect on the North Korean people.

Nowadays, pretty much everyone in North Korea can sing one or two South Korean songs and remember the lyrics. These days there are even dance instructors teaching the choreography of South Korean pop idol groups in North Korea.

Of course, many North Korean songs are about the crazed deification of the Kim family and the dictatorship. That's why people are inclined to be attracted to South Korean songs about love, romantic relationships and basic human feelings.

But just how much do North Koreans really like South Korean culture? Perhaps the following examples will give you some idea.

At times when there are electricity shortages in North Korea—when it becomes difficult to watch South Korean TV shows or DVDs—soldiers would disassemble tank batteries to provide the electricity needed to continue watching. I've also heard that even some guards on the North Korea-China border find solace in watching South Korean dramas and films.

Why are we so crazy about South Korean and Western culture?

Well, the new world we experienced through these foreign dramas and movies was much more affluent and free than we'd ever imagined. The confident expressions, behavior, and true love which the actors displayed were either the kinds of things we weren't allowed to have in North Korea, or simply things you wouldn't often see in public.

For us it seemed that when people in these movies were in love, they were not afraid to show it. They freely expressed their opinions. They didn't live in a totalitarian society where they were forced to obey rules. They were affluent, and their fashion and the towns they lived in were astonishing. Their world appeared like heaven to us, who were living in a society that seemed to control every human instinct. In this environment, people like me became fascinated by the outside world through film and TV. While we had next to nothing, foreigners had almost everything.

I realized after I left that it is understandable why the North Korean government fears the free flow of Western culture, a culture that does not discourage liberalism or human instinct. In short, the Pyongyang leadership knows that foreign culture could bring about a collapse of the dictatorship they have spent so many decades building.

But their control is not total and foreign DVDs and films continue to enter North Korea. Today I can't even begin to imagine how many young North Koreans will be enjoying the wild and racy pop culture of South Korea.

Freedom is something delightful and enjoyable for everyone, especially those who grew up under a dictatorship like in North Korea. Now North Koreans are in the process of rediscovering basic human instincts that were so long denied. I hope the spring of democracy and freedom will arrive for my countrymen, some of who have lived with less dignity than animals.

Do you learn much about the outside world from North Korean news?
DT: If you read a North Korean newspaper or watch North Korean TV news, you'll probably see a lot of Kim Jong Un, his father, and his grandfather. You'll see positive news about domestic matters, and occasionally, some foreign news—but not anything that might make you think that life is better elsewhere, or that the DPRK government could do better.

Kim Yoo-sung:
I think the majority of North Koreans don't know about the news that isn't covered in the North Korean media. In an isolated country like that, there is very little information coming in from the outside world.

A limited number of North Koreans do find out. They are the ones who frequently visit China on business trips, or who smuggle goods across the Sino-NK border. And there are others who hear news not covered in the North Korean media by secretly listening to South Korean radio.

So, would they hear of news like the actions of the pro-democracy Umbrella Movement in Hong Kong? There is very little chance of ordinary North Koreans finding out about these kinds of events if they aren't broadcast in the North Korean media. The only way for them to find out about anti-Chinese government protests in Hong Kong is by listening to South Korean radio in secret.

The North Korean government almost never reports any anti-government protest in other countries, because it is afraid the people would be encouraged to stage similar anti-government protests to end the dictatorship.

But can people spread news by word of mouth at the *jangmadang* (marketplace)? My answer would be no. It's impossible for ordinary North Koreans to talk to one another about news that's not officially reported by the government. Since there are informants present at the *jangmadang*, you could be sent directly to the State Security Department if you were ever overheard talking about such things.

North Koreans are therefore too afraid to talk openly about unofficial news in public places, such as the *jangmadang*. Even if they do talk about it, they make sure this is only with their family members in the home; they'd never talk about it outside.

So how do some North Koreans discover that the outside world is different? In my personal opinion, the majority of North Koreans already know that the outside world is different. They learned that other countries are very different by watching movies from South Korea, America and Europe following an influx of those movies in the early 2000s. Until my third year of high school, I believed North Korea was not that different from other countries and that in some aspects North Korea was superior.

Things changed in my fourth year. When I watched South Korean dramas for the first time in 2002 I was completely shocked, because South Korea was completely different from what I'd always thought it to be. From then on, I became curious about the outside world and wondered what it would be like to live in other countries. Day by day, my desire to visit other countries grew.

I think other North Koreans learned that the outside world was very different by watching movies and video footage. I also think that they hope North Korea will become like those other countries.

Do North Koreans know that freedom, liberty, human rights and democracy exist in some other countries? I think most North Koreans don't know that those values exist in other places. They merely learn that life in other countries is freer and more comfortable than in North Korea. They don't know that people can be totally free and have their human rights respected.

Ordinary North Koreans can secretly listen to foreign radio if they try to, and a minority of people do, I think. I imagine they stay up-to-date with international news by secretly listening to foreign radio every night.

But even if they do, they can't openly talk about it once they step outside their homes. It's therefore very hard for word about the outside world to reach a large number of people in North Korea. Also, some people are too afraid to listen out of fear of getting caught by the government. If you are caught, you'll be sent straight to the State Security Department or a political prison camp.

Greater access to news may help ordinary North Koreans, to some extent. But it will not necessarily bring democratic change to North Korea. To bring change to North Korea, the elites, rather than ordinary people, would need to change first. Even if there were greater international news coverage in North Korea, it would not necessarily lead to democratization. Nor would it change the miserable living conditions of North Koreans overnight.

What kinds of books are available in North Korea?

DT: Young people around the world read less and less these days, a consequence of the rise of new distractions, like the Internet and the smartphone. There are fewer such distractions in North Korea, so reading is as popular as ever. The kind of reading material available is highly limited due to censorship, but that doesn't necessarily mean that people will find the novels, non-fiction, and comic books available to them boring.

Jae Young Kim:
As far as literature is concerned, censorship and ideology direct everything in North Korea. Of course, we have many different types of books, but all are checked thoroughly for political correctness. However, just because a book conforms to those standards, it doesn't necessarily mean it is boring.

When I was little, like many other children I read a collection of books titled *Memoirs*. This long epic was about the birth, childhood, and death of our first leader, Kim Il Sung. It was eight volumes long and I read every page with fascination, despite the highly ideological subject matter.

Reading these books, I became very impressed by the heroine Kim Jong Suk. She was the first wife of Kim Il Sung. She was depicted as a selfless woman always making sacrifices for the leader, and I remember her drying Kim Il Sung's wet clothes with her own body and even making insoles for his shoes out of her own hair, to protect his feet. I felt so proud reading these stories about the Great Leader, and was inspired to behave like Kim Jong Suk. It was books like this, alongside *The Complete Works of Kim Il Sung* and *Immortal Leadership*, that taught us to praise the revolutionary history and great work of Kim Il Sung and Kim Jong Il.

It might sound strange to you, but these kinds of books were very popular and hard to borrow without a long wait at the library. Despite being distinctly political works, I guess that, ultimately, they were good reading.

Compared to South Korea and America, the contents of our novels did not vary much, it is true, but I do remember gripping tales about heroic soldiers or prisoners of war being returned to the country. Some might say we were being brainwashed, but at least it was done entertainingly.

Folk stories were the only popular books without any political ideology. I remember books like *Lim Kkunk Jung* and *Chun Hyang Jeon* were quite popular.

Regarding fiction, some of the best children's stories were imported from foreign countries—I especially enjoyed "Daddy Long Legs" and "Cinderella." The stories and pictures in these books fascinated us because they reflected the mindset of another world—although to us it was just fantasy anyway, so I guess they were deemed politically safe.

You'd need dedication to get hold of these books, however. I would always queue in long lines, and join long waiting lists to borrow books from the local library. When I got hold of a desired book, I'd have it for one week. Having had to wait so long for the privilege, I would waste no time absorbing it. For many North Koreans, reading is a real pleasure. That said, many people can't read at all.

Aside from children's books, we have access to foreign technical books and even a few translated novels, although these are mostly imported from China and Russia. Whatever comes over the border, however, is usually edited out of its original form.

Before publishing a book in North Korea, it is seriously censored by the authorities. As a result, nobody writes political books. Books or writings with "wrong" thoughts can end up with the reader facing serious investigation if caught with them. Now I am in South Korea I am so happy that I can read all kinds of books whenever I want.

How do people get access to foreign TV shows and movies? And, is the increasing access North Koreans have to such media likely to result in dissent, mass defections, or other actions that would weaken regime control?
DT: Technology is really making a difference to North Koreans' access to information about the outside world. Some lucky people in the border regions have long been able to receive TV signals from China or South Korea, but for the majority, it was first the DVD/CD and then the USB stick that opened up a new world for them. But while this development is certainly encouraging defections and

changing North Koreans' minds about the outside world, we should be cautious about making any assumptions that it will result in political change, as Jinhyok Park explains.

Jinhyok Park:

It took a couple of decades for ordinary North Koreans to realize that South Koreans and Chinese are much more advanced and wealthier than they are. This was due to the regime's strict ban on outside information: the North Korean government desperately wants to keep outside information from making its way to its people.

Many ordinary North Koreans believe that the Korean War was started by the United States, not the DPRK, and a lot of them aren't even aware of the genealogy of the Kim family they are forced to worship.

But outside information began to make its way into North Korea in the late 1990s. During the famine, it wasn't just humanitarian aid consisting of food and medical supplies that made its way into North Korea: Chinese goods and products were smuggled in, too.

The Chinese economy was progressing at a faster pace than ever and in witnessing this, North Koreans stopped looking down on Chinese people. In the early 2000s, dramas, movies and music from China, Hong Kong, America and South Korea became popular across the country, dramatically changing people's perception of the world. North Koreans began to look on the outside world with admiration, a tremendous change for North Koreans who grew up being brainwashed and doing only what they were told by the regime.

Until several years ago (when I was still living in North Korea), foreign movies and TV programs were distributed on CDs and USB drives that had been smuggled in. North Koreans living on the coastline and near the border would listen to Radio Free Asia, Voice of America and even had access to ordinary South Korean TV programs and anti-North Korean broadcasts by South Korea.

Shortly after that, the regime began to crack down on those watching foreign TV in Pyongyang, forcing people to tune into the same TV channel or radio station all day. People were no longer able to watch the channel of their choice, but the younger generation's desire for outside information never dwindled.

When I was still in Pyongyang, it took at least two to three years for South Korean hit movies to get to North Korea. My sources in North Korea now say it only takes a few days. People living in Kaesong and Wonsan record South Korean TV programs when they air, and sell copies on the black market the next day.

When I was still in North Korea, I only watched South Korean TV occasionally, and out of sheer curiosity. But these days North Koreans watch it almost every day. I wonder what is going on in young North Koreans' minds while they receive education under the socialist dictatorship and watch capitalist media and TV programs at night.

One thing I can tell you for sure is that the influx of outside information has played a role in shaping the way North Koreans perceive the world as well as the desire to escape the regime: I'm the perfect example. As I became more familiar with outside information, the society I saw in dramas and movies didn't seem that strange to me anymore.

After watching dramas and movies, I knew I desperately wanted to live in this world I had seen. It became one of the main reasons I left North Korea. While I was staying at a refugee camp in Southeast Asia, most North Korean defectors I met there were already knowledgeable about South Korean society.

Financial difficulty and hunger were not the reasons these people left North Korea: they made a decision to escape from North Korea for their children's future and due to the admiration they had for South Korean society. I think this wouldn't have been possible if they hadn't had access to information from the outside world.

At the same time, I don't think it will cause the collapse of the North Korean regime, and it won't bring any upheaval or demonstrations against the regime, either. Let me tell you why.

North Koreans can't process the information they get from the outside world. After growing up so strictly brainwashed by the regime, they often lack the ability to think critically and be creative.

The regime continues to wield a massive amount of power over its people through terror.

It doesn't matter that North Koreans now realize how irrational the regime is. There's absolutely nothing they can do. Even if a group of people wanted to gather and demonstrate against the regime, they would have to organize a meeting to make a plan: This just isn't possible in North Korean society.

In North Korean society, you never know who might be working as a secret agent for the regime. If you get caught doing something they don't like, your relatives will also be held responsible for your sins. So North Koreans rarely talk about their true feelings with other people: they do everything they can to appear loyal to the regime.

Of course, an influx of outside information is better than nothing. If information is steadily distributed around the country and the perceptions of North Koreans change, we could perhaps hope for the democratization of North Korea.

But just the fact that North Koreans can now watch South Korean TV drama and movies isn't enough: creating an atmosphere that will encourage transition would be more meaningful and effective.

What would North Koreans think if they saw Seth Rogen's movie *The Interview*?
DT: There is no doubt that *The Interview* is not funny. But what would North Koreans themselves think about the main concept of the movie, that of an assassination attempt on Kim Jong Un? It's a valuable question to ask, as the answer can tell us something about the extent of loyalty to the regime.

Je Son Lee:
Throughout watching *The Interview*, I wondered what the purpose was in making the movie. I pondered this for a while, but I will never understand why. I've watched lots of Hollywood films—even when I was living in North Korea—but this is the first time I've watched such a terrible Hollywood movie.

This movie has absolutely no consideration for its viewers. Making a movie that is worthwhile to watch is the least movie producers can do for their paying viewers. If they had this in mind, I believe they wouldn't have made such a lousy, terrible film.

Prior to the official release of *The Interview*, there had been all kinds of fuss over it. It received international attention when the personal e-mails of Sony Pictures executives were leaked and President Obama made a statement condemning the hacking, which was allegedly carried out by North Korea in retaliation for making a mockery of their leader. I'm not 100 percent sure if North Korea was really behind the cyber terror attacks on Sony Pictures.

I decided to watch *The Interview* as soon as it was released. After all, it was a major Hollywood film about North Korea, about a plot to assassinate Kim Jong Un. I wanted to see the movie for myself and was curious to find out how North Korea was depicted. So, I went straight to watch it as soon as the movie became available online.

Now, I want my two hours and money back.

I can summarize my thoughts and opinions about *The Interview* as follows: First, it's way too childish. Many parts in this movie are very different from the reality of North Korea. I guess I have nothing to say to people who insist that it is just a comedy that people would expect to watch while eating popcorn and sitting on the couch, and that no one expected *The Interview* to be anything more serious than *Meet the Parents*. Since it was the first major Hollywood film depicting North Korea, I just hoped that it would be slightly better than a B-class comedy movie.

Secondly, what do I think of the cyber attacks, if North Korea did carry them out against Sony Pictures? Well, for one thing, it is premature to blame North Korea for the cyber attacks. None of us definitively knows that North Korea carried them out. Even if North Korea is responsible for the cyber attacks, I think Sony Pictures got what they deserved. If they decided to make a movie about the Supreme Leader of North Korea, they should've seen what was coming.

And finally, what would North Koreans think of this movie if they watched it? They would feel resentment toward the producers of this movie rather than being critical of Kim Jong Un and the North Korean government. North Koreans are less loyal to the leader than in the past, and they fantasize about capitalism while being displeased with the North Korean government. But they're still confined to the territory of North Korea and Kim Jong Un is the Supreme Leader they pay utmost respect to.

The Supreme Leader is a father figure to all North Koreans. Thus, it will inevitably bring harmful consequences to satirize and lampoon him in a movie like that. For example, even if some children are deeply displeased with their parents, it doesn't help to make fun of their parents in front of them. No matter how lousy your parents are, they're still your parents.

The movie also portrays a reality that's very different from what North Koreans know. The movie will only make them divert their anger and resentment away from the North Korean government and toward the United States.

But please bear in mind that all of this is my very personal opinion.

Do North Koreans really believe the government's propaganda?
DT: This is a very complex matter, but in simple terms, some do and some don't. From my own research, it seems that those who live near the Chinese border or in large towns and cities, and who consume foreign media, are most likely to reject government propaganda. The elderly, and those who live in the countryside, are less likely to question it.

Mina Yoon:
I would say in North Korea, there are two sorts of people: Those who have no doubt that North Korea is the center of the world and its leader is superhuman, and those who do not. You might wonder, then, what the ratio of each is.

Unfortunately, I can't give you a clear-cut number. That's because in North Korea it is very hard to know what others are really thinking. Because of the strict regulations on speech, people cannot openly exchange their opinions with others. However—from my very subjective impression—around 70–80 percent of North Koreans are probably in the latter category.

Let me tell you why I assume this.

Before 1994, when North Korea was ruled by Kim Il Sung, people received food rations from the government. At that time, you really didn't have much to be worried about when you finished all your given work for the day. People believed that they were enjoying the happiest life on earth in return for their consistent loyalty to their leader. At that time, the government's propaganda seemed to be working pretty well.

However, the situation has since changed. Far from receiving regular food rations, these days, even the water and electricity supply is limited. People have to manage on their own through the markets, instead of depending on the government like they once did. Furthermore, there is so much information coming in now from the outside. As such, people don't believe everything the government tells them any more.

However, I would assume that 20–30 percent still take the propaganda as the complete truth. I myself used to be living proof of this. My father, who was a military officer, raised his kids as radical communists. Because what I learned at school matched with what my father told me, I did not need to question anything.

Father used to tell me that we North Koreans had been liberated from Japanese colonization and American threats only because the people had worshiped their leader so sincerely. He said without our leader, Kim Il Sung, we would have had to live miserably just like the Japanese or South Koreans—who were deprived of all basic dignities as human beings.

Growing up, I once heard horrible stories about a Korean girl who went to school in a *Hanbok* (a traditional Korean costume) and had her *Hanbok* ripped off with a knife by her Japanese classmates. I also heard about South Korean kids who had to shine the shoes of American soldiers to earn their own tuition. Listening to those stories of our fellow Koreans, my little heart was broken and I often thought about possible ways to bring all those people to

North Korea. But my father told me that it was because of the South Korean government and the U.S. that these people could not come to North Korea, even though they wanted to. He concluded that this was why we should drive the U.S. military out of the Korean peninsula as soon as possible and reunify Korea. That was the only way that North Korean and South Korean people could prosper together, he said.

When I was a kid, in my eyes my father was a truly great person. He always put other people's happiness before his own and he lived his life primarily for the community, society and nation that he belonged to. I was deeply proud of my father, a man who was so different from others. I often thought I wanted to be an even greater person than him, and from time to time, I pictured myself becoming a party officer or army executive member, even though I was a girl.

Looking back, thanks to my father's education, I was inspired to think thoroughly about the true nature of our society, community and nation, and agonized over what it means to live a meaningful and valuable life. My conclusion was that I should be loyal to the government. I believe this conclusion contributed to my later decision to serve in the military.

I know it may sound a bit silly, but we—I would like to use the North Korean military "we" to express what I felt part of—felt good that our work had a visible influence on the attitudes of the South Koreans and Americans. To be more specific, I was told that when we took a strong stance in developing cutting-edge nuclear weapons, then the U.S. would often propose a return to negotiations in response. At those talks we could then ask the Americans to provide us with rice or other scarce resources, or lead them to loosen the economic blockade against us. That's what I read from the education material, too. In short, I learned that "Our leader's courage and audacity conquered the world."

I remember there were stacks of corn sacks with "Gifts from the U.S." written on the bags. I later found out that these bags were actually donated by the U.S. and were not in fact an American tribute to us. I was told that the Americans gave us the rice because they were afraid of us! I had no idea about the truth then. I was simply proud to be part of the military in such a powerful nation, and when I sometimes ran into the posters saying "The world runs around Chosun," I felt very proud of myself—and my country.

Reading about the propaganda and ideological education in North Korea, you might start feeling a bit concerned. Well, I would say you don't really have to be. That's because more and more North Korean people are realizing that theirs is not a normal nation. Just look at me—someone who used to be truly loyal to the government but who eventually left North Korea. Am I not a living example of the recent changes in North Korea?

You see, these days, many North Koreans criticize their government in front of other people.

I once worked as a vendor in the market selling corn. I vividly remember a rumor once that there would be a distribution of food rations for a couple of days to celebrate Kim Jong Il's birthday. But when my colleague in the market—an older lady—heard of the rumor, she scoffed at it, saying:

"Oh…I do not buy it. Do they expect me to believe what they are saying after all these scams? How many times have we been deceived by the government?

"We'll only get rations after the grains are processed, cooked, eaten and pooped out—when I see the starving mutts trying to eat them.

"Look at the currency revaluation:* it's always the people who suffer. I don't believe anything or anyone any more… come to think of it, I feel so bad about your generation."

I thought her outburst was both amusing and realistic, but at the

---

* The currency revaluation she mentions was the 2009 decision to lop two zeroes off the North Korean Won, with citizens given just seven days to change a maximum of 150,000 Won in cash. The real value of that amount was just US$30, meaning that anyone holding more than that lost the remainder. The revaluation functioned as a cash grab against the emerging trading class, who held lots of Won in cash. Today, traders understandably use Chinese Yuan or other foreign currencies instead.

same time, her words made me feel depressed about the dark future lying ahead for our generation.

Writing this, I feel heavy-hearted. All those memories and the agonies that I went though—even after I decided to leave North Korea—are coming back to me all at once. But people say pain can be reduced when shared with others, and I think this is true.

Do North Koreans disapprove of the regime's nuclear program?
DT: It is a common criticism that the DPRK spends huge amounts of money on its nuclear program, whilst millions of North Koreans continue to live in abject poverty. It may surprise you to learn that despite this, most North Koreans seem to approve of the nuclear program. That doesn't necessarily mean that they support the government behind it, but rather, they believe that having nuclear weapons will prevent their country from being pushed around by others.

To understand how a state like North Korea can exist, you have to understand Korea's history and self-image as a small—and divided—nation colonized by Japan, and bullied by China, the U.S., and Russia. It is the people's sense of past humiliations, and fear of a repeat, that the DPRK government feeds off.

Je Son Lee:

No, to my knowledge most ordinary North Koreans don't have negative opinions of the regime's nuclear program.

When I was still living in North Korea, the regime had a successful nuclear test. People were very proud of it. We once had a town hall meeting where my neighbors talked about how the U.S. could not boss us around anymore. Most North Koreans are very aware of the fact that other countries make fun of and look down upon North Korea. North Koreans think that the main reason for this is our poverty. North Koreans are well aware of their country's status in the international community.

In fact, when North Koreans return after spending some time abroad, people are curious as to know how North Koreans are perceived in other countries. Those North Koreans would tell their neighbors that North Korea and its people are usually looked down upon. People take great interest in this and word spreads quickly among the people.

In my hometown, many of my neighbors frequently visited China, without permission from the government. Still, they eventually voluntarily return to North Korea because they get discriminated against in China. When you're a North Korean in China, they treat you as if you're always starving. The moment you say you're from North Korea, they would throw food at you, saying things like, "You poor thing, you must be starving! Here's food!" Incidents like this make North Koreans feel self-conscious.

Therefore, North Koreans become very proud when they hear that North Korea has become a *de facto* nuclear state. When North Koreans hear news like this, they tend to think: "Our nation may be poor. But we can be one of the most powerful and influential nations in terms of defense."

Unlike South Korea, North Korea invests heavily in history education, especially the period of Japanese imperial rule and the era following independence. As many people know, the Japanese committed unpardonable atrocities against unarmed, innocent Koreans. The North Korean government highlights these acts of brutality and the agony people face when they suffer the loss of their country. The North Korean government justifies nuclear weapons as a means of protecting the nation.

The brutality of the Japanese and U.S. military are depicted in textbooks. North Koreans read such textbooks from their kindergarten years. Pictures and graffiti of Japanese and American soldiers committing acts of violence are painted on the buildings of kindergartens, schools, and offices in North Korea. If you grow up being brainwashed and exposed to such an environment from kindergarten onwards, how would you feel? North Koreans grow up realizing the importance of protecting their own country.

This leads to the justification of the possession of nuclear weapons. The North Korean government doesn't teach its people about the negative side of the nuclear program. So, ordinary North Koreans have no way of finding out how dangerous nuclear weapons can be.

I'd like my readers to keep in mind that this is purely my opinion and experience from my time in North Korea. But from what I've seen, North Koreans are in favor of their government's nuclear program for one reason: It will prevent a return to the time when Koreans had to suffer under the U.S. military or Japanese imperialism.

Are North Koreans allowed to use the Internet? And can they communicate with the outside world?
DT: For a time, certain embassies in Pyongyang would leave their WiFi open so that passers-by could get online. The government put a stop to it, as they simply do not want their citizens to have free access to information. Internet access is strictly controlled, and despite persistent rumours of liberalization, no concrete reform has yet taken place. It is common for North Korean organizations to have one email address, which will be checked by one designated senior person. If you want to get in touch with someone by email, it may take months to receive a reply.

Je Son Lee:

Internet use is quite limited in North Korea. At least in my hometown, where I was born and raised, people didn't know what the Internet was. The Internet does, in fact, exist in North Korea, but not everyone has access to it.

In other countries, anyone can send an e-mail by a simple click. Until 2008, all you could do using the Internet in North Korea was log onto the library website of universities, such as North Korea's prestigious Kim Il Sung University. Still, being able to sit in a chair and view documents from Pyongyang online was a sensational experience.

What the North Korean government is most afraid of is the gathering of like-minded people who have the same opinions on social issues. That's because they never know when the people might decide to instigate an uprising. To prevent disorder, there are laws in North Korea against three or more people gathering together; of course, this law, like others in North Korea, isn't always enforced. Still, it is true that North Korea won't approve any kind of gathering of people not initiated by the government.

But still, the government allowed the people to connect with each other on mobile phones within the domestic network. I think it did so for the following reasons: First, they were still able to block communication with people from outside North Korea on the phone network. Second, although it has become easier for North Korean people to share their opinions by messaging each other, at least for now most people hold similar beliefs and opinions on many issues.

North Korea did its people a big favor by allowing them to own mobile phones and connect with each other within the domestic network. But the risk they were taking was not that great. One thing is certain: The government will keep an eye on its people.

However, there are other forms of media through which North Korean people can see the outside world: radio transmitted from South Korea; Chinese TV channels; DVDs (smuggled from the outside world, South Korean and American in particular); and magazines. Of course, all of these make their way into North Korea via

China. *Hallyu* (the spread of South Korean pop culture) in North Korea and North Koreans' love of imported goods have grown, well beyond what the outside world thinks. Thanks to all of this, authoritarianism in North Korea is gradually being eroded day by day.

This has also had an impact on colloquial language in North Korea. North Koreans have begun to copy South Korean accents and adopt more foreign words. For instance, there's a story that goes, one day, a phone rang in a North Korean house. The father of the household picked up the receiver and said, "Hello?" The next thing he said is, "Son, you have someone calling you from Seoul."

Do you understand what happened here? It was a female classmate of his son who was calling up and spoke with a South Korean accent. Of course, there's no way to confirm whether it really happened. But a story like this is an indication of how popular *Hallyu* is among the younger generation of North Koreans.

There is another example I can give you, and this I can confirm really is happening in North Korea. In North Korea, the word for bathroom is *uisaengsil*, while in South Korea it is *hwajangsil*. Young people in North Korea use the South Korean word to refer to the bathroom these days. This example shows how North Korean society is going through cultural change more rapidly than the outside world might think. North Korea is transforming so rapidly every day. I think it is unfortunate that people in the outside world are unaware of this.

It seems that people outside North Korea still picture the same country that went through the Great Famine of the 1990s. This makes it harder for people to understand North Korea properly. If you'd really like to know about North Korea, break away from the stereotypes you've created inside your head. That's the first step to understanding North Korea.

PART 4

Pyongyang vs. the Rest

[Introduction]

Kim Jong Il himself used to say that as long as he could control Pyongyang, his position would be safe. Pyongyang is the regime's fortress, and as such, only those who the government wants there can stay there. Over the years, Kim Jong Il moved hundreds of thousands of people he considered to be from "disloyal" classes out to remote provinces like North Hamgyeong, and brought those he liked better into the capital to replace them.

There is something like a "border" around Pyongyang. I've seen it with my own eyes—road signs tell you you're about to enter, but there are also three diagonal red lines through the word "Pyongyang" itself. This means you can't come in unless you have a permit. If you're caught in the capital without one, you can get into serious trouble.

You can also, of course, pay a bribe. The figure I heard for entrance to Pyongyang was US$30–50, though this may have changed. Some say this is more expensive than the bribe required to actually leave the country and cross into China!

Why is this? Anyone who has seen both Pyongyang and any other North Korean city will know the answer. Pyongyang isn't rich—there are still many poor people living there, and overall, it may compare to a third-tier Chinese city—but relatively, it is better off than anywhere else. Pyongyang also has status, as the capital city and as a center of culture and opportunity.

So Pyongyangites are the luckier ones, but what of other North Koreans? Read on, and you'll see that there are major differences between the different regions in terms of lifestyle, way of thinking and worldliness.

What is life like in the countryside?

DT: North Korea is obviously changing. But that change is not evenly distributed. Those living in Pyongyang or in those cities near the Chinese border tend to live much more "modern" lives and know more about the outside world than those in rural areas.

Please note that since Jae Young's piece was written, agricultural reforms have been introduced. Farmers are now allowed to keep the majority of what they produce, in direct contravention of standard communist practice (after all, North Korea is not really communist any more; that cannot be stressed enough). This is starting to result in better standards of living in the countryside.

Jae Young Kim:

Life in the North Korean countryside is difficult compared to life in the South Korean countryside. North Korean farmers just don't have access to good equipment or fertilizers, two things that make life considerably harder there. I lived in the countryside and people like me got used to working all year, adjusting to the seasons.

From a young age I had to help my parents with farming, and even during school days I would go to help in the fields between lessons. This is quite normal for a lot of kids, and at school there is even a one-month break for farming every spring and autumn! I hated it so much that I often skipped it, pretending to be ill.

Because we lived at a relatively high altitude, we grew potatoes and corn instead of rice. In addition, we farmed beans, barley, millet and other kinds of grains, while at home, we grew various vegetables on our small plot. So at least my family did not need to pay for fresh vegetables. And although farming takes place all year round, people can't rely on it to sustain themselves, so they have to make money on the side by rearing domestic animals. As such, most homes keep pigs, rabbits, goats or dogs, but in our home we had dogs and rabbits.

As North Koreans do not have modern equipment or much fertilizer, we got used to doing most of the work by hand rather than with the help of machinery. In spring when weeds began to sprout, it would be time to plow the fields. This can be done by oxen or with tractors. But in North Korea, in addition to fuel being too expensive, there aren't many tractors for farmers to use, so most of the plowing is done by oxen. As you can probably guess, oxen therefore were very valuable animals, and we needed to keep them healthy for the entire year's farming work.

While oxen could help plow the fields, they were useless at dealing with weeds. So when new weeds appeared in the fields, they had to be removed by hand because the chemicals we had were not sufficient. Between spring and autumn, we did back-breaking work, weeding the field about four times with a hoe. Not wanting to waste even the weeds, we also used a sickle to cut them down to make compost with them. This compost helped make the soil better, so every summer or autumn we made compost after doing the weeding.

I always helped my parents by sowing seeds in spring, weeding in summer and harvesting in autumn. It became a familiar rhythm to my life. Before school and after school, I tended our home garden. I often took my younger brother to the fields, but he would always disappear if we were weeding—it was hard to make him do any work! As he grew older though, he began to feel bad for our hardworking parents and started coming to work the field without being told to do so.

When it came to harvest time we collected the grains, made sheaves to carry them, then transported it all by oxen or tractor to the granary on the farm. After all of the grain was gathered, it was threshed and then distributed according to farmers' recorded attendance and work attitude. As we lived at a high altitude and had poor soil as well as poor equipment, we didn't end up with much at harvest time. And because farmers must sell crops to buy other household goods, we were always poor.

If we'd had our own private land for farming and were able to engage in market activities, things could have been different. But as you probably know, the North Korean government forbids private ownership of land, and even farming equipment may not be owned by individuals. The only land available for private use is the little bit of land that surrounds a house, and we did all we could with this tiny plot of land.

My parents put a lot of effort into planting vegetables and tending them. Fertilizer and pesticide was supposed to be provided by the state, but it didn't happen regularly. Instead, these chemicals were only to be found in the illegal market, but the government maintained tight surveillance on these kinds of private activities. If you were absent from work, you had to explain yourself and submit a medical report.

Life in North Korea was very communal, you had to work all the time, and the day was always long. Even on holidays or at weekends, you had to work in the garden at home. It was the only way to get by. Life in the South Korean countryside feels much easier, as here there is mechanized farming. I truly hope that agriculture will improve for North Koreans so they can enjoy a better life soon.

What is it like to live in Pyongyang, compared to the rest of the country?
DT: You might not envy someone for coming from Pyongyang, but a provincial North Korean probably would. It is often said that Pyongyang is more or less a different country to the rest of the DPRK. People there have a much better standard of living, but also, they are expected to show greater loyalty to the regime.

If you travel through North Korea, you'll notice the difference immediately. As soon as you leave the capital, the roads turn to dirt tracks, and most buildings are shoddily built.

Ji-min Kang:
When I tell people I'm from Pyongyang, it always raises their attention. People give me a surprising look and always show a keen

interest in learning about my life there. They seem to have this fixed idea of North Koreans from Pyongyang—they see us performing at mass games or wailing uncontrollably over the death of Kim Il Sung. Often I feel they see me as if I came from ancient Rome or another planet.

I have a lot of friends around me now, something I could never really have in North Korea. There, it's very difficult to form proper relationships with other people—when I lived there we were prohibited from privately meeting with more than five people and were under a surveillance system that made us monitor even our closest friends. So the friends I have here in Europe now make me feel so grateful and comfortable.

North Korea is a small country—you can reach anywhere by airplane within an hour. But countless people die there without visiting Pyongyang even once. That's because the government does not allow its people to move from one place to another without the relevant travel documents and a good reason for travel. It is very difficult to do so except on business trips or for family events. Entry into Pyongyang is strictly controlled due to the security of the Kim family and the dense military presence there. So Pyongyang is seen as a dream city that everyone wants to visit: The only city in North Korea that has a theme park and zoo; the only place you can enjoy culture, the arts, and sports. It's even home to the country's only bowling club!

People living outside Pyongyang have never had much of a modern lifestyle and probably won't for the foreseeable future, so it cannot be denied that Pyongyang citizens are a privileged class in this sense. For example, when millions of North Koreans starved to death during the Arduous March, the people in Pyongyang hardly suffered. And during that time I never saw any homeless kids in the streets.

So how did the people in Pyongyang survive in a period of severe nationwide famine? Are they really better off because they are a privileged class? Of course there are indeed a lucky few, such as high-ranking officials and their families, who live under armed guard. But what about the others?

North Korea once had a planned economy that included a rationing system that allowed many people to get their basic necessities from the government. But the severe famine, which followed natural disaster and economic crisis, meant that the government could no longer sustain the rationing system and the normal people outside Pyongyang were pushed out onto the street without being given a chance to adapt to such an abrupt change.

But Pyongyang was a completely different world. No one was dying of hunger, no one was homeless and the rationing system more or less continued to work smoothly, albeit with reduced quantities. Even though the electricity and fuel supply frequently cut off, at least in Pyongyang there was no sign of weakened government control. So while rations were not as abundant as they used to be, the fact that people got rations at all was a substantial advantage.

So what about other the other regions?

Since the rationing system stopped working, people began to embrace the concept of the market economy and gained first-hand experience of it. They were desperate to find food and needed money. So they went to the river or sea to hunt fish and sell in the market. Some people even bred domestic animals and butchered them secretly.

People running restaurants or hotels were often involved in prostitution and brewing illegal alcohol to make money. Some of them even tried to dismantle infrastructure, machinery and ammunition in order to sell the equipment off to Chinese merchants. Almost every market in North Korea became overflown with Chinese goods and consequently North Korea became economically closer to China. In my opinion it was this economic turbulence that ultimately opened the eyes of the North Korean people.

Additional contribution from Je Son Lee:
For many people in the countryside, Pyongyang is a place that is typically viewed more as the residence of the leader than as a traditional capital city. In a nutshell, if North Koreans were Christians, Pyongyang would be viewed in a similar way to Bethlehem. As a Christian might regard the place of God as a holy place, North Ko-

reans living outside Pyongyang perceive the city mainly as a place of holiness. However, these perceptions tend to be limited to those who only see Pyongyang on their TV screens.

Since TV is the primary distribution system for visual propaganda in North Korea, materials are only broadcast after a thorough and strict censorship process that ensures there is as much worship of the leaders as possible, and to reduce excessive information about other countries. As a result, Pyongyang on TV always seems heavenly and dreamlike. But the dream doesn't last forever. People who visit Pyongyang often discover the economic gaps there, and learn how many of the residents actually live in relative difficulty.

Many visiting North Koreans are rather relieved that they live outside Pyongyang. While people outside Pyongyang only need to sweep their streets three times a week, Pyongyangites are required to do so every morning. The reason? Because they live in the same city as the General (Dear Leader). While people in other cities hold small events to celebrate important days such as the birthdays of Kim Il Sung and Kim Jong Il, people in Pyongyang must hold much bigger events. As such, residents in Pyongyang are subject to a stricter and more intensive form of collectivism than those in the remote countryside.

Tell us about some of the different slang found around the country. What does this show us about North Korean society?
DT: What is interesting from the response below is that slang now seems to be national. With bad roads and poor communication links, it was natural in the past that slang terms would arise and be used in localized areas. Today, with the rise of the mobile phone, shared slang spreads throughout the country. Many other sources also state that South Korean slang is very popular among the young now, due to the availability of South Korean drama shows and pop music on smuggled USB drives.

Kim Cheol:
In any society, language reflects the spirit of the times and concretely expresses the people's sensibility in the quickest way. The most typ-

ical means is through slang, and North Korea is no different in that regard. However, the difference between North Korea and South Korea or other countries is that there is no Internet, so there is a clear difference in how slang is created and spread.

A typical slang term from the "Arduous March" [famine] in the mid and late 1990s is *kkotjebi* (flowering swallow). This metaphorical term references North Korean children wandering in search of food, as a swallow looks for a warm place. *Nojebi* (old beggar), and *Cheongjebi* (young beggar) were also in use. After Kim Il Sung's death in 1994, these terms spread along with food shortages.

Nowadays North Korean language is changing in many diverse ways. Slang is more common than in the past, and the increasing numbers of mobile and landline phones is resulting in the creation and spread of slang words nationwide. In the past many words were only known in specific areas.

One example is *Son Ogong*, an expression which can give you some insight into the daily lives of young people. You could say that a young person who doesn't know this word must be a (foreign) spy, such is its popularity. It is originally the name of the red monkey from *Journey to the West*, a Chinese story that is also popular in North Korea as an animation.

In North Korea, though, *Son Ogong* means something very different. *Son Ogong* is a word referring to the things a man looks for in a marriage partner. "Son" refers to a mobile phone, "O" to a motorcycle, and "Gong" to study.

In other words, the ideal marriage partner for a North Korean man is a woman who can provide a mobile phone and a motorbike, and can put you through university. In North Korea, a phone costs about US$200–500 and a motorbike around $500–1200. This might not sound like a lot in South Korea, but to the North Korean middle class it is no small amount.

Your social status is influenced by whether you have a phone or not, and possessing a motorcycle is a kind of display of financial power. Moreover, almost all students at top universities have mobile phones, so those who are relatively poor also feel the need to have one.

Through such slang words, we can see the values of North Koreans. In the past, the word *Gajaemi* (a flounder fish) was used to refer to the ideal bride. "Ga" refers to family status, "Jae" to money, and "Mi" to beauty.

As you can see, part of the definition of a perfect bride used to involve family and appearance, but these days it is all about material items, hence *Son Ogong*. This indirectly indicates that the underground economy is growing and the influence of the government-led socialist economy on the lives of the people is decreasing.

There is also a slang word, *Seokki*, which shows us the influence of North Korea's long military service on people. *Seokki* means an old-fashioned person who habitually interferes in others' lives and causes trouble, whilst being somewhat lacking themselves. This is a word often used by soldiers who have finished military service.

After serving for 10 years, discharged soldiers become ignorant of ordinary social mores and struggle to adapt to civilian life. But much depends upon what kind of military service they did. Those who had regular contact with ordinary civilians during their military service are able to keep up with the changing times and thus can find stable jobs, engage in business, and face no problems in interpersonal relationships after they are discharged.

But those who spent their twenties just taking orders from superiors and socializing with their military comrades face difficulties in their lives once they are discharged. Some become *Seokki* just a few years after returning to civilian life.

Do North Koreans get to go on trips and holidays?

DT: Recently, the government has started advertising holiday trips in newspapers. North Korea does have some very beautiful mountains, and decent beaches; but there aren't that many people with the money and free time to be able to enjoy these things properly. Getting there is difficult, too—trains are a real challenge (as we shall see in a later essay), and roads are often unpaved or cracked.

Jae Young Kim:

We don't get to travel much in North Korea, and during my time there I only went to two or three different places. I once visited relatives in Chongjin, a city in the northeast of the country, and once or twice went to a "revolutionary" town as part of a trip organized by my school. But like other North Koreans I got to explore through my television, learning about famous places like Pyongyang and Mt. Kumgang through a range of TV shows. I was always curious about these places and wanted to visit them, but I sadly never got the chance.

One of the few times I went to another town was on a school trip and it is something that will always stick in my memory. The "revolutionary" town we were visiting was some three hours away from my school, so we had to travel by road to get there. However, our school didn't have a bus and all they could get for the long drive was an old truck.

I remember it was a truck that would have normally been used for delivering coal and the exhaust was really smoky. We had to sit in the back for six long hours to get to and from the town that day. When I came back home, my nose and my white clothes had become black from the coal dust and I felt really travel-sick. This kind of thing was normal growing up in North Korea, with the economic problems affecting everything from school trips to even simple things like trying to go out for a picnic. But despite the problems, we genuinely enjoyed our coal-truck trip.

Moving from one city to another in North Korea is extremely inconvenient. Because of this, people do not often leave their home town unless there is an emergency. First of all, North Korea has pretty bad transport infrastructure; second, people don't have much time for travel; and third, it is not easy to get permission from the government to move from one city to another.

Some people do get to travel, though. My dad had a job that involved a lot of business trips, so he often visited big cities like Pyongyang, Sinuiju, Hamhung, and Nampo. However, these were all work trips and none were for pleasure, as far as I recall.

As I mentioned, we don't have much time for travel anyway. North Korea isn't as free as the outside world so it's a real privilege for anyone to go on holiday, assuming they can get enough time off work in the first place. However, occasionally the government does send a group of people who have worked really hard on special trips, but this only happens once or twice a year.

These kind of trips are not the leisurely holidays that you might enjoy overseas with your friends or family, but instead are more like group tours that follow a government-approved itinerary. On these trips people usually go to North Korea's main sites: Mt. Paekdu, Pyongyang, Mt. Chilbo, and Mt. Kumgang. Fortunately for those lucky enough to go on these holidays, the government pays for everything and all the facilities and services are provided for free.

My friend used to work in Dol Kyuk Dae, a government office, and went on one of these special trips as a reward for her hard work. She told me she really enjoyed her trip, having the chance to go all over the country to see Mt. Paekdu, Mt. Kumgang, and even a hot springs spa in Kyungsung! The government paid for everything to give her a great holiday and she only needed to bring a little bit of money for herself.

I know that there are some really fortunate people in North Korea who have enough time and money go to nearby beaches or valleys with friends or family. One household in my town was quite rich and they used to rent a car to go the beach sometimes. But, this is not a common situation and most people just go to the closest valley or mountain when they have free time, quietly enjoying the environment or spending time fishing.

I myself never got the chance to go to the beach in North Korea. I saw beaches on TV a lot but I didn't have a chance to go in person because I lived so far away from the sea. Maybe that is why I love beaches now and enjoy eating seafood so much! I am happy that I can now go to the beach anytime I want and enjoy holidays by going on trips, things I didn't get the chance to do in North Korea.

Are there regional rivalries in North Korea?

DT: If you took the average newspaper article on North Korea as a guide, you'd end up thinking that North Koreans are brainwashed robots who all think and act in the same way. It is bizarre to even have to point out that this is not true. One way of showing you it isn't true is by drawing your attention to the fact that North Koreans have different regional rivalries and stereotypes.

Je Son Lee:

Regional rivalries exist in North Korea, but not to the extent of those in the United States or South Korea. Regional rivalries exist between Northerners and Southerners in the U.S. and between Gyeongsang and Jeolla residents, for example, in South Korea. Regionalism in North Korea is not that prevalent.

But people do have names to call those from other provinces. It's hard to tell whether people from other regions in North Korea have the same opinion. But I'll tell you everything I know about the regionalism that existed in my hometown in North Korea.

First, Pyongyang: The image of Pyongyangites is that they are lazy people who like to have fun in life. I think there's some truth in this. I met many people from Pyongyang while I was in North Korea and most of them were more into enjoying themselves rather than working. People in rural areas are more honest about their feelings. Therefore, when they don't feel like working or studying, they speak their mind and say that they want to take the day off.

But people from Pyongyang aren't direct and they won't speak their mind. So, when they don't feel like working, they don't want to say it directly, probably because they don't want to offend you. But they will find a way to get out of work earlier, anyway. I'm not saying this applies to all people in Pyongyang. But this is the notion most North Koreans have about people from Pyongyang.

Second, people from Chagang Province: Again, I'm not saying this is true about everyone from Chagang Province, but people think that those from Chagang are more likely to be frauds than people from other regions. Back in my hometown, seven out of 10 people who were scammed, got scammed by those from Chagang Province. Chagang Province was not that far away from my province, but they spoke with a very different accent. People in my hometown sound very abrupt and stern. But people in Chagang Province speak very gently, which makes people feel comfortable. Thanks to this, those from Chagang Province find it easy to scam people from my province.

In fact, I got scammed three times in North Korea, and all three times it was someone from Chagang who scammed me. Fortunately,

I got my money back in the end, but it took lots of time and effort to catch them and get my money back. Since then, I have become more cautious toward people from Chagang Province. Of course, not everyone from Chagang Province is a crook, but I can't help but be suspicious and have low opinions of those from Chagang Province.

Third, people from Hwanghae Province: They're the most innocent, naïve people in North Korea. There's one legendary story: During the Japanese occupation, when some Hwanghae people were captured and being transported by a Japanese police officer, when he fell asleep on the way, they didn't even dare to run away. Instead, they would try to wake him up by telling him, "Mr. Police Officer, we won't get there in time. Please, wake up."

Next, people from Hamgyong provinces [north and south]: Women from Hamgyong tend to be more tough and aggressive than those from other regions. I think those are good qualities for women to survive in this world. But because of their nature, people don't want to deal with women from Hamgyong. Back in my hometown, we had a neighbor from Hamgyong. People didn't like her because she was loud and she would do anything to get her way. When she sensed that people started avoiding her, she tried to change her attitude and later, she became more accepted in my hometown. Still, most women from Hamgyong make good housewives since they're tough and they work hard to support their families.

Lastly, people from Ryanggang Province: Ryanggang Province is the most capitalist province in North Korea. Everything has a price there. People in Ryanggang must be very used to it, but to people in other regions this capitalist culture seems heartless. But surprisingly, Ryanggang people are the most giving people in North Korea. Ryanggang Province is where most *kotjebi*—homeless children who wander in search of food—settle, because people there are likely to give them more food out of generosity.

Because of the viciously cold weather in Ryanggang, it isn't the ideal place for farming or growing fruits. Yet, these *kotjebi* head to Ryanggang because people there are the biggest givers. In other provinces and regions, when *kotjebi* steal food, people are likely to chase after them, hit them, and take the food back. But in Ryang-gang, they don't. Most of the time, they'll voluntarily feed them. My own mother even took *kotjebi* to our house and invited them to have dinner with us. She also shared some of our holiday foods with them. One of them stopped by our house later and thanked us. He told us that he stopped begging for food and began running small errands for people, and even started a family. Before, I didn't understand why my mom would invite *kotjebi* to have dinner with us at our table. But after I met this guy, I changed my mind and realized that my mom had done the right thing and even changed the man's life.

What are North Korean trains like?

DT: The longest train journey in Korea is probably Seoul–Busan, a trip which can be made in around three hours on the fast KTX train. However, as Je Son Lee explains, an equivalent journey in North Korea takes 24 hours—and that's just when everything is working according to plan, which most of the time it isn't. That old line about dictators making the trains run on time has not been true of the three Kims.

Je Son Lee:

First of all, few people can afford to take a train purely for leisure. Train fares are expensive for most people. There are other obstacles, too: You need to obtain a permit to travel from one city to another. You're not allowed to simply hop on a train and travel to another city for sightseeing or because you just feel like doing it. You need to obtain a permit first. It takes a lot—and I mean a lot—of effort to get one, and if you're applying to get a permit to travel to Pyongyang or towns near the Chinese border, you need to pay a lot more money in the form of bribes to officials.

Most people travel to other towns for the weddings of relatives living in other parts of the country. But sometimes people lie about this. The government is highly likely to issue a permit if you state that the purpose of your trip is to attend the wedding of a relative. A bribe is still required, though.

North Koreans who travel on trains may fall into three categories. The biggest are vendors, then people on business trips, and then travelers. However, just because you have a permit doesn't necessarily mean that you can purchase a train ticket. In North Korea, there is only a limited number of seats you can buy at the price set by the government. For example, if there are 20 seats available, government officials take half of them and give them to people they know. Of the remainder, touts take five to seven of them in order to give them to people they know. Now, only three to five tickets are left for everyone else to purchase. At all times, there are more people trying to buy tickets than there are tickets available.

Some people then pay over the odds to get a ticket. You have to reward the tout handsomely, and even still this is almost impossible unless you are well-connected with the people working at the ticket booth. Basically, it takes a lot of money, effort, and connections to get on a train. Yet, there are some people who manage to get on without out a permit or a ticket—they just bribe government officials on the train by shoving a large amount of cash in their pockets. Bribing these people is the most hassle-free way to travel.

However, people working on the train regularly change shifts during each train ride. So you need to pay tips to the new employees every time the shift changes. It costs more money, but it guarantees comfort on the train. Usually, it is traders who choose to travel this way. Traders usually carry illegal goods such as drugs with them, so they have to hand out bribes. In return, their safety is guaranteed for the whole train ride. Since most crewmembers ask for a lot, ordinary travelers get permits and tickets through the regular process.

As far as I can remember, people weren't assigned seats until the year 2000. So, as long as you had a ticket, you could take any seat available, first-come, first-served. So as soon as the train pulled in, passengers would rush to get the best seats. There were more people coming in through the windows than the doors. Windows began to crack as too many people tried to climb through them while carrying big suitcases.

During the summer, it was fine without windows. But in winter, your hands and feet would freeze, as the temperature drops well below zero in North Korea. Often, people lost their belongings and it was usually well-built people who got the best seats on the train. Thankfully, assigned seats means that we don't have windowless trains now.

When I was a little girl, I went on a train trip with my uncles. Before that trip, I never knew how difficult it was to guard my seat and belongings on the train. Thanks to my uncles, we managed to get good seats. But four adults had to take turns guarding our belongings when one of us wanted to use the bathroom.

A train ride from Hyesan to Pyongyang usually takes 23 hours and 50 minutes, if the train leaves on time. But due to electricity shortages, it normally takes three to four days—and it could even take up to seven to 10 days. Once it took 20 days for the train to reach Pyongyang after it left Hyesan. Since passengers have to spend a lot of time together on the train, you end up becoming really good friends. Often, people make friends for life on the train.

North Korea doesn't have a proper banking system, so most people keep cash with them at all times. But due to delays, people often run out of money before they reach their destination. So people bring lunchboxes. In winter, they bring as many lunchboxes as they can, but in summer, food goes bad pretty quickly. So, people get out at stops and stock up. Restaurants and kiosks near the stations always overcharge people, so it is easy to run out of money.

If someone skips a meal one day, he'll pretend he isn't hungry. But if he starves himself for two or more days in a row, he'll begin to stare at you while you're eating. You would feel inclined to share some of your food with him. Plus, after staying on the train for days without a shower, he'll begin to look like a vagrant. After four or five days on the train, you cannot tell a passenger from a *kotjebi* (homeless child).

At the beginning of the journey the train is loaded with water. But it runs out of water on the way to the final destination, so people can wash their faces only when the train briefly stops at a station. It is a great relief if the station has a washbasin. If it doesn't, you have to buy a bottle of water. When people run out of money, they sell some of their belongings to other passengers onboard (but in this case, they get only one fifth of the original price). Or sometimes they borrow money from another passenger. But you never know whether they will pay back the money later. Of course, there are some bad people who don't pay back. But some people feel so grateful that they return the favor for a bigger amount later. When you build a friendship that way, it usually lasts a long time.

The Outside World

[Introduction]

At the heart of the DPRK myth lies the idea that the world outside Korea is a scary, barbaric, untrustworthy place. The essential social contract between Kim Il Sung and the people was that in return for absolute loyalty, he would guarantee both food on the table and protection from all those scary foreigners—particularly Japanese and American ones.

This is a product of Korea's history—one of division by the Soviet Union and the U.S., colonization by Japan, and vassalization by China. Of course, Korea isn't the only small country to have been bullied by bigger ones. But in both North and South Korea, governments have found it highly expedient to play up this narrative.

Even when Korea was still a monarchy, the country had a reputation as "the Hermit Kingdom." While Japan was busy modernizing and trading in the late 19th Century, Korea attempted to retreat into itself. This did not help prevent Korea from losing its sovereignty to Japan in 1910, as the country was militarily very weak and internally divided as well. The spirit of isolationism remains though, and North Korea's leaders seem to think that isolationism plus strictly enforced unity—and nuclear weapons—will preserve their nation as an island of pure Koreanness.

Today, it is only possible to leave North Korea if one has permission. Permission is only given to elites, or those with enough money to bribe their way out. The regime treats those who leave and don't

come back as traitors, and severely punishes the family members they leave behind.

Those who are denied something become more curious, though. Judging by the uncontrollable level of demand for foreign TV, music, and movies, North Koreans are extremely interested in what is going on beyond their borders.

What do North Koreans think when they see foreigners in their country?

DT: From my own experience, people in the main areas of Pyongyang aren't that surprised when they see foreigners. There aren't many tourists by Seoul's standards, but relative to 10 years ago, it is pretty easy to see a non-Korean face in Pyongyang these days. That said, when a group of five of us were allowed to take a jog around the city without guides, there were plenty of people who did a double-take at the sight of us!

Elsewhere, people will definitely stare. But that doesn't mean they dislike you. It's more a matter of curiosity.

Jae Young Kim:
It is easy to forget how big a country North Korea is. People's perception of foreigners differs dramatically, depending on which part of the country they are from. In the past, propaganda efforts were extremely successful at brainwashing most North Koreans, creating mistrust and suspicion towards foreign visitors. We were led to believe that foreigners were a real threat to national security, and that most of us would never see a foreigner in our lives.

The lack of foreigners would seem like proof of the government's ongoing protection of its people—the idea of meeting a foreigner would fill some people with fear! But growing up near the Chinese border, it didn't take long for me to realize that all this information was wrong. Chinese people often came into North Korea for business or other reasons, and I remember when I was little, meeting Chinese visitors amazed me. I would brag about it at school and my friends wouldn't know what to say.

But in the inland areas it is a different story. One of my North Korean friends living in South Korea still feels awkward meeting foreigners and often perceives them to be a threat, because people from his region were isolated for so long. This way of thinking remains intact among some North Koreans, due to the combined effect of intensive propaganda and a complete lack of contact with foreigners while growing up. Things like this go to show the brainwashing effect of the North Korean education system.

Our ideological schooling tells us from a young age that foreign countries—especially the United States—are the reason North Korea is so poor, due to sanctions. As such, North Koreans who only had this kind of education feel a stronger revulsion towards foreigners than those of us from the border areas.

An additional question: How do you feel about the small but steadily-increasing international tourism industry in the DPRK?
DT: I personally believe that increasing tourism in the DPRK would be a very positive move. Frequent visits by foreigners will help improve the perception of North Korean people toward foreigners

whilst promoting an opening and vitalization of the economy. North Koreans fully understand that their country is poor. They also know that foreigners are richer than them. So they hope to have a better life by interacting with the outside world—and tourism is one way they can do it.

Many North Koreans know well that areas that have a lot of foreign visitors, such as Mount Kumgang [though tourism from South Korea stopped in 2008], and more recently Rason, have a higher standard of living. Despite the effects of the propaganda, the average North Korean today isn't going to harass foreign visitors, despite the rumors some foreigners hear. If I were still in North Korea, I would not think in that way. Rather, I would believe that increased tourism will help make my life better. Of course, tourism will not affect the general public directly, but it will affect them indirectly by increasing job opportunities and raising the total income of the country.

So you see, international tourism helps many North Koreans and promotes the opening of the country. I believe North Koreans would agree with me on that. My personal opinion is that the expansion of the tourism industry will make the hard life of the North Korean people easier.

What rumors were there about the outside world when you lived in North Korea?
DT: Government propaganda famously used to tell North Koreans they had "nothing to envy," but these days, citizens are well aware that their country is very poor. Information about the wealth of China and South Korea does flow into the DPRK, but not in a complete and verifiable fashion. As a result then, it cannot be surprising that there are plenty of rumors about how neighboring countries are lands of milk and honey.

Jae Young Kim:
There were lots of rumors about the outside world when I lived in North Korea, usually focused on how much richer the rest of the

world was compared to us. Nobody knew where these rumors started, but they always left us curious and wanting to find out more.

With China being the closest neighbor, most of the rumors I heard about the outside world revolved around how much better life was there. It was common to hear things like, "China is so rich that you can't even compare it with North Korea," or "Chinese people own two cars per household and all live in two-story houses." Obviously it's not common to own a car in the DPRK, so it was intriguing to hear these kinds of things.

We also knew that Chinese people had food and clothes that would have been unimaginable for most North Koreans. There was one rumor which was especially crazy, that, "Chinese dogs sometimes refuse to eat because they are so full." But these stories weren't just based on rumor, because many of us knew people who had gone to work in China for a few months and come back with enough money to live like a king in North Korea for years.

Not everything we heard was good, though. We heard some pretty scary rumors about China, too. One was about a town called In-Dwejii (인돼지/Human Pig), where the Chinese were rumored to be growing human beings in a pigpen—just like animals. People said you'd be sent to that town if you accidentally crossed the border, and that if you went there you'd never come back. I'm not sure where these stories came from but I guess they weren't enough to stop a lot of people from crossing the border to China regardless.

Of course, rumors also swirled about prosperity in South Korea, too. There was a saying that South Korea was much, much cleaner than China. People would say, "When you travel three days on the Chinese train, your socks get so dirty. But even after spending a week on a South Korean train, your socks stay really clean."

These rumors about the outside world weren't things you could gossip about freely with friends. That's because if you said something "wrong" about the outside world, there was a chance you could be punished for promoting non-socialist influences. As a result, these rumors were only shared between close friends or family—people you could trust. And this being the case, it always blew me away that there were so many rumors to be heard about the outside world.

With all the stories I'd heard, it was easy to think that life would be full of luxurious comfort as soon as I left North Korea. But after crossing the border for the first time, the reality of China became apparent and things appeared very different to what I'd imagined. However, it was safe to say that the Chinese did have a richer life than we did.

The most impressive part about arriving in China for me was how bright the city was at night and how people could watch TV 24 hours a day. In North Korea, we had a serious lack of electricity and I could only watch TV on weekends or holidays. So words can't describe how amazed I was by the fact that you could use electricity all day and all night. And at the start, every day in China felt like a holiday because I was able to watch TV all of the time!

Another thing that really surprised me in leaving North Korea was that in all of the countries I went to, you could say whatever you wanted. In contrast, back home we always had to use proper terms for talking about the government and our leader. Naturally, it would also be impossible to even think about criticizing them in public.

When I finally got to South Korea, I was really shocked by the fact that you could talk about the president without using his formal title—and even talk badly of him openly! This was all very new to me. You see, when I arrived in China I actually had an argument with a local friend who was talking about Kim Jong Il without using his formal title. For me this was so shocking that I insisted he must always use Kim Jong Il's official title when talking about our "Dear Leader." He just laughed at me!

There were many differences between the rumors I heard in North Korea and the reality of life outside. Of course, there are also many poor people in South Korea and China, so it was incorrect to think that everybody would be enjoying a luxurious life in those places.

Sometimes I miss North Korea. Thoughts of my hometown and family trouble me a lot. The first thing on my mind is always my parents and my lovely home. Especially during holidays or birthdays, I feel a part of my heart is empty from missing my family as much as I do. I guess people call this homesickness. I just wish I could come home after a good day and share my news with my family.

When I see my friends in South Korea, I miss my friends back in North Korea and the great memories we have together. I do my best to keep the memories of my hometown fresh in my mind, so that I can be satisfied with my current life in South Korea.

What do people who live near the border think about China when they look across at the bright lights?
DT: There are places along the Korean side of the DPRK–China border that are close enough to literally throw a stone and hit a Chinese person on the other side. People even trade with Chinese by floating baskets of goods back and forth across the Tumen River, which is extremely narrow at some sections.

It is impossible for those living in border towns like Hyesan or Sinuiju not to notice that those looking back at them are much richer than they are. They also notice the 24-hour electricity and cannot help but wish that North Korea was more like China.

Je Son Lee:

Issues such as human rights or political systems are considered unimportant by most North Koreans. As a result, while those of us living along the border did envy the Chinese, it was usually for material reasons: jealousy of the bright lights and products we knew to exist there. Because access to electricity outside Pyongyang is not the best, most of us in the country are used to lighting up lamps with paraffin and gasoline to see in the dark, suffering from the heat of flames, unbearable smoke and nasty odors every single night. As such, the bright lights in nearby China made the country look like a paradise.

Of course, those living along the border are but a small percentage of all North Koreans, meaning that even the thought of seeing Chinese lights at a distance is inconceivable for the vast majority of people living in the DPRK.

Once, when my 10-year-old cousin came to visit my house from a small town far from the border, I took her out for street food at a kiosk in a night market. As it was at dusk, the entire town was getting darker and darker, but thanks to light from nearby China we could see where we were going. Suddenly, my cousin clapped her hands together and yelled excitedly, "Wow, that looks amazing! Je-son, what is that place? Can you please take me there and show me around?"

I was so shocked by her reaction to the lights that I started sweating! Because she responded to them in such an excited, high-pitched voice, she immediately grabbed everyone's attention. I felt so embarrassed that I grabbed her wrist and dragged her into an alley so no one would stare at us, but she looked up at me, wondering why I was so embarrassed and nervous.

"Eun-joo, that is China, not our country. You can be arrested by security guards [police] for saying things like that. Do not ever talk about that place. Do not ever stare at that place. Do you understand?"

But she snapped back at me, unable to understand why we weren't allowed to talk about it. "Je-son! Why is that that town is full of flashing lights when we don't have any here? Why are we not allowed to look at that town?"

I didn't know what to say to her. I didn't know how to explain to her that it can be a crime to be curious about cultures in other countries. So, I gave up and decided to bring her home for the night.

Later on, seeming to be lost in deep thought, she suddenly asked: "Je-son, have you ever been to that place?"

I told her I hadn't.

"Je-son, when I grow up, I will make sure I go to that place [China] for sure, even if it's just once. Will you come with me?"

I explained to her that China is not just a place where people can freely move in and out, and that if we were to go there we would be committing treason for having defected from our country.

After that night, my cousin would not see China again for another seven years. It probably was fortunate for her, because if she ever got caught trying to sneak over to China out of sheer curiosity, she may have been subjected to much greater suffering and pain than the conditions she was already living in.

As my story might suggest to you, China is often a place of wonder for North Koreans who don't know much about South Korea. And like my cousin, many North Koreans simply envy the fact the Chinese seem wealthier than them. They care much less about politics or human rights than you might think. Yet strange as it may sound, North Koreans become most envious of China when they are told extravagant stories by those defectors who are sent back after being caught illegally crossing the border. I'm talking about the kind of tales that describe Chinese people as skipping meals when they don't like what's on offer, and having electricity 24/7.

Can North Koreans study abroad?

DT: South Korea is the biggest exporter of students to the United States after China and India. Overseas study in a Western country is something that probably a majority of the South's social elite, and substantial numbers of ordinary people, undertake. This is a result of Korean society's huge focus on education. North Koreans prize education too, but overseas study is an activity barely even open to the "one percent." It may be something more like the 0.01 percent. Kim Jong Un was of course one of them, attending school in Switzerland. Those who do go abroad have their eyes thoroughly opened by the experience, but that does not mean that they can stay behind after graduation…

Kim Yoo-sung:

For most people the answer is a short one: No.

North Koreans cannot go to other countries to study just because they want to. Ordinary people in North Korea don't even know that people in other countries can go abroad for their studies. They wouldn't even know the expression *yuhak* ("overseas study").

There are, however, some people in North Korea who can study abroad—the chosen people. These are, as you may imagine, the children of elites in North Korean society. But even if those chosen children go to another country to study, the North Korean government makes sure to hold their parents hostage while they study abroad. This is to prevent their children from defecting to a third country and refusing to return.

Actually, when one of my South Korean friends went to middle school in Australia, she witnessed how one of her classmates, the daughter of a North Korean diplomat, had to leave her little brother in North Korea while her father worked as a diplomat in Australia. Her entire family went to Australia to stay for the duration of her dad's mission there, but they were forced to leave her little brother behind in North Korea.

If the North Korean government didn't keep her little brother in North Korea, her family could've been tempted to stay away after witnessing how free the outside world was. They could've simply gone to the South Korean embassy to gain South Korean citizenship or could've asked for asylum at another embassy in Australia. But since her little brother was being held hostage in North Korea, they couldn't take that kind of risk.

This is exactly why the North Korean government holds the remaining family members hostage when someone goes to another country to study or work. Those staying abroad know that their family members back in the North could face persecution if they decided to defect to another country.

Many North Koreans dream of traveling to a foreign country to see what it's like. Many of those I knew at home used to say that they would never ask for anything else if they could get on a plane to go to a foreign country once in their lifetimes. But most of them never get the chance.

Those of you reading this could probably get on a plane and go abroad whenever you wanted to. Your government couldn't stop you from doing so. Most North Koreans can't get on a plane even once before they die.

The reason why North Korea doesn't allow its people to go abroad is simple—they're afraid their people will find out the truth about the totalitarian regime. Should a North Korean visit another country, they would immediately find out that all kinds of propaganda in North Korea was outright lies. The North Korean government knows very well that it will bring an end to the regime if North Koreans can freely go to other countries and see the outside world for themselves.

People would realize what a brutal, ruthless dictatorship they live under. They would realize that people in democratic societies have the freedom to criticize and vote for their own presidents and lawmakers. People who have tasted such freedom will demand the same kind of democracy from the North Korean government, and maybe more than that.

Even if the chosen children of the elites get to study abroad, they're never free from the surveillance of the North Korean government. The State Security Department in North Korea watches every movement of North Koreans living and studying abroad until they return to the North.

Also, the State Security Department devises a system that makes everyone spy on each other. If one of them is reported to have made a plan to defect from North Korea for good, the North Korean government makes them return to the country immediately. North Korea makes every effort to prevent the children of elites from defecting.

What does the North Korean government tell you about neighboring countries?

DT: When I worked as a reporter for *The Economist* in Seoul, my bosses (who would fly in whenever "big" things happened involving North Korea) would always have a shock when they saw how North Korean propaganda dealt with the South's then-President Lee Myung-bak. They would release videos of dogs ripping an effigy of Lee to shreds, or of soldiers shooting at targets with his face on them. Sad to say, this is just the way North Korea is.

While South Korea's leaders are referred to as "traitors" and American sell-outs, South Koreans themselves are painted as victims in North Korean propaganda. The real "devil," though, is Japan, due to the colonial history between the two countries. A huge part of the legitimacy myth around Kim Il Sung is built on his anti-Japanese guerrilla years. It serves the DPRK very well to continue to demonize Japan.

Je Son Lee:

If you've read a little bit about North Korea, you'll know that the United States military is considered the main enemy by the government. The North Korean government is supposed to distribute equal amounts of the pie to everyone, but since it fails to do so, it strives to develop nuclear weapons. The North Korean government finds justification for this under the cause of protecting the nation against the United States—the hero North Korea standing tall against the world hegemon, which imposes its power on innocent, weak countries around the world!

The North Korean government strives to educate (or brainwash!) its people by providing materials showing war crimes the U.S. military committed against unarmed Koreans during the Korean War. This works every time. The main logic behind these educational materials is straightforward: Imperialist states such as United States and Japan are bigger in size and have a stronger economy than North Korea. Hence, we—North Korea—need to do our best to maintain our national security against those nations. We can live without bread, but we can't live without weapons (to protect ourselves).

Other than statues of Kim Il Sung, what is the most common sight in North Korea? The answer is war memorials and museums exhibiting the war crimes and atrocities the United States and Japan committed against innocent Koreans during the Korean War and the colonial era. From second or third grade, North Korean students go to those war memorials and museums on excursions. This is how young North Koreans learn the importance of national security. When they see the photos and archives of Americans and Japanese torturing innocent, unarmed Koreans, students are meant to understand that it is even more severe than how it is shown in their textbooks.

North Korea focuses on the importance of maintaining its national security against the United States. But young North Koreans feel more anger toward Japan. The Korean War lasted for just three years (1950–53), but Korea was annexed by Japan for 35 years (1910–45). There are more historical archives about ruthless Japanese imperialism than about the Korean War. Hence, despite the fact that North Korea works so hard to make its people hate America, young North Koreans feel more anger and resentment towards Japan and what they did to Koreans during the annexation and World War II. In this sense, the North Korean historical education system has been successful.

The North Korean government and its people have negative opinions of America and Japan. But North Koreans do not look badly on South Korea. What North Korea always says is, "South Koreans are the poor people we share blood with and who are suffering under American military rule. We shall be their savior soon!"

When two teenage South Korean girls were run over and killed by a U.S. armored vehicle (the Yangju Highway Incident), a public demonstration was held in North Korea, too. The main purpose of this demonstration was to help drive the U.S. military out of South Korea and make sure it didn't happen again. I'm not sure why the

North Korean government staged such a demonstration, but most North Koreans felt anger and sympathy for these teenage South Korean girls who lost their lives.

However, there are hardly any North Koreans who believe that South Koreans are starving under U.S. military rule. North Koreans are not dumb enough to believe that! When North Korean TV news reports on demonstrations staged by South Koreans, we pay more attention to how the South Koreans dress than why they're protesting or going on a strike. North Koreans can tell immediately that South Koreans are better dressed and look better off—they have far better clothes and shoes and are often very stylish people! Most North Koreans know that South Koreans are wealthier and have the freedom to protest against their own government and voice their opinions.

Anyway, North Koreans don't have a bad opinion of South Koreans, because the North Korean government educates them to believe that South Koreans are the people North Korea needs to save and help! North Koreans have a great interest in South Korean pop culture as its dramas, movies and comedy programs have spread across North Korea. In fact, there are many young North Koreans who would want to escape from North Korea if they could see South Korean actors just once in their lifetime. South Korea seems like a kind of heaven that most young North Koreans want to visit.

Now, what do North Koreans think of China? I'm not sure about what the North Korean government thinks of China. But most ordinary North Koreans don't like China that much. North Koreans know that China has a better economy than North Korea. But North Koreans think Koreans are a more civilized and cultured people, with better manners than the Chinese. North Koreans have this notion that Chinese people take a bath only once a year, don't keep their houses clean, wear shoes inside their house and so on—for these reasons, North Koreans think Chinese are filthy and therefore, less civilized than Koreans.

While South Korea is a heavenly place to North Koreans, North Koreans wouldn't ever want to live in China. Most of the time, North

Koreans think China is worse than North Korea. In North Korea, one can find derogatory terms and racial slurs referring to the Chinese and Japanese. But no derogatory terms about South Koreans exist in North Korea. Among South Korea, China and Japan, the North Korean government may hate the South the most. But ordinary North Koreans? They hate Japan the most, with China second only to Japan. But oh boy, North Koreans love South Korea and its pop culture and they want to live there!

What do North Koreans think about the United States?
DT: This is one of those questions where the answer depends entirely on who you ask. Generally, those who still trust in the government are more likely to hate the U.S., and those who do not are more likely to be neutral or positive about the U.S.

When I was in Pyongyang, I asked one of my guides their opinion of America. Her response seemed quite rehearsed, but was one which, I felt, also reflected her true feelings. She liked American people, but not the American government and its foreign policy. In that respect she may not be much different from many people around the world, plenty of Americans included.

Je Son Lee:
The North Korean government publicly declares that the United States is the main enemy of North Korea. But that doesn't mean that all North Koreans agree with them.

The regime incessantly lectures its people about ideology. Their top priority is to brainwash people to worship Kim Il Sung, Kim Jong Suk, Kim Jong Il and Kim Jong Un. But the North Korean government doesn't forget to spend a significant amount of time and effort teaching its people to hate Japan and the U.S. military.

But the regime doesn't succeed in completely brainwashing people all the time. Most people in my hometown, including myself, despised the Japanese and viewed them with disgust and hatred. But we didn't hate Americans. Older people who experienced the Korean War used to tell us that Americans didn't commit the horrible war crimes that the North Korean regime claimed. At least, the elderly in my hometown who were alive during the Korean War didn't witness things like that. The North Korean regime publicizes that U.S. soldiers tore off the limbs of innocent Koreans and cut off eyes, noses and lips and hung them on trees.

But I don't trust such rumors spread by the regime. Old people in my hometown used to tell us a different story. They said American soldiers adored Korean children and showered them with chocolate and gum. Those old people used to tell us that American soldiers were far more humane, and they didn't do heinous things like the Japanese soldiers. That's probably why they used derogatory terms to refer to Japanese whilst referring to Americans as "dear Americans." Since I grew up listening to stories like that, I never had a bad opinion of Americans.

Plus, American action movies and blockbusters were so popular in North Korea. The most popular movies in North Korea were the James Bond series, *Home Alone* and *Mission Impossible*. There were so many other American movies that were available in North Korea. And even if subtitles weren't available, we loved American movies so much we didn't care.

Many American action movies seemed far-fetched to us in North Korea. Those high-tech gadgets and touch screens were mind-blowing. We couldn't believe such technology could exist! We thought such things existed only in the movies. The reason we loved American action movies was because of their main characters. Most main characters in those American movies were always heroes and heroines who saved their town, or even the world, from villains. This is what captivated us.

North Korea teaches its people that those who can save their country and people are the true heroes. North Koreans grow up being taught about the importance of being one of those heroes. Thus, most North Koreans—especially men—always dream of becoming heroes by themselves.

But it's a dream that can never be realized if you live in North Korea. That's why we are drawn to American action movies. Since

North Korea is a highly patriarchal society, girls aren't urged to become heroines. I was just a little girl when I watched those American movies, but they left a long-lasting influence on me. While watching them, I dreamt of becoming a heroine myself to save North Korea! I always wondered: What kind of place is America? What would it be like to live in America?

I'm currently staying in America, taking ESL classes here. One thing that startled me is that Americans are highly individualistic. I know it's a capitalist country and that Americans aren't as collectivist as North Koreans. But Americans were so individualistic and selfish that I found it almost shocking. I even saw an American family at a restaurant that split the bill! As I got used to living in America, I began to think that it's just their culture rather than selfishness. After all, I never had a bad opinion of America in my life. Even when I was living in North Korea, I was always fond of American pop culture.

Now that I'm in America, I have grown to like this country a lot more. People are friendly here and the environment is great, too. On my way to classes every morning, people are mowing their lawns. Oh, how I love the fresh smell of the lawns!

Ji-min Kang:
North Korea teaches its people that the Korean War broke out when South Korea, under the United States' advice, decided to attack the North. It doesn't forget to teach its people that Kim Il Sung defeated the United States military—an army which had never been defeated until it encountered Kim. But none of this is true, of course. It's just propaganda.

My grandfather served in the Korean War. According to him, trains filled with soldiers and war supplies kept coming in every night near the 38th parallel. Immediately before starting the war, this is what North Korea told its soldiers: "According to intelligence services in North Korea, the U.S. and South Korean military are planning a major attack at around 6 a.m. on June 25. This is exactly why we need to launch a pre-emptive attack on them and unify Korea."

But for the first few days of the war, he did not see a single soldier in the South who was ready to fight. Why? Because they weren't planning on launching any attack on the North. You probably know the whole story and how the Korean War ended, destroying much of the country and separating families. But North Korea insists that it was the United States that was the core reason for all the pain suffered by the two Koreas.

In fact, there is an interesting slang phrase known by all North Koreans: "Yeah, I'm an American." It means you admit you're culpable for every fault and problem. In North Korea, the United States is considered the cause of every problem on earth today.

What is ironic, though, is that American pop culture is very popular among North Koreans. Hollywood films such as *Titanic* were a big hit in Pyongyang, too. I'm sure more and more Western pop culture has made its way into North Korea since I left Pyongyang.

Do you think North Korea could beat the U.S. and South Korea in a war?

DT: The DPRK likes to portray Kim Il Sung as having virtually single-handedly driven the Japanese out of Korea and having "won" the war against the Americans in 1953. The North Korea military today is well-manned, but very poorly equipped, so it is highly unlikely the Korean People's Army would be able to win in a conventional war.

The elephant in the room is the nuclear weapons program, which is Kim Jong Un's ultimate insurance policy. The goal is to possess a threat so deadly that the U.S. and South Korea would never dare to pursue "regime change," in spite of the weakness of the rest of the DPRK's arsenal.

Mina Yoon:

If a war breaks out, I don't see any chance for North Korea to win. I believe the morale of the North Korean army is not high enough to make up for the lack of modern weaponry and food. Extreme poverty in North Korea also has impacted the army. Most soldiers in

North Korea are more interested in dealing with hunger than fulfilling their duty. One of my colleagues once said, "I am hungry. I think the government shouldn't neglect hungry soldiers like this, because when people are starving to death, you never know where they might point their guns." Having been raised by a most patriotic father, I was shocked to hear talk of rebellion. But it was me who was different from others.

My colleagues also said, "When war breaks out, you know what I would like to do? I'll just play dead in the mountain of bodies;" or "I would rather be a dead hero than a living beggar." It was unthinkable to say such things back in the '90s. Back then, whoever made rebellious remarks like that was arrested without question. However, these days, it is the person like me, who cannot sympathize with such sarcasm, who is laughed at.

Things have changed in military placement, too. In the past, some people volunteered to join the most dangerous, hardworking troops because they believed it was an honor to lead the way in protecting the nation. However, people now seek to serve in safe units where they can get food rations throughout their 10 years of service. For that, they have to bribe the officers in charge of placement. Parents are willing to spend a fortune to get their children into a good unit, because that will decide the living standard of the recruit for the next 10 years. That is why only people who do not have money or strong family backgrounds end up in dangerous commando units.

Still, there are a few exceptions. One of my childhood friends decided to serve in a commando unit. His father and my father were fellow soldiers, and they both became professional military officers later. We were friends when we were kids, didn't see each other for more than 10 years, and then met up again when he was about to join the military. He said he wanted to go to a commando unit, believing it to be a big honor to serve in one.

When he applied, everyone was desperately opposed to the idea. No one could understand him because commando units were only for kids who have no other choice. His father also tried to stop him. However, he was very stubborn. This teenage boy had watched propaganda campaigns about commando units and their special training on TV and was mesmerized. He finally joined a commando unit, despite everyone's opposition. Unfortunately, the story did not end well: I heard a rumor that he escaped the barracks after a year and a half, and his violation of military rules eventually caused his father to resign from his position. The reason he ran away was the ruthless training and constant hunger.

This story captures the reality of commando units in North Korea. There isn't the special pride or sense of duty that there once was. Even the soldiers in leading elite units, who still get good rations, have changed. In the past, soldiers in elite units were ready to commit suicide for the government and the General. Nowadays, going back home alive is their one and only mission.

My conclusion is that morale of young North Korean soldiers is far too weak to overcome the military's obvious handicaps. Aside from the possibility that North Korea may use nuclear weapons, there is little chance, if any, that North Korea could win a war in light of its poor weaponry and unmotivated soldiers.

I truly hope everything settles down without a war. I know it might not be easy, but I believe there is still a chance to bring about the reunification of North and South Korea without using guns. Maybe the help of surrounding nations and allies could be critical in bringing a peaceful reunification to the Korean peninsula.

Currently, both South and North Korean men are obliged to serve in the military for a certain amount of time. When the two Koreas are reunited, we won't need to maintain compulsory military service. Then, we can convert to a voluntary military system under which only those who truly desire to serve in the military can fulfill their duty. Freedom to decide to go to the military—that would be another great benefit of a reunified Korea.

What should the world do to help North Koreans?

DT: The North Korea "question" is a very difficult one to answer. South Korea and the U.S. have tried both "sunshine" and hardline approaches, and neither has made much difference to the political situation, or to the human rights of North Koreans or the amount of food on their tables. There is also much discussion about China's role in reforming North Korea. There are those who say China has plenty of leverage and could push North Korea to reform if it wanted to, and those who believe that the Kim Jong Un regime will always just do whatever it wants regardless. There is also no guarantee that any humanitarian aid will reach its intended recipients.

So my own view on this is quite sceptical. I think we must *try* to help North Koreans as much as possible, but not get our hopes up too much. But let's see what a group of North Korean defectors think:

Jinwoo Ham:
North Korea's current rulers focus on developing nuclear weapons and missiles, while paying little attention to the well-being of their people.

The international community needs to place heavy sanctions on the DPRK as long as it continues to violate the human rights of its own people and remains unwilling to give up nuclear weapons. That is the only way to make North Korea collapse.

At the same time, the international community also needs to help North Koreans speak up and rebel against the current dictatorship. In order to achieve this, it is necessary to take advantage of all kinds of media including broadcasting, publications, and video to raise public awareness.

Sungha Joo:
This is not an easy question, as the North Koreans need all the help they can get. At this point, however, the kind of help required can be divided into the aid that is required now, and that which will be needed post-unification.

Currently, it is important to put more pressure on North Korea over its human rights abuses. The regime should be made to understand the necessity of improving human rights to develop the country.

After unification, North Korea will, however, need substantial

TOP AND BOTTOM: Kim Il Sung and Kim Jong Il, the first two leaders of North Korea. Unique among the socialist countries for developing a family dictatorship, North Korea is now essentially a feudalistic monarchy with some emergent capitalistic characteristics thrown in. Kim Il Sung, though dead, is "eternal president" of the DPRK, and following his own demise in 2011, Kim Jong Il has been elevated to semi-godlike status as well. It is common to see pictures and statues of both of them together throughout the country. *Photos: Marcel Pedro*

Provincial roads in North Korea are, like this one, not generally busy. The average person may be able to afford a bicycle, but certainly not a car. Things are different in Pyongyang, however. It is even possible to see small traffic jams there these days. *Photo: Marcel Pedro*

TOP AND BOTTOM: Farming is still mostly done with traditional methods, and much of North Korea still has many of the characteristics of a traditional rural society. It is common to see oxen, as was the case until around the 1970s in South Korea. If one visits the North Korean countryside, one will also see children playing in rivers, and their mothers beside them, doing the family washing. *Photos: Marcel Pedro*

TOP AND BOTTOM: Typical houses of rural people in North Korea. Things would not have looked much different fifty years ago. *Photos: Marcel Pedro*

TOP: Laborers working on a railway line. On the building behind are pictures of Kim Il Sung and Kim Jong Il. The text says "long live great leader Kim Jong Un, long live the glorious Workers' Party." *Photo: Marcel Pedro*

BOTTOM: A typical fishing village. Fishing represents about 4 percent of national exports. North Korea sells well over US$100m of its catch to China each year. Some of this is resold to other countries as Chinese, due to UN sanctions against North Korea. *Photo: Marcel Pedro*

TOP: A moped parked on a street in the city of Pyongsong. Mopeds are considered a status item, even to the point where men say you should try and marry a woman whose family can buy you one. These days, they're a valuable business tool for market traders.
Photo: Daniel Tudor

BOTTOM: A fisheries manager oversees work whilst having a cigarette. Note his lapel badge, which portrays Kim Il Sung and Kim Jong Il. All North Koreans are supposed to wear such badges, and place them on their left lapel, close to their heart. *Photo: Marcel Pedro*

TOP: Cosmetics on sale at a street market. The main item you can see here is sun cream, made in North Korea. Most products at such markets are imported in via China, though. *Photo: Marcel Pedro*

BOTTOM: North Koreans taking a photo with a smartphone. Though ordinary people do not have Internet access on such devices, smartphones themselves are becoming popular, especially in Pyongyang and border cities. *Photo: Marcel Pedro*

TOP: An old lady sells cigarettes on the street. This is not technically legal, but if she bribes inspectors with a portion of her earnings, she'll be left alone. *Photo: Daniel Tudor*

BOTTOM: A small street market, where locals can buy meat, vegetables, drinks, and so on. *Photo: Daniel Tudor*

TOP AND BOTTOM: Common street scenes in North Korea. Traders with bicycles carrying goods to market. Note the poor quality of the road in the top photo—most places outside Pyongyang are like this. *Photos: Daniel Tudor*

Young women wear traditional dress (**chima-jeogeori**, or '**hanbok**' in South Korea) and dance.

Displays such as this are very common in North Korea. *Photo: Marcel Pedro*

The Pyongyang skyline, with the famous (or infamous) outline of the Ryugyong Hotel, a still-unfinished 105-story building that symbolizes both the government's ambition and the failure of its economic policies. *Photo: Marcel Pedro*

TOP: A couple walk by the monument to the founding of the Worker's Party, in Pyongyang. It is a common sight to see women in traditional dress in North Korea; the practice is more or less dead in the South (though weddings would be an exception). *Photo: Marcel Pedro*

BOTTOM: These days, Pyongyang looks something like a third-tier Chinese city, rather than the odd place many expect. Apartment complexes like the ones in this photo are being built at a rapid rate. *Photo: Marcel Pedro*

TOP: The Haedanghwa Department Store. Haedanghwa used to be owned by Kim Jong Il's sister, Kim Kyung Hui. These days there is plenty of conspicuous consumerism in the big cities of North Korea, with the new moneyed elite buying designer goods at places like this. *Photo: Marcel Pedro*

BOTTOM: Taxis drive by the People's Palace of Culture in Pyongyang. These days there are something like seven competing taxi firms in the capital. One of these is owned by Air Koryo, the national airline. *Photo: Marcel Pedro*

TOP: The famous Pyongyang Metro, which has two lines and carries around half a million people per day. It's also extremely cheap at 5 won per journey—at the real market rate, this is less than a tenth of a US cent. *Photo: Marcel Pedro*

BOTTOM: A train at standstill in the countryside. North Korean rail journeys are notoriously difficult—a trip from one side of the country to the other could take several days, or even a week. *Photo: Marcel Pedro*

TOP AND BOTTOM: Propaganda posters are everywhere in North Korea. The first promotes reforestation, a major issue for the country. North Korea is one of the most deforested places in the world; this also exacerbates flooding, leading to deaths and the loss of viable farmland. *Photos: Marcel Pedro*

One of North Korea's most famous propaganda images, Kim Il Sung and Kim Jong Il stood at Paektusan, the tallest mountain on the peninsula and one which has huge significance in national myth and folklore. *Photo: Marcel Pedro*

TOP: Factory workers. North Korea is a heavily sanctioned country, but its cheap labor means that there is still plenty of demand. Note that the workers are all female, and supervisors in the background all male. *Photo: Marcel Pedro*

BOTTOM: North Korea is slowly embracing the information revolution. A small number of elite people have Internet access, but for the majority, there is a national intranet named Gwangmyeong. One can even now book Air Koryo flights through it. *Photo: Marcel Pedro*

TOP: School children singing and dancing. The Kim family monarchy is ever-present: the text above them reads, "Thank you, Dear General Kim Jong Un." *Photo: Marcel Pedro*

BOTTOM: Children at an elite school studying foreign languages *Photo: Marcel Pedro*

TOP: A child of the new elite. She has her own bedroom, a TV, and lots of toys; her life may not be so different to a youngster's in South Korea. *Photo: Marcel Pedro*

BOTTOM: A tourist tries out skateboarding at a new facility. The DPRK is trying to promote tourism these days, though the detention and subsequent death of tourist Otto Warmbier gives obvious grounds for pause. It is still fair to say that most North Koreans will have never spoken to a foreigner. *Photo: Marcel Pedro*

TOP AND BOTTOM: Children in school stage shows. The standard of such performances would seem scarily impressive to non-North Koreans, and reflects a great deal of rehearsal. *Photos: Marcel Pedro*

A girl studying English at an elite Pyongyang school. The English taught in North Korea is British rather than American, owing the the US' status as main enemy. North Koreans who study English will be familiar with classic authors such as Charles Dickens or Jane Austen. *Photo: Marcel Pedro*

TOP AND BOTTOM: School calligraphy practice. *Photo: Marcel Pedro*

ALL PICTURES: North Korea is home to many Buddhist temples, including Anguk-sa, the oldest on the entire peninsula. Many are in a poor state of repair, however.
Photos: Marcel Pedro

TOP: Life is tough for the average person, so tourism isn't something most people get to do very much of. Here we can see members of one family out at a scenic location, taking photos. The presence of the smartphone would suggest they are better off than most. *Photo: Marcel Pedro*

BOTTOM: Portraits of the Kim dynasty in a family home. The gaze of Kim Il Sung and Kim Jong Il are everywhere in North Korea. If one were in a strongly Catholic country, one may expect to see crucifixes in people's homes; North Korea effectively has its own state-created religion. *Photo: Marcel Pedro*

TOP AND BOTTOM: Football practice in North Korea. This is a country that takes sports quite seriously; considering its size of population and lack of resources, they tend to outperform on the international stage. *Photo: Marcel Pedro*

A major sporting event can make an awesome spectacle in North Korea. Here, the crowd is as much part of the show as the actual game itself. It also attests to the regimentation of North Korean society. *Photo: Marcel Pedro*

TOP: Foreign businesspeople enjoying a lavish Korean meal in a private room. The elite of Pyongyang can eat like this too, with karaoke machines also available for those who wish to sing. *Photo: Marcel Pedro*

BOTTOM: Waitresses preparing a meal at a high-end restaurant, of the kind favored by political elites and the emerging capitalist class. These waitresses will also be able to entertain guests by singing. *Photo: Marcel Pedro*

Old ladies take part in national holiday celebrations. *Photo: Marcel Pedro*

TOP: Alcoholic drinks on sale in a supermarket. Here you can see typical North Korean drinks alongside imported ones like Bavaria Beer. *Photo: Marcel Pedro*

BOTTOM: North Korea is heavily sanctioned but for those with the money, almost any foreign product can be bought. Here you can see imported, high-end cognac and whiskey among other drinks. *Photo: Marcel Pedro*

international assistance. This international assistance should not be made in a way in which only a few major party members receive the majority of aid money.

Hyunmoo Jung:
The DPRK's leaders are obsessed with developing nuclear missiles, while the North Korean people live in agony.

The international community therefore needs to have stricter sanctions—both political and economic—as North Korea continues to violate the human rights of its people whilst maintaining its nuclear capabilities. This is the only way to make the North Korean regime collapse.

At the same time, the international community should help North Korean people rebel against the dictatorship by educating them through media sources such as radio, broadcasts, and books.

Sehyok Oh:
The international community needs to let North Koreans know that it has a continuous and long-lasting interest in them. One method of achieving this is through humanitarian aid—though only under certain conditions.

The North Korean government doesn't want its people to know that the international community is providing so much humanitarian assistance. As a result, I suggest that the United Nations and other organizations which provide humanitarian aid ask Pyongyang to ensure the people of North Korea know the origin of all the aid being given.

The international community needs to let North Korea know that there are many opportunities to make positive changes. Therefore trade, cultural and academic exchanges should all be encouraged.

Soon-kyung Hong:
The most important thing the international community can do is to speak out for the human rights of ordinary North Koreans. It is the only way to rescue them from the current dictatorship.

Also, the international community should impose additional sanctions on the North Korean government, as well as do more to publicize the human rights issue.

Jihyun Park:
The biggest help the international community can give is to be considerate and sympathetic, while simultaneously taking a sustained interest in the North Korea situation.

Even if the international community isn't continually taking direct action, they need to remain interested in North Korea in order to encourage it to open its doors to the outside world.

At the same time, it seems to me that the international community isn't doing enough to ensure the implementation of human rights in North Korea, instead being more focused on North Korea's nuclear weapons.

PART 6

Comparing North and South

[Introduction]

When I visited North Korea, I was not surprised to see that a lot of people's mannerisms, expressions, and ways of thinking reminded me intensely of South Korea. Foreign visitors to either Korea are endlessly told of Korea's 5,000-year history, and seen in that context, the seven-decade division of the country is not such a great length of time. Plenty has changed, of course, but the underlying characteristics remain the same.

In almost all ways, North Korea today is a much less successful country than South Korea. It made me sad to see people I recognized as Korean—from a culture I've come to love over the seven years or so I've spent in the South—living such tough, impoverished lives. Per capita income in North Korea is roughly 3% of that across the DMZ.

It is commonly said that defectors from the North will be one of the "keys" to reunification. They are the only group of people who can truly understand Korean as it is spoken in both states. (As you will see in this chapter, North Koreans and South Koreans have diverged quite a lot.) The defectors are also the only group of people who have a full understanding of both societies as they are today, and as such, they will be a bridge between the two in the event of a major political change.

That said, defectors do not necessarily have easy lives in the South. Increasingly, Southerners view North Koreans as foreigners, and worse still, poor foreigners—economic migrants, even. North Korean women are sometimes even treated as mail order brides; one can see adverts by marriage agencies offering this, proclaiming *nam-nam-buknyeo*, an old pre-division saying to the effect that the best men are from the south of the peninsula, and the best women are from the north.

Lacking a South Korean education, defectors also find it hard to get decent jobs. On a few occasions I have seen North Koreans doing casual work at restaurants, for instance, and then heard customers talking about them behind their back.

How different are the versions of Korean spoken in the North and the South?

DT: In South Korea, I can probably understand about 70–80 percent of what people say, what is written in newspapers, and so on. When I went to North Korea though, I understood less than half. That's because there are real differences between North Korean and South Korean. Certain words, such as *Geonbae* ("cheers"), will instantly produce a response like, "That's what they say in the South!" (In the North, the word is *Chukbae*). For those used to the South, North Korean generally feels a little old-school—Korean as it used to be spoken, uncorrupted by the myriad loan words that South Koreans use.

Kim Yoo-sung:
North and South Koreans use a common language, Korean, and the same writing system, *Hangeul.*

However, more than half a century has passed since Korea was divided. Since the two Koreas have been separated for so long, the way South Koreans speak and write greatly differs from the way North Koreans do.

Following the end of the Japanese occupation in 1945, Korea was divided into two countries under different governments and ideologies. While South Koreans can freely travel to other countries, there is one place on earth they aren't allowed to visit—North Korea. While South Koreans were allowed to consume popular culture from places such as the United States and Western Europe, they weren't allowed to watch movies, listen to songs or read books from North Korea.

This long separation has resulted in a number of differences. First, North and South Korea have different ways of spelling. For example, the "r" sound can come at the beginning of a word in North Korean. However, the "r" sound can never come at the beginning of a word in South Korean. One notable example is the word *ryori/yori*, which could be translated as "cooking" in English. Therefore, it's *ryori* in North Korean but *yori* in South Korean. This is just one example. Think of it as being like the difference between American and British ways of spelling.

Second, North Koreans and South Koreans speak with different accents and intonation. Actually, North Koreans and South Koreans already spoke with different accents before the Korean War. In fact, different accents and dialects exist just within South Korea. So, it's not surprising that North Koreans and South Koreans speak with different accents, right?

Think of it this way: In the United States, northerners speak with a different accent from southerners. Americans, Canadians, British, Australians and New Zealanders speak a common language, English, but they speak with different accents. Koreans living in the northern part of Korea speak with a different accent to Koreans living in the south.

Third, the South Korean language has an abundance of slang and abbreviations that North Koreans can't understand. The younger generation in South Korea gets these from the Internet and instant messaging. Slang is made up of words that have come into use recently, so it's no surprise that North Koreans who have newly arrived in South Korea have a hard time understanding South Korean slang.

Lastly, the most striking difference between North Korean and South Korean is the existence of loanwords. South Koreans have borrowed many words from the English language. Also, South Koreans still use words made from Chinese characters, while the North changed those words to pure Korean ones. The North Korean government has continuously made efforts to get rid of words influenced by foreign languages and change them to pure Korean words.

When South Koreans read or hear those words, they can't understand them at all.

There are many English words that have been taken into the South Korean language, such as "shower," "cafe," "radio," "hairdryer" and so on. North Koreans have made extra efforts to "purify" their language and thus haven't adopted any words from English. However, despite these efforts at purification, there are some North Korean words that sound similar to English ones, but were actually acquired through Russian. For example, "group" is *group* in South Korean. But, it's *groupa* in North Korean. "Tractor" is *tractor* in South Korean, while it is *trak-tor* in North Korean.

Such striking differences will be an obstacle to communication between North and South Koreans. There are other things to be taken care of before the unification of Korea, but such differences in the languages of the two Koreas should definitely be given careful consideration.

Is it true that there's no *tteokbokki* [the ubiquitous South Korean street snack composed of rice cakes in spicy sauce] in North Korea? What kinds of street food do exist in North Korea?
DT: If you've been to South Korea, you'll be able to appreciate the significance of this question. Street food is a big deal there, and the king of street foods is *tteokbokki*. It would seem strange to me to walk around a city full of signs written in *hangul* and not see *tteokbokki* on sale somewhere.

Kim Yoo-sung:
Tteokbokki does not exist in North Korea. Before I came to South Korea, I had never heard of such a thing. Only after I came to South Korea did I see *tteokbokki* for the first time.

When I finally tasted it, I couldn't understand why it was such a popular street food and why people would enjoy eating it. It was very different from the kinds of food I was used to. But as I got used to South Korean food day by day, I grew to like *tteokbokki* so much. Now I must admit that I've become a big fan.

Near my home in South Korea, there is a very famous *tteokbokki* restaurant. My wife and I go there at least once a week. That's how much we enjoy eating *tteokbokki* these days. Our daughter was recently born, and we can't wait to take her with us on our weekly visit. I'm sure our daughter will grow up to like *tteokbokki* just as much as me and my wife, when she's big enough to eat it.

If you haven't tried *tteokbokki* yet and just looked at pictures of it, you'd probably wonder if it would be delicious at all. But let me assure you: It is one of the best street foods I have ever had.

The *tteok* in *tteokbokki* refers to the rice cake, its main ingredient. *Tteok* is very sticky and tasty itself, but when chili pepper paste *(gochujang)* is added, the dish has a richer, spicy and sweet flavor. People who love *tteokbokki* do so because it's spicy and sweet at the same time. *Tteokbokki* is my comfort food: When I eat it, it seems to relieve my stress right away. Do you know what's even better? *If you eat tteokbokki* with a bowl of hot soup, *it t*astes heavenly.

Other kinds of South Korean street food, such as *hotteok* and *odeng,* do not exist in North Korea either. I have never seen them there. Instead, there are other kinds of street food in North Korea: *Injo gogi bap* (artificial meat rice), tofu *bap* (rice) and *soondae* (Korean traditional sausages).

The most popular street food in North Korea is *injo gogi bap*. It is as commonly found in the streets as *tteokbokki* is on the streets of South Korea. The term *injo gogi* may sound strange to most South Koreans. But *injo gogi* would be called soy sausage in South Korea and Western countries. The period from 1995–1999 was the hardest time for all North Koreans, as they were affected by economic difficulties. Remember the Great Famine? During this time, North Koreans didn't let any food go to waste. People used leftover soybeans and turned them into soy sausages. This became popular all over North Korea. At first glance, these soy sausages, called *injo gogi,* look like *odeng* in South Korea. People stuff *injo gogi* with rice and spicy sauce. This became a delicacy and a popular dish in North Korea. I often saw people eating *injo gogi*, tofu *bap* and *soondae* at street kiosks when I was living in North Korea.

After I arrived in South Korea, I saw that street food also exists in the South. But street foods in South Korea are nothing like what I saw in North Korea. Among South Korean street foods, *tteokbokki* and *hotteok* are my favorites. I eat both pretty often. But *odeng* … I don't enjoy eating it just yet. But who knows? I never thought I would like *tteokbokki* when I first arrived in South Korea. Now, I love it so much that I eat it every week. Someday, I may like *odeng* just as much as I love *tteokbokki*.

When Korea becomes unified, I bet South Korean street foods such as *tteokbokki*, *hotteok* and *odeng* will appeal to North Koreans. And, of course, South Koreans don't know North Korean street foods such as *injo gogi bap* and tofu *bap*. I look forward to the day when Korea becomes one country again and Koreans from both sides of the country can enjoy these street foods with each other.

Do North Koreans listen to K-pop?

DT: South Korean pop music is absolutely huge in China, Thailand, Japan, the Philippines, Malaysia, and many other places. K-pop is slick, its performers having perfected their dance moves and voices through years of training, and their appearances through years of workouts, makeovers, and plastic surgery procedures. North Korean pop singers are also well-trained, but in that boring socialist/militaristic way—they sing about being good citizens, and how wonderful Kim Jong Il or Kim Jong Un are. In a straight match-up between South and North Korean pop music, there's no way that young North Koreans would choose the latter. And many are finding ways to access K-pop.

Je Son Lee:

I have heard that there has been a growing interest in K-pop idol groups such as Girls' Generation in North Korea recently. However, there was little interest in such K-pop idol groups prior to 2012. K-pop idol groups look stunningly glamorous and beautiful. They're often featured in flashy video clips, as well. But I think that North Koreans are very sentimental people, so, they pay more attention to the lyrics and voice of singers. They think lyrics and the voices of singers are far more important than appearance.

Also, North Koreans were born and raised in a very patriarchal society. K-pop idol groups are mainly teenagers clad in skimpy clothes and North Koreans find this socially unacceptable. In North Korea, people who can afford to watch video clips from South Korea and other countries are the ones with money. Hence, it is mostly adults who can afford to consume K-pop culture. Teenagers aren't likely to have enough money to consume whatever they like, unless their parents are affluent, high-ranking officials.

When watching the South Korean dramas or movies, adults and teenagers react to the same scenes differently. Grownups like scenes such as when the male character donates his corneas to the female lead, or when the two of them get married right before the death of the female lead. If you have watched this particular K-drama, you probably know which scenes I'm talking about.

Teenagers pay more attention to the amusement park (Seoul's Lotte World) featured in the drama. They are far more interested in the fashion style of the main characters—jeans and short skirts, etc.

When it came to the background music of this K-drama, grownups like "Kal-muri," sung by the famous trot singer Na Hoon-a. Teenagers like the song "Bogoshipda (I Miss You)" by Kim Bum-soo. It doesn't mean that teenagers don't like the trot song "Kal-muri," but they do prefer the latter.

The grown-ups, though, don't like "Bogoshipda" at all. They say it sounds like a poem, not a song. Also, they never like the fashions shown in South Korean dramas. Adults often criticize the miniskirts and skimpy clothes worn in them. Still, they are crazy about those South Korean dramas because they like the storylines so much.

North Korean dramas and movies are all about making sacrifices for the leader. Even if the main character dies in the movie, they died for our leader. Yet in South Korean dramas, people make sacrifices for someone they love. This was fresh and shocking to most North Koreans. Likewise, South Korean dramas are more realistic and down-to-earth. This is why grownups love watching them, even though they don't like the skimpy clothes! Teenagers and children love the storylines, too. But they also love copying the Seoul accent, as spoken in K-dramas.

"Bathroom" is *wisaengshil* in North Korean but *hwajangshil* in South Korean. Due to the popularity of South Korean dramas, the younger generation of North Koreans has begun to use the South Korean term. They adopt new words and new culture from South Korea more quickly than adults. It is possible that K-pop idol groups may have gotten more popular in the North by now.

But up until 2012, people didn't feel comfortable about any of those recent South Korean songs. They preferred old songs to new hits from idol groups. In 2012, the most popular South Korean songs among North Koreans included old K-pop such as "Friend," "Private's Letter" and "For Love." Later on, when the South Korean drama *Sweet 18* became popular in the North, South Korean singer Chang Nara, who sang on the soundtrack, attracted much attention from North Korean viewers.

I'm not sure how the K-pop scene has changed since I left North Korea. But I can tell you that those singers and their songs were popular among North Koreans while I was there. In my case, my favorite K-pop song was "Like Being Shot by a Bullet," by Baek Ji-young. But since my mom didn't like that song, I couldn't sing it at home. One thing is for certain: The taste of the young generation in North Korea is very wide and diverse. You never know, North Korea's teenagers might be dancing to EXID's "Up & Down" at this very moment.

What did you think about South Koreans when you were in the North?
DT: Every week, the North Korean government conducts *kangyeonhwe*, or lectures, that disparage the South. Some North Koreans may believe such propaganda wholeheartedly, but most of them take it in one ear and let it out of the other. Where the lectures portray the South as evil and impoverished, some North Koreans see evidence to the contrary in the form of the food, fertilizers and medicines that

come from the South. As a result, many North Koreans know that the South is wealthy, and feel envious. Strict North Korean laws keep them from expressing any such knowledge and feelings about the South, however. Lots of information about South Korea has become available and made many North Koreans change their image of the South, so in general, positive feelings about the South outnumber the negative. I also believe that the growing positive image of the South is causing more North Koreans to defect.

Jae Young Kim:
Those who live near the border with China know a lot about South Korea. Information about South Korea flows in along with the Chinese products, video and radios that are smuggled into North Korea. Many South Korean TV programs are also smuggled in video file form, and surprise the North Koreans, who obtain and watch them secretly. However, people in areas far from the border do not know much about South Korea. A North Korean who became a friend of mine during the process of escaping from North Korea told me he only learned about South Korea after arriving in China. People in most inland areas do not have much access to transportation or outside communication, and receive ideological education through state TV, the North Korean government's propaganda tool. As a result, information about South Korea cannot reach them, even through word of mouth.

I was in high school when I was first exposed to news about South Korea. I went to visit my uncle's home, where I watched a South Korean TV drama called "The Staircase to Heaven." It was the first time ever I saw a South Korean drama, and I was very surprised. I could feel for the first time that South Koreans were living much better than us. It was shocking to see that young South Koreans of about the same age as me were living a completely different lifestyle. The sophisticated atmosphere of the city streets and the actors and actresses shown in the drama were enough to excite me. I was so saddened by the heroine's death in the drama that I had a mild case of depression for three days, and my heart pounded a bit when I saw the male lead. It was such an unforgettable experience that I searched for that same drama as soon as I arrived in South Korea.

That first experience opened my eyes to South Korea and kindled my curiosity. I began listening to South Korean radio broadcasts. I was able to pick up Chinese and South Korean radio channels where I lived. My parents tried their best to stop me from doing so for fear of getting caught, but I was magnetically drawn to South Korean radio news, even though it all began through simple curiosity. I still remember it so vividly; every night after 10 p.m. I would take out the matchstick that was put into the radio in order to block foreign channels, and listen to them at low volume, all the while looking out to see if my parents were watching me. The hassle of having to put back the matchstick into the radio during the daytime was nowhere near enough to dampen my curiosity.

I had to ensure the security of our home before I listened to the radio. All lights had to be turned out, all the curtains had to be drawn, and the radio volume could not be louder than the whisper of an ant. An occasional barking of a neighbor's dog would cause my heart to drop to the floor and my eyes to double in size. It was like something from a movie. Radio sounds were clearer on cloudy days. I was so taken by these accents that were so different from ours that I even tried to repeat words in a Seoul accent, all at a very low, barely audible level.

What caught my ears especially in those days was the news. Unlike North Korean news, South Korean news discussed events happening in real time. It also included news about various food and medical supplies that were being sent to North Korea as aid. I was confused for a while when I realized that South Korea and America were sending aid to North Korea; that was so different from what the government was telling us. I began wondering who was telling the truth. Meanwhile, I also enjoyed writing down the lyrics of songs, and singing along. Once, my parents even joined me and sang along.

What did you think when you saw election campaigns in South Korea?

DT: According the *The Economist's* Democracy Index and many other measures, North Korea is the least democratic country in the world. Meanwhile South Korea has recently shown itself to be one of the world's most robust democracies, as the events surrounding the downfall of former president Park Geun-hye in late 2016 and early 2017 demonstrate. The difference between the two Koreas is jarring, and so it is surely interesting to ask what a North Korean arrival to the South might make of that great symbol of democracy, the election.

Je Son Lee:

Election campaigning doesn't exist in North Korea. So, when I witnessed election campaigning with my own eyes for the first time in South Korea, I didn't understand what they were doing. Candidates and their supporters made so much of an effort to speak to people on the streets. These people distributed the candidate's business cards and flyers to passersby. When I witnessed all of this for the first time, I thought, *these people have too much time on their hands, don't they?* At that time, I didn't know anything about the role of politicians, or what kind of power they could exercise.

In North Korea, politicians are nothing more than puppets for the regime. Of course, top officials in the Supreme People's Committee may exercise limited political power while closely assisting Kim Jong Un. Apart from these top officials, the people chosen to serve on most provincial committees in the DPRK are puppets. They don't exercise any political power. Nor can they "motion" for or oppose any legislation.

More importantly, they don't have any competition, either. Once they become a candidate, they automatically get elected. That means they don't need to go out in the streets to beg citizens for votes. After all, there's no need to take any time and effort to campaign. Once the Workers' Party of Korea appoints you to be a candidate for your district in the upcoming election, you're going to be elected 99.9 percent of the time.

If you're a North Korean with political ambition, all you need to do is to win the hearts of top officials at the Workers' Party, not the voters. You shower the top party official with extravagant presents and money in order to be nominated. Even if you succeed in becoming a member of the committee, which is the legislative body, there's nothing you can change about the way North Korea is. So, if anyone wants to invest in bribery just for the nomination, that probably means they're just out for fame. They just want to brag about the fact that they're "honorable" committee members.

These are normally the kind of people who don't even possess basic qualifications to be a good politician. They just want the status. Of course, I'm sure that not all committee members are pompous or arrogant. But, at least those who I met wanted to brag about it. That's all I knew about politics back in North Korea.

When I witnessed the election campaign in South Korea for the first time, I was blown away. Everything they did looked so crazy to me! At first, I didn't understand why they were pouring so much money into their campaigns. I thought, why don't they spend that money on the elderly and other people living in poverty? However, after I began to understand more about the election process, I learned that not all these candidates get elected. They have to compete with others. That's why they were spending so much money. But what caught my attention was a list of policies they pledged to carry out once elected. I believed they would carry them out, but it didn't take me long to realize that they were all false promises. I don't know if these politicians are bad for being pathetic liars, or whether it's my fault for believing them in the first place.

It left me in complete shock. I became confused. It crossed my mind that South Korea's election system could be more dangerous than North Korea's. In the North, no matter who gets elected, they're given no political power. Therefore, they cannot implement any laws or regulations that could put people in danger.

However, people in South Korea have freedom of speech and can express their political stance and opinions freely. It is an amazing thing that South Koreans can vote for whoever they want. No one forces them to vote for a particular candidate.

When an election comes up, I do wonder who I should vote for. I'm still not knowledgeable about the electoral system, the role of politicians, or what the candidates are like. Some people vote for the political party the candidate represents. Others vote for candidates based on their capabilities, even if they don't necessarily endorse the candidate's party. Either way, one needs to take an interest in politics.

But South Korea's election campaign looks too extravagant and luxurious to me. It looks like they're all spending way too much money.

How do South Koreans react when you tell them you're from North Korea?
DT: I have a few North Korean acquaintances in South Korea, and generally, they will say they feel discriminated against by South Koreans. If they are sat in a restaurant and speak to each other in North Korean accents, people sat at nearby tables will stare, or start talking about North Korea themselves. Some older people even consider North Korean defectors as potential spies. That said, I doubt that most regret coming to the South.

Kim Yoo-sung:
When my family escaped from North Korea, our intended destination was America, not South Korea. The reason we initially chose to immigrate to America was because we received help from an American civic group called LiNK (Liberty in North Korea). At the time my family left North Korea, it cost about US$3,000 to get one person out and bring them to the immigration office in Thailand. So, it cost approximately US$9,000 for the three members of my family to escape from North Korea. Even when I was arrested by the Chinese authorities, this American civic group paid to rescue me from the Chinese detention center.

For these reasons, I'm still thankful for all the Americans who helped me. I think they literally saved my life. I'm opening with this story because, if I could turn back time, I would choose to immigrate to America instead of South Korea.

I've now been living in South Korea for over six years. Most South Koreans treat North Koreans with prejudice, stereotypes and discrimination. Within the first month of arriving in South Korea, I got a part-time job at a company that made small parts for smartphones. That company had its headquarters in Seoul and a factory in Suwon, an hour south of Seoul. There were eight workers at that factory, including myself. Five of them were women.

When ten days had passed, a new college graduate joined. When he found out that I came from North Korea, he stopped calling me by my name. Instead, he started saying "Hey, you! You come over here!" He became very rude and he started treating me with disrespect and ridicule just because I was from North Korea. Every morning I took a shower before going to work. But he kept telling me that I stank. I couldn't stand being discriminated against like that. So, I left that job after a month. Ever since, I have stopped telling people that I come from North Korea.

According to a poll, only two out of 10 North Koreans reveal that they come from North Korea. North Koreans constantly feel that it is better for them to conceal their origins. I wanted to work in sales most of all. I applied for numerous vacant positions in sales, but I could never pass the first round. When my application passed the first screening process and I was called in for an interview, I was told that I had little experience in South Korea. I was confident that I could do very well in sales, but the recruiter told me that they would only consider my application again once I had gained two years work experience in South Korea.

So, I chose plan B. I decided to work really hard for the first company that would hire me. I've successfully landed a job with a South Korean company now. At first, I was worried about how they would treat me, knowing that I am from North Korea. I was relieved when they treated me very well. They didn't ridicule or shun me. When I started working for them, the tasks were very challenging and demanding. However, I didn't quit, because they treated me the same as they would South Koreans. After two months, I became used to the work and would even whistle on my way to work every morning. I don't know how long I will work for this company. But since I'm highly satisfied with my workplace, I would love to work for them for 30 years or more, until I retire.

We see and read news reports about racism happening in America today. In South Korea, it's the same; both prejudiced and tolerant people exist. And so it will take time before discrimination against North Koreans disappears. South Koreans and North Koreans are of the same race and we share blood. Still, we have to face discrimination in South Korea.

I had a chance to visit America in August 2014. To be honest, I didn't love New York City, because it was too crowded, hectic and flashy. But I absolutely loved other parts of America I visited. It felt like paradise to me. If I could speak English and if U.S. Citizenship and Immigration Services would allow me to immigrate to America, I would live in the U.S. rather than South Korea. I don't know if it will ever happen. Right now, I will continue to work hard for my company so that I can be a valuable employee.

What should South Korea do to prepare for reunification?
DT: Reunification is an awkward topic. South Korean politicians pay lip service to the importance of reunification, but increasingly, the South Korean public lacks interest in it. When I visited North Korea, I got the sense that reunification is a much bigger deal there. Perhaps due to propaganda, or perhaps due to other reasons, I was told several times there that it was the dream and destiny of Koreans to be reunited. One rarely sees this kind of fervency in the South.

Sung-ha Joo:
South Korea simply wants to avoid reunification. That's because South Koreans are scared of the potential tax burden and of what it will be like to live side-by-side with North Koreans.

Because of this, I believe it is important for the South Korean government and NGOs to make efforts to change South Korean attitudes. South Koreans need to be open-minded about living with North Koreans, and in particular understand that unification is coming and has to come, no matter what they want.

I believe the current discourse about unification focuses too much on economic issues and does not focus enough on pointing out that above all, unification is about living together.

Mina Yoon:

The South Korean government needs to take the lead in inter-Korea relations. To help this process, South Korea needs to recruit more experts on North Korea.

NGOs and organizations need to raise awareness of the importance of unification for South Koreans, especially the younger generation, as well as inform North Koreans about the outside world. The government has a limited role and limited abilities. But NGOs and other organizations have more to offer.

Ji-min Kang:

In North Korea, you are either the oppressor or the oppressed—there's no middle ground. But things might turn around if there are radical changes in the North. Indeed, there will be countless people who hold grudges against the government for its ruthless and oppressive rule.

So without adequate measures after a regime collapse, North Korea could become a stage for bloody retaliation. Revenge will beget even more revenge. If we don't prepare beforehand, the country will turn into a bloodbath within a few months of any major transition.

I have heard that people in North Korea's security forces say that they may one day need to escape into China. I think this shows just how strong people's hostility could be—and the level of fear in the North Korean government. North Korea will therefore need international assistance, especially in dealing with security problems and food shortages.

Also, people who have suffered in the political prison camps will need quite a bit of help—including, possibly, therapy. Medical facilities in North Korea have undergone extreme deterioration. Medication and medical equipment are all lacking and many people are dying from various diseases. Medical aid is therefore another area where there is a dire need for assistance.

Ji-hyun Park:
One of the major things South Korea needs to do today is to help defectors living in South Korea adapt to the capitalist system. Once North Korea collapses, the defectors will be the ones leading the North Korean people. However, even they find difficulty in gaining a foothold in South Korean society, and so they are forced to go to foreign countries. NGO groups should provide support so that defectors are able to achieve refugee status.

Hyun-moo Jung:
The first thing South Korea should do is to make efforts to understand North Koreans better. Don't we have almost 26,000 defectors here in South Korea?

Still, South Koreans cannot judge all North Koreans by looking at these 26,000 people. Most defectors who have made it to South Korea are the ones who almost starved to death or who were subject to political oppression back in North Korea. In other words, they're mostly either top elites or from the lowest classes—there aren't many from the middle class.

PART 7

Health and Welfare

[Introduction]

From my time spent in North Korea, the impression that stays with me the most is that of the tough lives led by the majority of the people. One day we took a drive from Pyongyang to another nearby city, Pyongsong. Though Pyongyang is not rich by international standards, and Pyongsong is certainly not the hardest-up place in North Korea, the difference between the two places was stark.

The citizens of Pyongsong lived in decrepit old apartment buildings where electricity looked to be in short supply. They were scraping a living by trading basic goods on the street, or by engaging in related work—transporting goods around by bicycle, or fixing said bicycles, for instance. The clothes they wore were rather shabby, and generally people looked weary and weathered. One can only imagine what it must be like to live in this way during the deep sub-zero winters.

People living in such circumstances are naturally more susceptible to illness than you or I, other things being equal. But what happens when you fall ill in North Korea? Technically, free healthcare is available for all. Anyone can see a doctor. However, in practical terms there is a huge variance in quality, depending upon who you are. The Pyongyang elite can enjoy a reasonable standard of treatment, whilst the masses may have to just take a few aspirin and hope for the best.

It wasn't always like this. Healthcare is another aspect of life that has changed since the famine of the 1990s. As with food, shelter, and education provision, the standard of healthcare enjoyed by the general population was much better and much less dependent on how much money one had. But as mentioned previously, the government's social contract with the people—obedience in return for guaranteed welfare and security—has completely broken down. Rule now is the result of fear, and residual positive feelings about Kim Il Sung.

And how about old people? Elderly North Koreans simply have to keep working. There is no concept of a pension. Or, indeed, welfare payments for those who fall ill and cannot work; there is little help for the disabled either.

As one may imagine, the need to survive has made North Koreans become extraordinarily resourceful and resilient. In the event of reunification, I would definitely want to invest in North Korea—very few people could compete with North Koreans in creative problem-solving on low budgets, and sheer hustle. In a better world though, they wouldn't have needed to develop such skills.

What was it like to live through the famine?
DT: In the mid-1990s, North Koreans experienced a devastating famine that left hundreds of thousands, possibly even more than one million, dead. I can clearly remember my shock when a defector acquaintance told me that he saw bodies literally piled up in his hometown during that period. It is truly strange and horrifying to think that this was going on just 50 kilometers from a city like Seoul.

Mina Yoon:
Based on North Korean standards, not many people suffered from malnutrition. Or, I should put it this way: The North Korean people do not have any standards when it comes to malnutrition. That's because it was such a common condition. In this situation, anyone who could walk was considered "normal." Even now, my rough guess is that based on global standards, more than half of North Koreans would be considered malnourished.

Thus when I lived in North Korea, I never thought I was suffering from malnutrition—even though I was not very healthy at the time. And compared to my younger sister, who suffered from critical malnutrition, my health was not a concern.

My little sister went to kindergarten then, and she occasionally collapsed just while walking on the street. Then one day even her eyesight started deteriorating. She could not see anything at night. She could not even pick up her rice bowl. My mother could not do anything, but shed tears looking at her, and my father did not know because, as always, he was away (with the military) and busy with work.

My friends and I went out to the hills and fields nearby, and collected shepherd's purse, a herb known to be good for night blindness. My kind-hearted friends filled my basket with shepherd's purse all day long, which could have made a decent dinner soup for their hungry families. However, even this could not save my little sister. There was no progress in her condition, and my mother finally wrote a letter to my father, who eventually managed to get pig's liver and sent it to my mother. She steamed it and fed it to my sister with salt, and fortunately it worked. My sister gradually recovered her eyesight.

At a time when a kernel of corn seemed more valuable than gold, I think the biggest victims were the children.

In my hometown, there was a little girl named Soon Yi. I often saw her drawing something with a broken branch on the ground, waiting for her dad, who was out looking for something to feed her. Because she was four years old, the same age as my own little sister then, I was a bit attached to her. Then, one day, I woke up and heard the sad news that she had died. Her mother passed away when she was still a baby and her father was the only one looking after her. It was not easy to find food then.

Because of the long-lasting famine, it was tough to find anything edible. When you went out to the mountains, plenty of people were already competing to dig out edible herbs. Farmland was another battlefield for digging out the rice roots remaining in the soil.

These rice roots would be ground into powder and made into porridge, or maybe some noodles. Though not as good as rice itself, the roots still contain some useful nutrients. Food made from rice root tasted so awful, though, that for the first time in my life, I realized that some foods are tasteless even for starving people.

The most popular substitute food in those days was rice bran cake, pine bark cake, wormwood cake and cake made with wine lees. Rice bran, which is called *Mi-Gang* in North Korea, is the powder produced in the process of polishing brown rice. My grandmother kneaded the powder and made us rice cake in a cauldron. We waited for the rice cake to be cooked, and because there was not enough firewood, the flame was not strong. My little brother, who could not wait for the cauldron to finally boil, started saying, "You no good ass, you'd better boil soon..." but eventually he fell asleep before the cake was done.

Even in those hungry, painful days, there were some happy events worth waiting for.

The days we ate pine bark cake were like Christmas to us. If you remove the thick, tough outer layer of pine trees, there's another layer before you get to the white flesh of the tree. There's a thin brown film between the outer skin and the white core. People peel off that thin film and pound it into fine powder. Then they add a couple tablespoons of flour to make a cake. So, basically, it is a cake made with tree bark and it actually tasted quite decent. However, it had one severe side effect: My little brother, the youngest, ate the cake and got constipation that was so bad that it caused him to burst into tears. Remembering my little brother sobbing loudly, now my heart aches again because he is still in the North. He was only four then, way too young to understand the hardships of life.

I sometimes wonder how I could live in such a world. I then remind myself that others were in an even worse situation than me.

Anyhow, none of our family died of hunger. My father's social status as a military officer was of no help, but we three children survived all this with our sick mother. I was the eldest, and I wanted to find anything to feed my little sister and brother, even little pieces of herbs. I sometimes went out wandering around hills and fields nearby with some of the old ladies in the village. As a nine-year-old girl, there was no herb that I didn't know. I can still recognize all the herbs on the mountain. Fern, bracken fiddlehead, bonnet bellflower, Solomon's seal, mountain wormwood, victory onion, clavaria, nae-matoloma…all of these now have become a memory of those times.

Now I can say I am in good shape. But when I left North Korea I was very weak. My mom visited me when I was receiving social adjustment training right after I arrived in South Korea, and when she saw me, she could not hold back her tears.

Can you take your pets to a vet in North Korea?

DT: The concept of pet ownership is not so common in North Korea, just as is the case in any poor country. When humans do not have enough for themselves, the idea of keeping a dog purely for companionship is a luxury. One hears of members of the new Pyongyang rich keeping pets these days. But for the average person, an animal is usually an asset to be put to work or eaten.

Je Son Lee:

When I was growing up in North Korea, I never saw any veterinarians or animal hospitals in my hometown. That's not to say that they don't exist. There may be animal hospitals in Pyongyang, or elsewhere, for all I know.

Now, while people don't talk about veterinarian clinics in the North, that doesn't mean that veterinarians don't exist in North Korea. During the Great Famine, North Korea tried to overcome food shortages by breeding a large number of animals that live on grass. That's when vets rose to prominence in the North. Most vets seen in the public eye at that time were all wearing thick glasses and they looked like giant geeks.

Vets in TV dramas or movies were no different. In films, they merely wrote prescriptions for sick animals in need of treatment.

By contrast, in those stories young, creative people in the neighborhood came up with a better way to treat the animals and they went on to become heroes. That was the typical line of such movies and TV dramas.

Vets studied and took examinations at institutions. On TV, I saw vets visiting sick animals to treat them at homes and farms. I have no way of knowing whether such a system exists in every neighborhood in North Korea. I only saw vets on TV. I never saw them in person while I was living in North Korea.

Of course, some dogs and pigs fell ill in my neighborhood. Under such circumstances, people went to doctors rather than vets. In North Korea, as long as you have money, you can buy pills and medicine that you need from the market without a doctor's prescription. When livestock or pets fall ill, people buy penicillin and inject it into the sick animal. If the animal doesn't get better, then they go to seek help from doctors.

I grew up in a city, with no farms nearby. However, some families in my city kept several pigs and dogs. I don't have any memory of any contagious diseases breaking out among the animals, but there were occasions when a male pig's urge to mate would get out of control. In such cases people would get a doctor to come and partially castrate the pig. On the same evening, men in the town would have drinks with the pig's testicle as a side dish. Dads in my old hometown used to say it was the perfect food to go with drinks.

As I'd seen veterinarians on North Korean television, I assumed that there would be medical schools for students who wished to become veterinarians in North Korea. But I never met anyone who studied veterinary medicine while I was in North Korea. I didn't hear of any vet schools while I was in the North, either. I can only assume that there would be one or two in Pyongyang.

Maybe I wasn't able to meet any veterinarians in North Korea because it isn't common for people to have pets there. Instead of small dogs such as a Maltese, big ones such as shepherd dogs are more commonly found in North Korea. Shepherd dogs are not only expensive to buy, but it's expensive to feed them the meat they need.

You have to be rich to keep such a dog. Ordinary North Koreans usually keep mongrel dogs to watch the house or to eat as *boshintang*. When they fall ill, people would rather eat them than provide treatment for them. They wouldn't go and see a veterinarian.

North Koreans would probably think it nuts to take your dog to a veterinarian when there's a shortage of physicians for people. They don't understand how you can spend so much money on going to a veterinarian for your dog. When North Koreans hear of the existence of veterinarians in other countries, they think it is only possible because these are capitalist countries. They assume that people seek help from a vet in a capitalist market not because they care so much about their dogs or that the dogs have become a part of their family, but because money can buy anything in a capitalist market.

When I first arrived in South Korea, I laughed so hard at the wide prevalence and existence of animal hospitals in South Korea. In North Korea, I was told that nothing is impossible in a capitalist market as long as you have money. Me and my friends often imagined how life in a capitalist society would be different from our lives in a communist state. In North Korea, we couldn't even imagine taking our dog to a veterinary clinic. Animal hospitals only existed in our imagination. Suddenly, they were everywhere in South Korea.

That's when I finally realized that I was living in a capitalist society. To me it was interesting to witness with my own eyes that money could buy anything. At the same time, I was confused and daunted about the unpredictable future that lay ahead of me. Several years have passed since then. I have a poodle at my home now. It breaks my heart when my poodle gets sick. I realize that veterinarians exist to ensure your companion animal—which has become a family member—gets the care it needs.

Do North Korean women use sanitary pads?

DT: I must admit this is a subject I know very, very little about. But given the general difficulty of daily life North Korea, and the male-first nature of society there, Je Son's answer below is exactly what you might expect.

Je Son Lee:
What pleased me most about leaving North Korea was that I didn't have to worry about sanitary pads anymore! In North Korea, women

make sanitary napkins out of white cotton. We wash and use them again and again. Some women buy cotton from street markets and make their own sanitary napkins. Some women buy pre-made sanitary napkins. Either way, they are not like the disposable ones you use in South Korea or America. Of course, North Korea produces disposables called "Daedong River" sanitary napkins, but they're so expensive that most North Korean women cannot afford to use them every month. Women choose to use such disposable sanitary napkins only when they go on a trip or when they're in a situation where they cannot wash sanitary pads. Washing them every month is the hardest task, one you want to avoid at all costs.

I once heard that Daedong River sanitary napkins were produced solely for female soldiers. But delivery drivers sell some of them to vendors on their way to military bases.

Recently, I saw adverts for "eco-friendly sanitary napkins, good for skin and good for the Earth." It is true that using cotton sanitary napkins reduces garbage and therefore, is good for the environment. But I cannot agree when these advertisements claim that using such sanitary napkins also reduces period pain. I got my first period at 14 and I had to use cotton sanitary napkins for the next 17 years in North Korea. I suffered from terrible pain every month during this time. Perhaps it had nothing to do with the napkins. Maybe my period pain got worse and worse because I was under constant stress from having to wash and dry the sanitary napkins in secret. To make it even worse, drugs for period pain don't exist in North Korea. When the pain becomes unbearable, some women buy aspirin, but that doesn't help much.

The very last thing I want to remember about North Korea is the sanitary napkins I used over there. In summer, it was slightly better as it took less time to dry. But in winter, it took forever. The water pipes froze and it was always difficult to find a place to dry them. Because they're usually made of white cotton, we had to use a lot of water to wash the blood away. Warm water isn't suitable for removing bloodstains. Thus, we always had to wash them in icy cold water while blowing our hot breath on our hands. It was always stressful for women to hang sanitary napkins under other pieces of washed clothing so that men would not see them. Not many people owned washing machines. Even if you owned a washing machine at home, you might not have been able to use it due to electricity shortages. So women had to wash sanitary napkins with their own hands in cold water.

Of course, there are many hard things in life. But dealing with sanitary napkins was the hardest thing about living in North Korea as a woman.

When you have to go to school during your period, it gets even worse. Most high schools in North Korea are co-ed. You have to take extra care so that boys in your class don't notice, using a cotton sanitary napkin 20cm in length and 10cm in width. There is no fixture to fasten your sanitary napkin onto your pants. If you don't take extra care, the sanitary napkin could slip out. I always had to walk with extra care so that boys wouldn't make fun of me. If you have never used one, you have no idea how stressful it is. At that time of the month, I was so envious of boys because they don't have periods.

But since the moment I left North Korea, I have been free from all the pain and stress of "reusable" sanitary pads. Whenever I see disposable sanitary napkins, which are so affordable and available everywhere in South Korea, I'm reminded of my old memories and feel bad for women who have to wash their sanitary napkins during the icy cold winter in North Korea. When I see news about sending USBs or flyers to North Korea, I cannot help thinking it'd be better to use that money on sending disposable sanitary napkins to North Korean women.

Does North Korea look after its elderly?
DT: Traditionally in Korea, it was a big deal if someone reached 60 years old. Thus South Koreans still have 60th birthday parties, even though average life expectancy there is now 82. According to the World Bank though, the average is just 69½ in North Korea, testament to the huge economic divergence between the two countries. And for those North Koreans who do manage to live long enough

to be "elderly," there is no such thing as a pension.

Kim Yoo-sung:
To tell you the conclusion first, I think there is no such thing as welfare for the elderly in North Korea. Actually, I had never heard of the term "welfare" when I was living in North Korea. I only learned that such a concept existed after I came to South Korea.

Of course, the North Korean government puts up a façade and says it takes care of its people. However, the government cannot afford to provide welfare benefits for those in need. In South Korea, everyone who is 65 and over can ride the subway for free and receive a monthly stipend from the government. But as far as I know, the North Korean government provides none of those benefits for the elderly. The community may try to help them, but their ability to do so is limited. Just like everywhere else, both sympathetic people and selfish people exist in North Korea. Good people try to help the elderly who get sick or injured, but since many people in North Korea are starving, it is not possible to help everyone.

Also, people in North Korea try to save up for retirement. Since there is no government support or welfare for the elderly or the disabled in North Korea, it is only wise for people to save up.

My maternal grandparents still live in North Korea. They have to make a living by themselves without receiving any government support, even though they are in their 80s. Life isn't very different for most other elderly people in North Korea, as far as I know.

In South Korea, people of 65 or over are entitled to free rides on the subway, but the elderly in my North Korean hometown weren't entitled to such welfare benefits. I'm not certain whether the elderly in Pyongyang can benefit from free transportation. But people in my hometown never heard of such benefits. In regions outside Pyongyang, public transportation hardly exists. You don't see a subway or buses outside Pyongyang. My mother is highly satisfied with South Korea's welfare system. She always says, "I would bring your grandparents to South Korea if they were 10 years younger."

I will admit, South Korea doesn't have the best welfare system in the world. Still, I think its welfare system for the elderly is good. Meanwhile, North Koreans in their 60s and older still have to work either on the farm or at the market in order to make ends meet.

It is widely known that the North Korean government spends an immense amount of money on the development of nuclear weapons, while its people are starving. A good government would take care of its people. But the North Korean government does not.

As I write this column, I wonder what my grandparents are doing up there, where they don't even have electricity. I wonder if they've already eaten their dinner. When I was still a college student in the North, my grandparents gave me a bunch of 1,000 won notes, telling me not to skip a meal. It was their hard-earned money and they gave it to me because they were worried I might miss a meal or two while in college.

It's getting so cold these days, and it must be a lot colder up there in North Korea. I wonder if they're still working such long hours. I would like to get a job as soon as possible so that I can help my grandparents, even in a small way. When unification comes, I hope all elderly people in North Korea can benefit from the same welfare system as the elderly in South Korea.

What is a North Korean funeral like?
DT: As Mina says below, North Korean funerals typically last for three days. This is, of course, a culture that existed long before the division of Korea, and as such, South Korean funerals also last three days. Main family members stay there throughout, and receive guests—old friends, relatives, co-workers, and so on. Korea is small, and in the South, transport links are excellent, meaning that those who care for the deceased will be able to attend on one of those three days. Things are quite different in North Korea though, due to logistical and bureaucratic barriers.

Mina Yoon:
Funerals in North Korea are not like in South Korea, where most of the bigger hospitals and chapels provide venues for funerals. Most

North Korean funerals are held at home, though there are a couple of exceptions. There's an old custom that the body of a person who died in a foreign land cannot enter the house. So, if someone dies while they're out of the country, the funeral will be held in that person's workplace, either in a hallway or an office.

High-ranking military personnel don't have funerals at home, either. In such cases, a funeral committee is set up and students and residents in town are mobilized to hold a grand memorial service. These kinds of funerals are usually held in a spacious hall at the central offices.

North Korean funerals usually last for three days. However, a special adjustment is made when someone dies at the end of the month. In North Korea, there is a superstition that the coffin has to leave the house in the same month in which the person died. If a person dies on the 29th, the coffin has to be out of the house on the 30th, or the 31st at the latest. However, this custom is not strictly followed.

Because of travel restrictions, people have to wait for permits to be issued. This usually takes at least two or three days. Plus, North Korea's outdated transportation system makes it impossible for many people to arrive quickly. Funerals sometimes have to be postponed while they wait for the immediate family to arrive. If guests are coming from far away, some people will extend the funeral to accommodate them.

Sometimes, people miss their own parents' funerals because they can't make it in time. They have to carry these painful feelings of guilt for the rest of their lives. If someone dies while doing military service, the parents are notified of the death shortly afterward, but usually they can't make the funeral. It's especially hard if the parents live in the countryside, where telephones are a rarity. They get notified by telegram, which generally takes seven to ten days to arrive. These parents cannot do anything but go to their child's gravesite, long after the funeral is over, and cry. After my grandmother passed away at my uncle's house, my mom and dad had to wait for the local government to issue their travel passes. My parents used all their resources to get the passes issued faster, and just barely made it to the funeral before the coffin was lowered into the ground. You know what? My uncle only lived 100 miles away.

There is really no concept of an "undertaker" in North Korea. You can find one or two in town if you ask around, but they are mostly elderly people who just happen to have experience of taking care of corpses; they are neither certified nor licensed. My uncle found an undertaker for my grandmother this way. We could not afford to buy new clothes to bury her in, so we dressed her in her old, thin summer blouse. My mother suffered from nightmares for a while after that; she said grandma appeared in her dreams, saying it was too cold. Mother felt heavy guilt that she couldn't get her a winter coat for the trip to heaven.

There's no particular dress code for funeral hosts. My uncle was the host at my grandmother's, and his colleagues helped him. At night, they played cards to stay awake. I helped my aunt cook rice and side dishes for guests. It was a good thing that the funeral was in winter. During the summer, corpses start to decay when the room gets hot.

In North Korea, there is no disposable cutlery or dishes, so you have to borrow from your neighbors. Funeral guests usually bring some food, maybe some corn or beans, with them. Some people give cash to the host to express their condolences. In return, funeral hosts pack up food from the service so the guests can take it home for their families. To North Koreans who are already suffering from economic hardship, you can imagine what kind of financial burden funerals can bring about.

My uncle's friends were able to secure a gravesite for my grandmother. Certain mountains are assigned by local authorities to be used as cemeteries, and I heard they pick the best for themselves. It was winter, and the ground was firmly frozen, so it was hard to dig. People usually use a truck or a cart to carry the coffin. In our case, we used a truck. In North Korea, no one owns their own vehicle, so our family went to the truck factory and begged the manager to rent us one. Of course, we paid for the rental, gas, and the driver. My aunt said it would take more than a year to pay that debt back. My father offered to pay half, and I remember our family's lives were harder for a while after that.

My family was never rich, but could live on corn soup or rice. We could only just afford the funeral expenses, but there are many people for whom even this simplest farewell is an unattainable luxury. They keep the ceremony among family members, set a table with a freshly cooked bowl of rice, then transport the coffin to the mountain in a cart, where they bury it themselves. Thinking of this, it's not only the living in North Korea who are pitiful, the dead are, too.

Will I see my grandma when I go to heaven? It still breaks my heart that I had to bury her in thin summer clothes, but I hope she is now enjoying all the luxury in heaven that she couldn't dream of while she was alive.

My grandmother always told me she would to live into her 80s, so that she could see me get married and have kids. She was only 61 years old when she died. In North Korea, when you enter your 60s, people think you have lived the natural span of your life. It makes me sad to think of people dying in their 60s as something normal. I can't help thinking that if my grandmother had been in South Korea, she would have lived longer.

What is childbirth like in North Korea?
DT: At 19.3 deaths per 1,000 births, North Korea's infant mortality rate is almost 10 times higher than South Korea's. This is the result of poor facilities and a lack of money available for investment in maternity care. Of course, Pyongyang mothers have better options than those in the regions, as Yoo-sung explains.

Kim Yoo-sung:
I would divide North Korea into two republics—the Pyongyang Republic and the Regional Republic. Residents in the Pyongyang Republic have access to obstetricians, pediatricians and facilities of higher quality, while residents in the Regional Republic are denied access to all of these. My aunt moved to Pyongyang after marrying someone from there. Once she came to visit us in our hometown.

She said she had her children at Pyongyang San Won and was delighted with it.

When my aunt told me how much more comfortable it was to have a baby and raise it in Pyongyang, I realized that the Pyongyang Republic was far superior to the Regional Republic I was living in. People in North Korea said that Kim Jong Il made sure that the medical service provided at Pyongyang San Won would be of satisfactory quality because he was heartbroken when he lost his mother due to gynecological disease.

In this column, I would like to talk about nursing and parenting in the so-called "Regional Republic" (rather than the Pyongyang Republic), and my own experiences in raising my baby daughter in South Korea, where I gave birth.

In South Korea, you can buy a pregnancy test kit from a drug store, meaning you can be almost certain you're pregnant before receiving ultimate confirmation from an obstetrician. But it is uncommon for North Korean women to do this. They only go to see an obstetrician when they begin to get morning sickness or when they're late with their period.

After a woman in South Korea finds out that she's pregnant, she goes to see an obstetrician on a regular basis. Throughout every stage of their pregnancy, women get ultrasounds and regular checkups from experts. Ultrasounds do exist in North Korea and expectant mothers can have them several times throughout their pregnancy. But they cannot benefit from the regular medical checkups South Korean women have easy access to.

Also, South Koreans are more considerate of expectant mothers. This is not true of North Korea, unfortunately—they puff cigarettes without caring whether a pregnant woman is nearby or not.

In South Korea, when a woman in labor feels excruciating pain, she can choose to have epidural anesthesia. In North Korea, many women these days deliver their babies at hospitals. However, there are still a few women in rural farming towns who give birth at home. This isn't a preferable way for most women. Also, when a woman wishes to get an abortion in the Regional Republic, sometimes nurses perform the procedure, which is illegal, at the woman's home. Even in my old hometown, there was a nurse who performed abortions near my house for women in desperate circumstances.

South Korean parents use disposable diapers for their babies. But North Koreans still use diapers made from pieces of cloth that you have to wash over and over. South Korean mothers who simply choose not to breastfeed have access to a wide variety of powdered baby formula that they can easily buy from a supermarket. But in North Korea, women who cannot breastfeed their babies have to resort to goat's milk from the farms, or any other edible food, in order to feed them. Affluent North Koreans buy South Korean baby formula when they cannot breastfeed. Even in the Regional Republic, people with money can benefit from services provided at hospitals from pregnancy to delivery.

When babies are 12 months old, they stop being breastfed and begin to eat the food grown-ups eat. Around this time, North Korean babies start going to nurseries. When the North Korean economy was better, almost everyone sent their baby to a nursery. But as the economy got worse and worse, people began to have their babies taken care of by grandparents instead.

Another major difference is that the South Korean government gives subsidies for parents with children aged up to seven years. The North Korean government provides no such subsidies. In North Korea, rich people benefit from various facilities and medical care. But people with less money have no choice but to raise their children in such unfortunate circumstances.

However, it occurs to me that the medical care rich North Koreans receive seems inferior to that which ordinary South Koreans receive here.

Can you get regular health check-ups in North Korea?
DT: Basically, North Korea follows the law of "one law for the rich, and another for everybody else." In theory, everyone has access to free medical care; indeed, a poor person may be able to see a doctor, but that doctor's access to good equipment and medicine might

be severely limited. But if you are part of the new *donju* ("masters of money") elite, or are a senior official, you'll have access to good enough healthcare. For those at the very top, hospitals like Bonghwa in Pyongyang offer healthcare services that are considered on a par with any decent Western hospital.

Kim Yoo-sung:

Honestly, I don't think I ever heard the phrase "regular health checkup" in North Korea. They weren't very common in my hometown. You would just go to see a doctor in town when you felt ill. Of course, everything—all the treatments and surgery—are provided free of charge in North Korea.

However, while there is medical insurance in South Korea, there's no such thing in the North. Until the early 1990s, all kinds of medical treatments and operations were absolutely free in the North. Despite the collapse of the North Korean economy in the late 1990s, it is still free to go and see a doctor, receive treatment and undergo surgery. But you have to pay for the medicine by yourself.

Article 56 in the North Korean constitution reads: "This nation strives to consolidate free public health care for all, and to focus on preventive medical treatments and to protect the lives of the people, and to improve the health conditions of the workers." Since 1969, specialist doctors have been assigned to every city and county in North Korea. Doctors were specially assigned to mines around the country as well.

From 1990, general practitioners took on duties, such as researching the existence of contagious diseases, writing prescriptions and connecting patients with specialists. North Korea boasts of this, saying, "This system enables people to see a doctor who knows their medical backgrounds throughout their lives, and this also enables doctors to provide more systematic and sophisticated medical treatment suitable for people in their districts."

North Korea's medical institutions fall into two categories: ordinary hospitals and special hospitals. Also, there are hospitals called "hygienic preventive hospitals." Among ordinary hospitals, "*Bong-*

hwa Hospital" and "*Namsan* Hospital" are for the elites of North Korean society. Ordinary North Koreans who are not elites can go to the Red Cross Hospital, the First and Second People's Hospital or Pyongyang Medical School Hospital. Isn't it interesting that you have to go to different hospitals because of your social status?

Zainichi Koreans from the pro-North Chongryon organization in Japan have built and opened the Kim Manyu Hospital, which is still operating in North Korea today. There are specialist hospitals, such as the Pyongyang OB/GYN Clinic and Pyongyang Central Tuberculosis Hospital.

Outside Pyongyang, people's hospitals and medical school hospitals exist in every province of North Korea. People's hospitals exist in every city and town across the country as well.

Universities in North Korea train medical students to qualify as doctors. It takes seven years for medical students to graduate with a degree. No national exams exist after graduation. As soon as you graduate from one of those medical schools in North Korea, you can practice as a doctor. But you have to pass all the exams in order to graduate from seven years of medical school.

There is only one school of medicine where you can study to become a pharmacist in North Korea. It's called Hamheung School of Medicine. That degree also takes seven years. However, it only takes two years to graduate with a degree in nursing in North Korea. There are even some nursing schools in North Korea where the degree can be completed within one year.

At first glance, the health care system in North Korea may look appealing, even flawless. But the quality of health care seriously deteriorates when there is a cut in the government budget. The most horrific thing is that there is no compensation in the event of medical accidents.

But, to answer the question, there are no regular health checkups. Therefore, the healthcare system in North Korea fails to prevent diseases that are really preventable. In conclusion, I don't think the healthcare system in North Korea is attractive at all.

PART 8

Defection from North Korea

[Introduction]

There are now 30,000 North Koreans living in Seoul, 2,000 in Europe, and many other small pockets of defectors dotted around the world. There are countless more living in China.

Widespread defection is a relatively recent phenomenon; yet again, the famine of the 1990s played a crucial role. When the DPRK's state ration system failed, most people were forced to fend for themselves. For some, this meant crossing the border into China. At the time, border security was lax, and those who made the journey found a land of relative plenty. Some went there to make money and return home, and others decided they would be better off never coming back.

China, though, is dangerous for defectors. The Beijing government is a historic ally of the DPRK, and will send defectors back to meet a cruel fate—a labor camp, or worse. This fact leaves escaped North Koreans in China vulnerable to exploitation. North Korean women are often sold as wives, or forced into prostitution or to work as online "cam girls" for the entertainment of men in South Korea, for instance.

For most, South Korea is the intended final destination. To get there, defectors must escape twice—once from the DPRK, and once more, from China. This involves dangerous border crossings into countries like Mongolia or Thailand. Once they arrive, they turn themselves in to the authorities, and are handed over to the South Korean embassy, which arranges for them to be taken to Seoul.

Those who make it this far are sent to a place named Hanawon for three months. Hanawon serves as both an educational institution, teaching North Koreans how to use ATM machines for instance, and as a place of interrogation—South Korean agents want to be satisfied a particular defector is not a spy before letting him or her loose in South Korea.

As mentioned, North Korea's harsh economic reality has historically been the main reason for defection. These days, however, there are many for whom this is not the case. I know of one defector, for instance, who made the move after becoming captivated by South Korean drama shows, fashion, and pop music. Another simply says, "I couldn't develop myself in North Korea." In the DPRK, you cannot simply do whatever you want with your life, unless you have a lot of money and/or connections.

Once in South Korea, however, many defectors have a rude awakening. They arrive in a country that seems more selfish than the one they came from; they find that their education is useless to employers; and they suffer discrimination from South Koreans, who see them as either pitiful, suspicious, or exotic. That said, there are relatively few who want to go back home, despite the obvious pain of being separated from family and friends.

There is another option, though. Some move on again, to a third country. The UK is the most popular option, with 1,000 North Koreans living there. Most live in London, which compared to Seoul is a multicultural Mecca where even those with the most exotic origin can find a degree of acceptance.

One of those people is Ji-min Kang. Ji-min is outspoken and eloquent on all matters related to defection, and as such, we asked him to contribute most of the essays in this chapter.

Why do North Koreans defect? And how difficult is it?

DT: Defection became a major issue in the mid-1990s, due to the famine. People simply left North Korea because they were starving. Today, there are almost as many reasons for defection as there are defectors. It is getting harder to leave, though. One of the major changes from the Kim Jong Il to the Kim Jong Un era is increased border security.

Cho Ui-seong:

One reason travel is so attractive is that you can always return to where you came from. But this is not the case with defecting from North Korea. Rather, it is a sad experience. So why do people make this painful, scary, tough, dangerous choice?

Since defection became a thing, it has occurred for various reasons, depending on the situation in North Korea, the methods and intensity of state control, and the changing mentality of North Koreans.

Those who came down to South Korea, who were once known as "soldier defectors," started to be called *talbukja* ["person who has escaped the North"] from the mid-1990s, during the period of extreme food shortages. Before then, most people who defected did so for political reasons; but following the famine, most people left to escape starvation.

Due to the collapse of Eastern European socialism, the death of Kim Il Sung, repeated natural disasters, and the economic blockade from the West, the North Korean authorities lost the ability to enforce border control. Even if they had, they wouldn't have been able to stop the irresistible force [drawing people away from North Korea]. This sums up the way people thought at the time: "Instead of staying here and starving to death, I'd rather get shot crossing the river." This attitude, and the authorities' poor border security, led many people to leave, and the number of those ending up in South Korea was not insignificant.

The authorities gradually realized the seriousness of the situation and in the 2000s began to tighten the border and mete out strict punishment to those attempting to defect. They also conducted public executions by firing squad to create an atmosphere of fear, and began monitoring the families of defectors.

People were learning how to live without government rations, and this made them think twice about defection. But defection couldn't be stopped completely. Meanwhile, news from the families of defectors and those who had been caught in China and repatriated began to spread, even to regions far from the border. Stories of the material wealth of other countries and how people there were free of starvation began to shake North Koreans—a people who had believed their country had one of the best standards of living in the world—to the core. This pushed more people to the border, to the Yalu and Tumen Rivers.

When people cross the river, money comes too. This money goes through the hands of a broker and into the pockets of the border guard and state security officer. Due to this trend, defection has become an industry in the border area. This illegal industry has grown steadily, steeped in women's tears and with medieval torture and public execution excreted as its byproducts.

The commercialization of defection adds cost as another hurdle. Defection has become a luxury product that can only be enjoyed by those brave enough to mortgage themselves to the brokers. It is so expensive that the only way an ordinary person would be able to af-

ford it would be if they were to rob a bank or sell drugs. What I'm saying is that without outside help, it is almost impossible to defect. This situation has led to serial defections of family members, who are assisted from outside by relatives who defected previously. This trend still continues.

Recently, other reasons for defection have emerged. The increasing number of mobile phones and other electronic devices has created an environment in which people can easily access external information. When young people whose blood boils for justice access such information, their desire to defect reaches extreme proportions.

I lived far from the border, and first heard news about South Korea via the radio. I listened to South Korean radio for a long time, and became convinced that if I went there and worked hard, I would have a chance in life. I resolved that I would go, even if I died in the process. And after undergoing tribulations worthy of a novel, I finally arrived in South Korea.

Having come to the South and met young [defectors], I saw that they had used many varied ways of escaping—via the East and West seas, over the DMZ, and by plane, boat, train, and bus. But we all had one thing in common: the dream of a better life.

Despite the heartrending inability to see them again, parents see defection as a blessing for their children, and this outweighs their fear of the dangers of escape. This is because they know it is a better choice for their children. There are middle and upper class parents in North Korea who pay the defection expenses and push their children to leave. There are increasing numbers of people who are leaving North Korea, in spite of the fact that they have enough money to survive. The 18-year-old student who recently defected while in Hong Kong for a Mathematics Olympiad, and Thae Yong-ho [who defected from the North Korean Embassy in England in 2016], are good examples of how the reasons for escaping are changing.

From the simple reason of survival to the desire for a better future, everyone has a different reason for defection. They all just have one thing in common, and that is the sadness of leaving behind their loved ones in their hometowns. When reunification comes and they can visit their loved ones whenever they like, they will be able to look on their defection as a proud decision. I hope that day does not come too late.

Why doesn't every North Korean who travels abroad just defect?
DT: North Koreans who go abroad are usually from the elite. They therefore have less motivation to defect. It is also of course the case that, as with anywhere, a better life elsewhere may be outweighed by the attachment to family and friends. However, there is a darker, additional reason: Whole families are very rarely allowed to leave. Those left in North Korea would be swiftly dispatched to a prison camp if their family members did not return home. This awful rule is being applied even more strictly these days, in the wake of the defection of Vice-Ambassador Thae Yong-ho, his wife, and children from the North Korean embassy in London in 2016.

Ji-min Kang:

There aren't many ways of traveling outside the country, especially for those who are not in the privileged class. In most cases, those who can go to foreign countries are diplomats and students, as well as athletes who participate in international competitions. In other instances, people who want to visit their relatives in China or work as a logger in Russia can do so, but these are rare cases.

North Korean society maintains its rigid caste system, and while the ruling class inherits all the privileges of their fathers' generation, it is as difficult for children of ordinary citizens to become a diplomat as it is for a dragon to be born in a ditch, as we would say in Korea. In order to be a diplomat you have to be intelligent, good-looking and have an impeccable family background. Among ordinary people, there is hardly anyone who can fulfill these requirements.

In Pyongyang, there are many sports organizations that have a lot of talented athletes picked from all over the country. Sportsmen and women are potentially less loyal to the government than other elites, and being a sportsman does not always require a spotless family background. This is pretty much the only way ordinary people can go abroad. However, this is only possible after winning countless national competitions, and even then, if their class background is very bad, they will eventually be barred from their organization.

How about overseas students? As a matter of fact, the government did not officially acknowledge the need for such education while Kim Il Sung was alive. Egalitarianism, based on socialist doctrine, did not recognize individual abilities and talents, since everyone is equal. Everyone had the same kind of education. Consequently, studying abroad is considered an advantage given to a lucky and privileged few.

Do you think that such students will be "workers of the country" after coming back? Often, students who come back to North Korea from overseas studies have to endure monitoring, wiretapping and harassment from government intelligence institutions. If they say too much about what they saw and heard in foreign countries, they will face consequences from the government.

This monitoring system indicates how terrified the government is regarding the flow of information from overseas. The reason why they block the border between North Korea and China and punish defectors is also because freedom of movement can undermine the establishment.

Let me tell you bit more about athletes in relation to this issue. I have many athlete friends who were able to go to foreign countries several times. Even though they did not achieve great things internationally, they were really proud of their experience. All of them, however, were very reluctant to talk about the world outside North Korea.

Or maybe they had nothing to talk about, as they were not allowed to see anything. I heard that team buses taking athletes from the airport to the hotel would have their curtains completely shut. Looking out of the window or waving at people is prohibited, not to mention switching on the hotel room TV. All these actions can result in punishment. The only places the athletes can visit are the hotel, training area and stadium. For this reason, they cannot even buy a little souvenir for their family on the way home. Therefore, their memories of other countries are limited to the time on the bus and in the hotel, training camp and stadium. Surely the magnificent stadium filled with so many spectators and flashy advertisement boards will be unfamiliar and marvelous for them, though.

What is worse, they even have to swear on an oath that they will not disclose what they saw to anyone after returning, as well as having their fingerprints taken. For a long period of time they will be under close government surveillance. Nonetheless, fragments of the outside world are by no means meaningless to these people. The liberating sense of freedom and wealth of the society seen through the little gap between curtains makes them realize they aspire to the same, and the much more scientific and advanced ways of training shocks them.

However, the fear that surpasses the desire for anything mentioned here is the pain that can result from seeking one's own happiness. North Korea has long had a law of guilt-by-association, and punishes its people accordingly. I cannot think of any other government that utilizes such a savage and cruel system. When I was living in North Korea, if someone defected, it was inevitable that their family, including distant relatives, would be jailed and sent to a camp. Because of this barbaric law, no one in North Korea ever thought about opposing the government through real action.

So why do they need this system? In North Korea, there is no one more aware of the absurdity and irrationality of the North Korean system than the diplomats themselves. In this respect, the government is well aware that brainwashing diplomats and asking for their loyalty will be ineffective in reining them in. Alternatively, the authorities use parents' love for their children as leverage. As such, it is obligatory for North Korean diplomats to leave at least one of their children at home when going abroad. Those children who stay at home are then looked after by relatives.

I'm sure that North Korean diplomats feel ashamed of their own government. It cannot afford to pay full wages to diplomats and even shamelessly and openly orders them to finance their operations abroad through drug dealing and counterfeiting. It cannot be any more shameful.

What will North Korean citizens think once North Korea is open to the outside world? Do you know that most North Koreans have never seen commercial airplanes? They are not even allowed to travel around North Korea without government-approved travel documents. I really wish that one day everyone in North Korea will be able to enjoy freedom of movement and the joy of travel.

As a defector, would you ever return to North Korea?
DT: For most, the answer would be a definite "No." However, life for North Koreans in the South is tough, and there are some who do regret their choice. In recent years the North Korean government has been making great use of "re-defectors" as propaganda tools, having them appear in videos criticizing the South, and thanking the Dear Leader for forgiving their apparent treachery. The regime sometimes coerces defectors into returning; if a defector's cover in

the South is blown, authorities in the North may threaten the safety of his/her family members back home.

Ji-min Kang:
Many people often ask me: Would you ever go back to North Korea? If so, under what conditions?

I'll admit that I have mixed feelings towards North Korea, but it is impossible to put all of my memories behind me and move on. It would've probably been a lot easier for me to forget all about North Korea if I didn't have such horrific memories of it.

North Korea is where my father still lives. Some friends of mine do not want to go back to North Korea. There they've lost their parents and friends, and suffered all the sorrows a human being possibly can. Life in North Korea was a nightmare, and they don't ever want to go back.

Still, it's a country in need of a lot more attention from the outside world. It'll require a lot of help from the outside world in order to rebuild the country after the collapse of the dictatorship. They'll need to model it after an already-existing democratic form of government, with new methods of public education and a thorough introduction to capitalism. North Korea will have to start off with a clean slate, and it'll need help and guidance in almost every aspect.

But before I go back I'd like to point out three things in particular that North Korea will need right after the collapse of the current dictatorship.

Firstly, what does North Korea need most following the collapse of the totalitarian dictatorship? Some say democratization, but I can't agree. They say democratization will be a true blessing for all the people in North Korea after suffering under dictatorship for decades, but I have a slightly different answer. I'd like you to understand that this is my very personal opinion: North Korea will need Leviathan. Of course, I'm not saying the country should have another brutal dictator like Kim Il Sung or Kim Jong Il, who were hedonistic and extravagant. I'm saying it should have a highly patriotic leader. I will give you two examples: Park Chung-hee of South Korea and Lee Kuan Yew of Singapore.

Of course, all North Koreans, including myself, eagerly await the arrival of democracy in the land of North Korea. However, who can guarantee North Koreans will have absolutely no difficulty in adapting themselves to democracy after experiencing decades of dictatorship and brainwashing? Take South Korea, for example. South Korea has one of the 15 biggest economies in the world. South Koreans also invest a lot of money in education. Yet many scholars say South Koreans are yet to possess a mature civic awareness, and they're not as cultured as those in other developed countries. I cannot say with confidence that North Koreans would perfectly understand democratic governance if democracy were introduced right now.

Secondly, North Korea will need a whole new education system. The best adjective to describe the education system in North Korea is "Spartan." North Koreans are taught to monitor one another while growing up and they're not taught qualities such as compassion and perseverance in school. Terrifying and horrible slogans such as, "Be a sniper to shoot a bullet right through the chest of an American with one shot," are what kids in North Korea are told in schools. Kids are deprived of opportunities to nurture their creativity and, instead, they're taught to develop hatred.

While growing up and being educated in the North, I was never taught to question. The authorities want obedient people who will acquiesce to the dictatorship, not people with curious minds who will raise questions. Because I was never taught to think critically in the North, I made many mistakes while adapting to the capitalist market, and I was ridiculed and shunned in the process. Other North Koreans have gone through the same experience.

Ninety percent of North Koreans who have escaped from the country suffer from various forms of mental illness. It's a result of living with extreme fear and tension while in China and North Korea. Those fears we had to live with were too horrible to even describe or recall. For this reason, many North Korean defectors are highly sensitive to even minor insults or stresses that others would shrug off, and so South Koreans avoid dealing with them. This is a microcosm of what will happen during democratization and the transition to capitalism in the North.

Lastly, we need to understand where we come from and we need the outside world to be more compassionate toward the ordinary North Korean people. It is not a sin to have been born in North Korea. All the mistakes we make are the consequences of what we learned in the North. And it is not within our power to change any of that. Due to decades of brainwashing, we surely will be different from you. Sometimes, you will think we're weird and awkward. However, we learn while making mistakes in the capitalist system. The remaining North Koreans won't be very different from me when North Korea opens up to the outside world. North Korea requires a great deal of effort and perseverance.

I will return to North Korea when it becomes full of love and hope and a proud part of the free world.

What were your first thoughts upon arriving in South Korea?
DT: It is hard to imagine two countries that are so different, and yet so similar, as North and South Korea. As a visitor to Pyongyang, I found this jarring; having lived in the South for a number of years, North Korea had a "parallel universe" type quality to me. Had I grown up in Korea, I imagine the shock would have been much stronger.

Ji-min Kang:
After receiving three months of training at Hanawon (a center that helps newly-arrived North Koreans adapt to South Korean society), I was finally able to join South Korean society.

No one welcomed us, though. The extent of the freedom and the affluent economy in South Korea were noticeable, but they weren't mine. Even after leaving North Korea I still had to worry: Of course I wasn't going to starve to death in South Korea, but I hadn't come all the way there only to stand in line for free meals for the homeless.

But the biggest worry of all was that I'd finally become responsible for my own life. I bet many of you don't understand when I say this: Why would I be afraid to finally be in control of my own life?

Before arriving in South Korea, I'd never made a choice for myself, even once. It isn't just me; North Koreans graduate from the schools we are allocated by the government. We only read books approved by the government. We work at places assigned to us by the government. We get married and have families that way. Most of us never feel the great, rewarding feeling of achieving our goals through our own efforts.

However, most North Koreans don't have a reason to worry about their future, since every part of their life is under the control of the government. Of course, we never find out what we're good at or what we can do, and no one ever taught those of us who leave North Korea how we should live in a society like the South. Does this sound like an excuse to you?

In the world we live in now, people are expected to develop their own skills and strengths to stand out from the crowd. One must improve one's skills and differentiate oneself from others, to earn respect and succeed in life. I wanted to live and succeed that way, too. I'd relinquished everything I had to come here, so no wonder I wanted to live like that in this free society. I loved that I was finally given freedom, as well as the happiness I could gain from even the smallest things.

The first job I had in South Korea was part-time work at a small convenience store, and it wasn't even easy to get that. I made a number of calls to classified ads listed in the newspaper, but was rejected because of my awkward North Korean accent and low confidence in the way I talked. I had never been rejected so many times in my life before. While working that first part-time job at a convenience store, I began to learn how things worked under capitalism.

In North Korea, where we were told we owned our lives, no one worked as if they owned their own lives. We were expected to work equally and split the pie equally, so people would think, "What will happen even if I don't do my best at work today?" Doing my first part-time job in the South made me realize that what we learned in North Korea had become a problem. I realized how hard it was to earn money and why I had to do my best in the job I was given.

Freedom was sweet and beautiful, but capitalism was a different story. Highly stressful competition, the pain you feel after losing, and the inability to maintain innocence are all part of the capitalist system. Also, the emotional stress from my time in North Korea and China had a traumatic effect on me that remained even after arriving in this free society. Many people suffer from traumatic events in their past and aren't able to live well. Many of them live in agony, both because they hadn't been able to save their family members, and from the resentment they felt after realizing that they had been tricked and brainwashed in North Korea.

Also, because we were exposed to the successful precedents of North Korean defectors, we didn't see the upcoming difficulties most defectors experience. Of course, North Korean defectors who have made successes of themselves have every right to be proud, and they can be role models for other new defectors. But not all defectors can be successful like them; the difficulties and pain most defectors experience are very real. Of course, everyone is responsible for their own choices, but life can be very cold.

I believe unification isn't far away. This means that North Koreans will be able to have their freedom, but they'll need to learn how capitalism works. If they don't dispense with their old ways of thinking, living with South Koreans in a unified Korea will create serious conflicts. Freedom is great and beautiful, but it's only self-indulgence if it doesn't come with responsibility.

Many defectors end up leaving South Korea for other countries. Why?
DT: Though the South Korean government welcomes defectors, giving them citizenship and a certain amount of financial support, South Korean society in general isn't always as friendly. Thus, despite having a shared language and culture, many defectors end up moving on elsewhere.

Ji-min Kang:
Questions like this always make me feel ill at ease. To be honest, I'm not proud that I left South Korea behind me and moved to a different country. Now I live in London.

The prosperity, wealth and freedom you're entitled to in South Korea is inconceivable, more than anyone in North Korea could ask for. No one in the North would complain about the wealth and freedom they could enjoy if they came to live in the South. Yet, there has been a growing number of North Korean defectors who have emigrated to a third country. Whenever I'm asked why this is I feel slightly embarrassed.

In fact, many people want to live in South Korea and there are numerous people who dream of becoming naturalized citizens of South Korea. Many foreigners come to South Korea and say it is a very convenient place to live. To North Koreans, South Korea appears to be luxurious, even extravagant. The infrastructure of South Korea is so reliable and well-structured.

Have we become too greedy? All North Korean defectors ever asked for when they arrived was a roof over their head and three meals a day. Of course, these two humble demands were met and satisfied automatically when they arrived in the South. However, South Korean society wasn't that welcoming to us. It was highly competitive and it bred the cruelty that comes from hurting others to stand above all others. But I was willing to accept that. Being from North Korea, we weren't able to compete with these South Koreans, anyway.

North Korean defectors are provided with free housing, and even if they don't make enough money, they can still get by and support their family members in the North. Of course, their initial wishes and dreams are achievable and realized in South Korea. It takes time for them to get used to South Korean society, but they can never be the same as people who were born and raised in the South. In South Korean society, North Korean defectors are not even B-class, but C-class people, the underclass. Of course, I'm well aware that our status wouldn't be any higher in other developed countries, either.

South Koreans are closely connected based on their hometowns, academic backgrounds and the important people they know. In South Korea, even if you graduated from a good university, if they don't like your accent or hometown, they might not hire you. In South Korea, people are cliquish and they seem to think that everyone conforms to stereotypes reflected in their background. South Koreans judge all North Koreans as one, although North Korean defectors come from different regions with different upbringings. They are human beings with different characteristics and personalities. It isn't fair to observe the behavior of one North Korean and then judge and criticize all North Korean defectors based on that.

What appalled me was that it even led some South Koreans to perceive us as people representing North Korea—the North Korea we despised so much that we fled from it! Whenever North Korea's military provocations occurred, we felt as if we were responsible for it in some way. We took extra precautions not to stand out in public.

Also, it is very stressful to live as a child of North Korean defectors in South Korea. These children feel as if they don't completely belong to South Korean society. As they feel self-conscious, it is not easy for them to make many friends. South Korea has one of the most competitive education systems and private education there is very costly. North Korean parents aren't able to afford expensive private education. North Korean education is behind that of South Korea. North Koreans children cannot catch up with their South Korean classmates. So, the second-class status of North Koreans gets passed onto children.

Like I said, South Korea is a very convenient place to live. It has the world's fastest and best Internet connection. Convenience stores are everywhere. Food can be delivered anytime during the day. Yet, many North Korean defectors decide to emigrate to a third country, and the reasons I've offered are some of the major factors behind it.

I moved to London. There, I didn't need to worry whether people thought North Korea was a poor country, or a rogue state, or a villain in the international community. In London, they don't judge other human beings solely on which university they attended. They don't perceive me as someone who is representative of the entire North Korean community.

Most importantly, England isn't as competitive as South Korea. South Korea's competitive society was hell. Even South Koreans agree. North Koreans could never win the race in that competitive society. At least in London, I don't have to feel constant pressure or frustration just because I was born in North Korea, something I never chose.

Of course, the cost of living is very high in London. By the end of the month, I'm left with little money to save up for the future. I know as long as I live in London, I'm not going to become rich. But at least here in London, I don't have to feel self-conscious about myself and where I come from. South Korean society is excessively competitive. There's little chance of North Koreans becoming upper class citizens or members of that society.

Group discussion: What do you miss about North Korea?

Nayoung Koh:
I miss my friends and the innocence of people in North Korea. Although we were poor, we were friends with all our neighbors and we all were very close.

Life in South Korea may be affluent and wealthy, but South Koreans aren't as innocent or sympathetic as North Koreans. This was the most difficult thing about starting anew in South Korea.

Back in North Korea, people always shared food with each other on holidays. But South Koreans are individualistic, and they don't even know the person who has been living right next door to them in the apartment complex for 10 years.

Ji-hyun Park:
What I miss most dearly are the times when I would sit around the table with my whole family and laugh, even though the only things on the table were a bowl of broth and a bowl of rice.

All I want to do is to call out loud to my father, mother, sister, and brother. If you mention the word "longing," I immediately think of my home, where our memories, happiness, and joys all remain.

During the time I wandered through foreign countries like a vagrant, the time I had to live under an alias, and the time when I had to live like a slave in someone else's home, I looked back on those memories and found solace in them.

It was because of these memories that I was able to make it through all the dangers to reach freedom. The longing is always in my heart, and I keep it there so as not to lose it. The power and love of my family is what made me who I am today. I always keep a room in the corner of my heart for this longing.

Prof. Inae Hyun:
What I miss most about my life in North Korea are the strong bonds and friendships I had with people. Of course, I have friends here in South Korea. But it isn't the same. It feels more special to have a strong bond with people from the country where I was born.

Also, another thing: People in a socialist state don't own property. Because of this, they are more innocent.

Soon-kyung Hong:
What do I miss most? First, let me remind you of one thing. North Korea is a totalitarian society that completely ignores the individual's life, preferences, and tastes. It is a suffocating society where politics governs individual relationships. As I enjoy my individual freedom in South Korea, I don't really have any nostalgia for North Korea.

However, it's true that I miss the family and friends who I left behind in North Korea.

Se-hyok Oh:
All people want to have treasured and innocent memories—memories with parents, and of course, memories with friends. Though it might sound strange, I have more good memories from North Korea than unpleasant ones. Even though I like living in the free South Korean economy and may become rich, I still have memories of the time when I couldn't live freely.

However, while difficult memories in North Korea come to mind, South Korean life is tough, too. If I think about my uncertain future, I think life will become even tougher. Will I become greedy? Rather than longing for family, I would say I have nothing to long for, as my family doesn't exist to me any more.

PART 9

Religion and Spirituality

[Introduction]

Due to its Communist roots, North Korea is officially an atheist country. But it is natural, especially in such a difficult environment, for people to develop religious or spiritual beliefs. It is impossible to know how many North Koreans believe in a particular religion—it isn't as though you could go and conduct an objective survey of them—but it is certainly the case that there are North Koreans who follow Buddhism or Christianity; there are also many more who believe in the native folk spiritual practices collectively known as *Musok* (shamanism).

Though the regime discourages all religion, it opposes Christianity the most actively. There are several likely reasons for this. The most important would be that Christianity holds that there is only one god, and that all humans are equal in the eyes of God; in a country where a human being named Kim Il Sung has been made into a god, this is something of a revolutionary message. Furthermore, Christianity is a Western religion, and a relatively recent import. Finally, *Musok* and Buddhism have much deeper roots, and are therefore near-impossible to eradicate.

Ironically, Kim Il Sung himself grew up a Christian, serving as an organist in his family's church at a time when Pyongyang was one of the most devoutly Christian cities in the world. There are definite parallels between Kim Il Sung's ideology and Christianity, as we shall see later in this chapter. In a sense, Kim Il Sung took a lot from Christian teaching, and simply replaced God with himself!

During a visit to North Korea, I was taken to Anguksa, one of the oldest extant temples on the Korean peninsula and a designated national treasure. It is clear that the DPRK does not want to hide Korea's Buddhist past, but at the same time, it does not see the religion as something that should guide people in how they live today. There are Buddhist associations—and, indeed, there are Christian associations, too—that the government likes to talk up; however, it is highly likely that these are "fake" organizations designed to make foreigners think that North Korea offers freedom of religion, as is officially enshrined in the national constitution.

If you ask about *Musok* in North Korea, you will likely be told that it is an illogical, superstitious practice. However, *Musok* is not going away. It has a 30,000-year history on the peninsula—far older than the concept of "Korea" itself. There is no guide to moral action in *Musok*, but rather, it is merely about communicating with the spirit world, often for the purpose of gaining good luck or driving out bad. Any village will have its fortune-tellers, who will be called upon in the midst of tragedy or ahead of important decisions, such as the selection of a name for your new baby. It has been this way for centuries, and I would imagine it will continue this way for centuries after the DPRK is gone.

The same is true in South Korea, actually. For many years, the South Korean authorities also tried to discourage *Musok*, and indeed, many people there do also consider it somewhat irrational. However, as a deeply ingrained part of the nation's heritage, North and South Koreans of all social classes still find comfort and guidance in *Musok*.

Do North Koreans believe in ghosts or spirits?

DT: The answer is often "yes." I don't know if there is a country in the world—rich or poor, developed or not—where there is not an abundance of ghost stories and a great number of people who believe in the spirit world. Despite the Marxist legacy of the DPRK, there is no doubt that North Korea is no exception.

Ji-min Kang:

North Korea's ruling principles are based on *Juche* ideology, which is itself based on Marxist materialism. As you may know, Karl Marx was a sharp critic of organized religion, saying it was "the opium of the people." In essence, then, the basic principles of North Korean socialism are strongly opposed to and incompatible with religious beliefs.

Even though the North Korean constitution officially states that it allows freedom of religion, this freedom simply does not exist. As such, I had to learn continuously about the negative effects of religion while growing up in North Korea. This environment makes many North Koreans agnostic, but some conduct religious activities behind closed doors, often with serious consequences.

So, given that the worship of a god is very difficult in North Korea, does this mean we don't believe in spirits, ghosts and the afterlife too?

Although Christianity is almost non-existent in North Korea, you might be surprised to learn that we actually do have very strong concepts of ghosts or spirits in the DPRK. And in fact shamanism, or human communication with the spirit world, is something that is very popular in North Korea, where it crops up most often in the form of fortune-telling.

Like anywhere in the world, when things get too much and life gets unbearably hard, people like to know what is ahead in their future. Spiritual beings can help in this regard, and as a result, many North Koreans invest their money in fortune-telling. North Koreans, you see, would rather trust the spirits than the party or nation.

Some North Koreans are so engrossed with folk religion and the spirit world that they even ask fortune-tellers to advise them on the best dates to move house or to get married. And many North Korean defectors speak to fortune-tellers in advance to ask them for advice on the best dates to bring their remaining families across the border to South Korea.

Sometimes fortune-tellers tell horror stories, or stories about life after death; also, those being told of their future tend to pass on to others what the fortune-teller told them. You see, North Koreans who weren't taught about Marxist theory tend to find these stories particularly captivating—and they want to believe them, for numerous reasons. So while Marx's theory of materialism says that there is no afterlife, the spiritual world simultaneously talks about reincarnation—something which many North Koreans find to be comforting. And like anywhere else, North Korean people are of course most afraid of death, so these tales are popular in many circles.

As you might expect, the North Korean government tends be insecure about shamanism and fortune-telling. Officially they try to discourage people from paying visits to fortune-tellers through special propaganda campaigns. But fortune-telling is so ingrained in Korean society that it is too late for this propaganda to have any impact: Even government officials feel skeptical about the propaganda, for a story about ghosts or souls is nothing strange to them.

But despite the official line, North Korea's top elites are known to invite famous fortune-tellers to Pyongyang with warm hospitality, often in order to find out more about their future. What's more: even the very top of the leadership is said to consult with fortune-tellers! Obviously, I can't guarantee that this is true, but one fortune-teller I used to know in Pyongyang once told me that Kim Jong Il used to get fortune-tellers to pick the dates he would go out and make visits to places!

Personally, I paid numerous visits to fortune-tellers when I lived in Pyongyang. One of the most famous fortune-tellers I remember was called the "baby fortune teller." He was a grey-haired old man and every night in his dream a spirit appeared who would tell him who would visit him the next day—also informing him of their entire past and future.

Because he became so famous, some people traveled for days from far-away rural areas to see him. Sometimes he would go missing. But when he returned, he would often come back in an expensive car with lots of gifts. According to the fortune-teller, he was visited by the wives of all top elites.

In a way, North Korea became one big religious nation—but it also became a mass of lies. That's because North Korean propaganda is like its own religion. The propaganda suggests that immortality is possible through the endorsement of Kim Il Sung's ideology. The propaganda says that while your body will perish after death, your political life is immortal. Such beliefs made Kim Il Sung the only god in North Korea—a belief system that would sometimes demand people's lives.

So North Korea refuted Marxist materialism—its official ideology made Kim Il Sung a god—and, it left its people to be captivated by folk religion.

How religious are North Koreans really? And is it true that there is an underground church?
DT: The answer Jimin offers below deals with a lot of the history of religion, particularly Christianity, in Korea. But this does inform part of the answer—that there certainly was a lot of underground religion, in spite of the official communist ideology, but that over time, the authorities have stamped most of it out.

Jimin Kang:

This is just my opinion, but Koreans seem to be a people with a deep sense of religiosity. Many of the foreign religions that have entered Korea have become prevalent and enjoyed great success. The history of our country has unfolded alongside the rise and fall of these religions, which of course include Buddhism, Confucianism, Catholicism and Christianity (Protestantism).

Maybe it's because of this devout religiosity that the Kim family can command so much loyalty, and a worthless novice can be subject to such flowery praise and rule the whole country, just because he is from that family.

In the past, Chinese emperors used superstition to emphasize their legitimacy and command the loyalty of the people, and would call themselves sons of heaven. Hundreds and even thousands of years have passed since then, and a new era has come in—one of science, technology and logic. Ironically, there is still someone in North Korea who designates himself a son of heaven, and there are ordinary people who show religious zeal towards everything he does. Of course, there are all manner of reasons and conditions that make this possible, but the loyalty of the common people who love him cannot really be explained with logic. Especially in the only communist country in a materialist world.

Actually though, North Korea was a land of very devout Christians before Kim Il Sung's communist regime came into being. Sungsil College in Pyongyang was the best seminary in the whole of Korea. This school was the alma mater of Kim Hyung Jik, father of Kim Il Sung.

Even after he moved to China, Kim Il Sung served as a Sunday school teacher. The given name of his mother, Kang Pan Seok, was a Koreanization of Peter. She was a church deacon. Kim Il Sung's grandfather and uncle were also pastors at the same church.

As such, North Korea was a religious land in which Christianity was prevalent. But following the establishment of Kim Il Sung's communist regime, Christianity was subject to brutal repression. Korean Christianity is still so conservative and firmly against communism because of this history, which is traced in tears of blood.

After the establishment of the communist regime in North Korea, all religions declined and most believers were killed in prisons or camps. After liberation and the Korean War, the remaining religious people moved to the South, where they and their descendants formed the foundation of Korean Christian society that exists to this day. Ironically, Christians who fled south due to persecution by the North Korean authorities turned South Korea into the world's second largest exporter of missionaries.

The underground church in North Korea has been almost completely destroyed. There were families who practiced small-scale worship. But when such people were caught, they were executed by the authorities.

Families of believers used the covers of novels to disguise their bibles, and sat together and worshipped quietly. Of course, the children were sworn to secrecy, but occasionally, the authorities would find them out by chance. There were cases were those caught starved themselves to death in prison.

The biggest problem for the authorities, however, was that of North Korean refugees who had escaped from North Korea after the economic crisis and had become Christianized by meeting Korean missionaries and pastors in China. They were protected by the church, and learned Christianity at the same time. Such people vowed they would preach Christianity. And hundreds of them re-entered North Korea.

As a result, when State Security Department agents arrest a defector, they focus their investigation primarily on whether he or she has been in contact with Christianity or attempted to go to South Korea [nb. obviously, the North Korean authorities are hostile towards South Korea too]. If they find either to be true, the arrestee will undoubtedly be killed.

North Korea's economic difficulties have also brought about a revival of shamanism. Because people were worried about their future, they began to search for shamans who could tell them their destiny or read their fortune. As a result, shamanism became a very popular religion. Even high-ranking North Koreans are attracted to shamanism, and there are rumors that Kim Jong Il went to see *Mudang* [shaman priestesses], too.

Anyway, anxieties about an uncertain future have made North Korea into a religious nation, but even now people are living from day to day without religious freedom.

Why do so many North Korean defectors become Christians?
DT: As Yoo-sung states below, there is plenty of overlap between North Korea, Kim Il Sung, and Christianity—despite the state persecuting anyone who follows the religion. But not only that, many of the groups who help defectors are very overtly Christian in nature. I have even heard of defectors who pretend to convert, in order to be helped out of China and on to South Korea by Christian groups. This is, of course, entirely understandable given the nature of their situation.

Kim Yoo-sung:
In North Korea, we were forced to study and believe only in *Juche* ideology. Though *Juche* is the one and only religion in North Korea,

I think many of my fellow countrymen were always curious about new ideologies and religions.

The North Korean regime places strict restrictions on Christianity in particular.

This is interesting because Kim Il Sung comes from a devout Christian families on both paternal and maternal sides. His father had been educated at mission schools before Kim was born. His maternal grandfather was Presbyterian and taught local people about the Bible in his town. As a devout Christian, his mother took little Il Sung to church on Sundays, even after the family moved to Manchuria. In Pyongyang, she took him to Chilgok Church, which still exists today. Kim Il Sung's uncle on his mother's side studied theology at university and became a pastor. In North Korea there are the Ten Principles for the Establishment of the Monolithic Ideological System; it is pretty obvious that the Kims got the idea from the Ten Commandments. Pyongyang was once referred to as the "Jerusalem of the East."

While the regime cracks down on all religions, it attacks Christianity especially harshly. Because the North Korean regime launched vicious verbal attacks on Christianity, I wanted to learn about Christianity more than any other religion. I think many North Koreans are especially curious about Christianity among all the religions that weren't available to us. I'm sure it wasn't just me.

While I wanted to learn about Christianity, I was never allowed to do so in North Korea. I was not allowed to read or study the Bible. There were no church services I could attend on Sundays.

Then, unexpectedly, I happened to leave North Korea for South Korea with my parents. When I first found out about my parents' plan to escape, the first religion I wanted to learn about was Christianity. While we were in Thailand, I saw a Bible placed on a desk at the police station. In North Korea, it is a crime to be in possession of the Bible or read it even once; you could be sent to a political prison camp for that. As soon as I caught a glimpse of the Bible, I immediately picked it up and began to read. It was my first time reading the Bible.

It wasn't easy to understand it. I got through the first few pages, and then stopped because I couldn't understand it very well. I thought I would study about God and Christianity in more detail after entering South Korea. At Hanawon, pastors, priests, nuns and monks from the church, cathedral and Buddhist temples came to speak to us every weekend.

Among the religions, Protestantism was the most popular, Catholicism second, and then Buddhism. Hanawon, which accommodates female defectors, had a pastor who was assigned by the Christian Council of Korea to give sermons every morning throughout the week. I don't know if these sermons are the reason, but I do know that many defectors commit to Christianity. After attending church services and hearing sermons every morning for three months at Hanawon, North Korean defectors begin attending church services in their new towns at the invitation of the pastor at Hanawon.

After leaving Hanawon, I also began to attend Sunday services at a mega church (which I prefer not to reveal the name of) that my pastor at Hanawon introduced me to. In the first year, the number of Christian defectors increased and, from the second year, it gradually decreased. Seven out of 10 defector friends of mine have stopped going to church, for example.

At the time though, I was so eager to study the Bible and learn about God's word and Jesus Christ. I lived as a committed Christian for the first three years before I stopped attending church. The reason why I stopped going to church had nothing to do with my Christian beliefs. There was a pastor whom I looked up to, but I soon found out that he was so fake. The pastor was married with two kids. But whenever he saw pretty North Korean defectors, he would tell them that he was single.

It didn't end there. He would often invite beautiful North Korean women to sit in his office with him alone. He would go to their homes to convince them to go on a trip to Jeju Island with him. I felt very disappointed and betrayed. Before me and my wife met each other, my wife almost went on a trip with him because she didn't know he was married and he persistently asked her to go with him. As we began dating, my wife told me all about this and I stopped going to church.

Although I have stopped attending church, I respect all kinds of religions in this world. When reunification comes, if some South Korean pastors and missionaries continue to betray God like my former pastor did, there may be an increase in the number of Christians among North Koreans in the beginning, but a sharp drop in the long run.

Is Christmas celebrated in North Korea?

DT: There was no strong cultural history of Christmas on the Korean peninsula, so it is not necessarily a surprise that North Koreans today do not celebrate it. The authorities wouldn't want people celebrating it either, though. This is in contrast with South Korea, where presidents offer Christmas wishes, and companies jump on the Christmas marketing bandwagon almost as enthusiastically as their Western counterparts do.

Kim Yoo-sung:

No, we don't have Christmas in North Korea. Therefore, it isn't a public holiday; Christmas is just another weekday when everyone goes to work or school, unless it falls on the weekend. However, Christmas does appear in our dictionaries and encyclopedias, along with Christmas Eve, but people don't really think much of it. It seems to me that Christmas is a big holiday for people in capitalist countries, mainly. I imagine people in those countries always spend Christmas in a highly festive mood.

Most North Koreans don't know Christmas is celebrated with such great enthusiasm in other countries. But I do believe diplomats and their children who travel abroad would be well aware of it. In a country such as North Korea where Kim Il Sung is the only god and people are brought up under *Juche* ideology, Christianity is not typically practiced or tolerated. Therefore, they don't teach children about Christmas at schools and they never tell people what Christmas is about. It's no wonder that most North Koreans don't know anything about Christmas or Christmas Eve, right?

Yet, December 24 was a public holiday in North Korea when I was living there. December 24 is the birthday of Kim Jong Suk, the mother of Kim Jong Il, so they declared it a public holiday. On December 24 every year South Koreans celebrate Christmas Eve, while North Koreans celebrate the day thinking dearly of the mother of Kim Jong Il, as it is the holy day on which she was born.

In South Korea, children wake up on Christmas morning to look for Christmas presents delivered by Santa Claus. I learned about this only after I arrived in South Korea. South Korean children fall asleep on Christmas Eve waiting for presents to come the next day. But December 25 is just an ordinary day for North Korean children.

Now I have a daughter who was born in and is being raised in South Korea, I will celebrate every Christmas with her from now on, as I adore her so much. It was at a church in South Korea where I celebrated my first Christmas. I felt somewhat awkward and uneasy as it was the first time I celebrated it and I didn't know what to expect. Four or five years have passed since I arrived in South Korea.

Now, I don't forget to celebrate Christmas and spend the holiday with my family. My daughter is 10 months old now. I expect that she will begin to have a concept about Christmas from next year. I will surprise her with a Christmas present and tell her that it is a gift from Santa Claus, for having been a good girl over the past year. As I'm writing this down now, I'm already looking forward to every Christmas I will spend with her, and I'm already thinking about what present I should give her.

In South Korea, young people seem to celebrate Christmas with their girlfriends or boyfriends. That was what everybody seemed to be doing on Christmas day. So, I was planning to spend Christmas just like everybody else. I met my wife on a blind date last January. We dated for six months before getting married in August of the same year. Thus I never got to spend Christmas with her while we were dating, since we couldn't wait to get married. But we spent Christmas together as a married couple last year.

My wife was already pregnant by Christmas last year. For that reason we decided to spend Christmas at home, instead of going to a restaurant. But I invited close friends of my wife to throw a Christmas party at home in order to make my wife happy.

This Christmas, I'm planning to have a big Christmas dinner with my wife, daughter, and my parents. After Christmas dinner, I would like to take my family to see the Christmas lights around Seoul. By Christmas next year, my daughter will be able to walk by herself. I'm looking forward to taking her and my wife to the beautiful Christmas lights at Seoul's Cheonggyechon stream and taking my daughter to a playground and playing with her there and being a good dad.

I hope all North Koreans get to celebrate Christmas like us sooner rather than later.

Love, Sex, Relationships

[Introduction]

N orth Korea is probably best characterized as a very conservative society when it comes to relationships. Sex before marriage does, of course, happen, but it is frowned upon, as is
something so innocent as holding hands in public. Most people will
have had few partners before getting married, and will probably
know a lot less about "what to do" than young South Koreans.

It may be that the DPRK authorities consider sexual liberalism
as a potential gateway to free-thinking in other areas. But more importantly, the North's conservatism is really a continuation of Korean tradition. The Korea that has changed greatly is the South,
which has become rather liberal in the past 10 or 15 years. In the
past, you'd rarely see public displays of affection there, and now, it
is quite normal. When I first lived in South Korea in 2004, probably
a majority of people despised international dating and marriage, and
homosexuality. Nowadays, the former is broadly accepted, and the
latter by about half the population, according to surveys.

The essays in this section are to some extent a reflection of each
author's background, and North Korean society at the time each of
the authors left the country. Different people have different experiences. Generally it can be assumed that city life in North Korea is
more liberal than country life. It can also be assumed that those who
defected a long time ago will have a more conservative idea of their
country, as more recent reports suggest that things are changing.

The section on pornography is interesting in that regard. While
it is certainly true that the authorities want to stamp it out, current

sources say that the rise of the USB stick as the primary means of spreading foreign media has led to an explosion in the sharing and consumption of pornography from abroad.

Another interesting development not mentioned in the essays is the practice of renting homes to young lovers, by the hour; this certainly represents a step in a non-conservative direction. During the course of researching my book *North Korea Confidential*, my co-author James Pearson and I heard from completely separate sources that this practice was going on in most towns. During afternoons when the kids are at school and the husband is at work, there are housewives who will take cash payments from young couples and vacate their apartment for an hour or two. Appropriately enough for the "new North Korea," the money received will most likely end up being spent at a semi-legal *jangmadang* street market.

How do you find love in North Korea?

DT: Korea has a tradition known as *jungmae*, where families would ask a local matchmaker to find a suitable partner for their son or daughter. Marriage was (and largely still is) a union of two families, rather than just two individuals. Although the "love marriage" is the standard these days, couples will meet for the first time via intro-

ductions from either friends or family friends. Suitability with one's own family and social status is crucial. Since division though, the South has become a little more liberal, and the North has largely kept its conservative attitudes.

Jae Young Kim:
While you might not think it possible, love exists in North Korea just like in any other country, and people are free to have relationships. However, the norms and social perception of relationships are different to South Korea and other parts of the world.

Romance and relationships in North Korea tend to be quite different, depending on the province. Country areas tend to be very conservative—there can be quite a lot of problems for a North Korean girl if she gets pregnant before she is married. But we don't have as many problems in the urban centers, where attitudes are quite different. Here, kissing is viewed as quite normal (although not so much in public), and you even find the odd girl who has had a child before marriage. Sex before marriage does take place, but it is not that common.

Although everyone has some idea about what happens when you've been dating someone for a while, the way relationships develop in North Korea is far less agreed upon, as it is hard to find scenes on TV or in movies where people physically express their love. As a result, you don't find many couples willing to express their affection in front of other people, who regard such behavior as awkward. When I first came to South Korea, I was so surprised at seeing couples kissing and cuddling on TV or in public places, but now I'm getting used to it.

My parents married for love. My grandmother (on my mom's side) didn't approve of their marriage, but they ended up getting married anyway and went on to have me. This has always interested me, because their relationship grew at a time when North Korea was highly conservative, and yet it still succeeded.

Although things are changing, until very recently the country did not have mobile phones, and still doesn't have the Internet. So, unless you could plan in person, you'd have to write letters to each other if you wanted to organize dates. I used to help one of my best friends, acting as a "correspondent" for her and her boyfriend, delivering letters between them whenever they wanted to meet. This is so common in North Korea that there is even a song called "*Bbukkugi*" ("Cuckoo") about this kind of love story.

When I wasn't there to help out, he would visit her house and make a signal outside that only she could recognize. But everything was made easier by the fact that both sets of parents knew about the relationship, allowing them to visit each other at their houses before getting married. I heard they had their first kiss in high school.

When I ask my other North Korean friends about their relationships, there are so many different answers. One of them had no boyfriend back home, but another had so many relationships that the stories she told never ceased to amaze me. I enjoy listening to her stories, since I myself was quite behind on "the relationship thing" in my life in North Korea. She used to brag to me about going on dates to theme parks, historical sites, battlefields, and our local park; she was even given gifts like a necklace, watch, or ring.

Like I say, I was quite late with all this stuff. When I think about my first love, all I remember is that my heart went pit-a-pat when I saw him for the first time. My love was a military guy and I found him very attractive in his uniform.

We met during the holidays (the only time the soldiers could leave base), and I got to know him through singing and dancing together. He was able to come out to my area quite often, because of his higher rank. Fortunately, my parents liked him as well. However, it was obviously not as easy for me to contact him as it is for couples in South Korea. Even now, I still remember holding hands and walking along the river with him. It was not a long relationship, but whenever I see guys in military uniform, they look very attractive to me because of him!

In short, I believe love and human nature is the same, regardless of whether you are in South or North Korea. All it comes down to is a difference of expression.

Does North Korea have sex education?

DT: North Korea is very "small-c" conservative and as such, you won't even see couples kissing on television. As may be imagined, then, sex is not something that will ever be discussed by schoolteachers with their pupils.

Ji-min Kang:

To be honest, questions about anything related to sex in North Korea always make me feel awkward.

In North Korea, sex is restricted and taboo. As such, there are only a few very limited, very exaggerated stories that get shared, as sex is not something that is talked about much in the open. Still, North Koreans are people just like everyone else, so things like affairs and abortion do take place. However, sex is the "forbidden fruit" that can destroy one's wealth and power.

North Koreans are never given sex education or an explanation of why such pleasure is something they should not know about. When I was in high school, if a boy held a girl's hand, it could become a big issue, and a very embarrassing one, since everyone in the school would always find out. Plus, no one really told us what the big deal was. Was it because students who become sexually aware could cause problems? Or was it, perhaps, because sexual freedom could make it difficult for the dictatorship to continue?

North Korea is different from Muslim countries, as North Koreans purportedly believe in materialism, not religion. What, then, is the rationale behind their suppression of this basic human instinct? When I was in school, I never received any sex education at all. I was amazed when I heard that sex education is provided in most countries, and saw students taking classes in it.

After I left the North, I was especially shocked when I learned how in many countries teachers would utilize models of genitalia to frankly discuss sex with students. For North Koreans, everything to do with sex is filthy and embarrassing and you are supposed to hide it. Boys therefore cannot understand the biological changes in their bodies and are not aware of why they start having desires for girls. Nor are girls informed about the changes in their bodies, except from their mothers.

North Koreans are barely aware of the concepts of abortion or contraception. However, I suppose human beings cannot hide every aspect of their desires, and we always need someone who can satisfy our sexual curiosity. There were always guys who were slightly older than their peers in the village that enjoyed telling filthy jokes. But even though the stories they told us were not accurate biologically, this was the only form of sex education we ever received. Whenever one of my friends had a wet dream, everyone gathered to console him over his "unknown disease." I didn't know where a baby came from until I had turned 13.

Due to such ignorance, I was very passive when it came to talking about sex, and people often mistook my awkward attitude for naivety. Boys normally learn about masturbation around the end of their teenage years, as they hear about it from their mature peers or older friends. The distribution of porn magazines or videos is abundant elsewhere in the world but is prohibited in our country, and would surely cause a sensation if discovered.

I guess the North Korean government is afraid that people would be able to resist their authority if they were also free to pursue sexual freedom. If caught looking at or passing around porn, you and your family might be imprisoned—or in the old days, executed. In North Korean movies, there are hardly any scenes that show actors kissing. Foreign films imported into the country are censored, and sex scenes are removed.

For instance, there was a big difference between the version of *Titanic* that I watched in North Korea and the one I watched after I left—I assume you can guess which scene was cut. Porn videos that North Korean diplomats sometimes brought into North Korea upon their return therefore became the privileged class's property, forbidden for ordinary people.

However, as government control became weakened due to economic difficulties, there were increasing numbers of prostitutes on the street. What's more, problems such as sexually transmitted diseases and abortions started occurring more frequently. There were also problems between rich and powerful men and the women who try to benefit by having relationships with them. The problems mentioned here might not sound unusual, as they happen all around the world, but when there is no sex education it can be very serious.

Of course, the extremely closed environment in North Korea worsens these situations. Due to such restrictions, homosexuality essentially doesn't exist in the North; hardly anyone understands the concept. Not only are people with this preference able to openly reveal their sexuality, but there is actually no way they can fully understand their own desires.

However, North Korea is going to face an inevitable time of transition. Due to the inflow of Western culture and other environmental factors—such as the rise of prostitution following times of economic hardship—people are gradually opening their eyes, discovering their own sexuality and finding out how repressed they are. Despite the taboos, many people are seeking sexual freedom; rumor has it that 80 citizens were publicly executed recently, supposedly for the distribution or watching of pornography.

I hope one day that freedom, and sex education, will arrive in North Korea.

What happens to gay people in North Korea?

DT: It would be ridiculous to say there are no gay people in North Korea. Going back centuries into Korean history, there are records of homosexual relationships, for instance, amongst members of the *namsadang* traveling drama troupes of the Joseon Dynasty. King Gongmin of Koryo kept a coterie of male lovers, following the death of his wife. Homosexuality, however, was never discussed widely, and those who had such feelings usually had no context to put them into. This has continued into present-day North Korea. It is only in the past ten years or so that South Korea has been any different.

Je Son Lee:
Personally, I never knew anyone who was gay in North Korea, but I've heard a lot from grownups about things that happen in the military.

Unlike South Korea's two-year mandatory military service, North Korean men are obliged to serve in the military for 10 long years. This is tolerable for soldiers stationed on the military bases near neighborhoods. But soldiers who are stationed in the middle of the mountains do not get to see women for 10 years.

In my older brother's case, he says he hardly saw a woman during his 13 years of military service. He says he probably would have had to climb between seven and 10 mountains to get sight of a woman.

That's why senior officers have been known to take charge of "pretty-boy privates." Some of them might have been gay. But others may have done so not because they were gay but because there were no women around.

In my teenage years, I went to do volunteer works in a farming community. High school students in North Korea are obliged to volunteer at farming communities for one month each year. That's when I went to a remote village in the mountains for the first time, and it was there that I saw a gay man for the first time in my life.

You could tell even from a distance that he was a man, but he was sitting on a stone by a brook with thick makeup on. I thought it was so weird and peculiar, that I asked local people living in that neighborhood about him.

It turns out that he was a man, but he always put on makeup and lived as a cross-dresser in the city. So his parents sent him to this remote village deep in the mountains.

Of course, I didn't hear this from the guy himself since I never spoke to him in person, but I often used to watch him from a distance with my friends. We thought it was a bit weird, but still very interesting.

How about lesbians? I'm not sure if it's because I'm a woman, but I've met and hung out with many of them! Most of my lesbian friends loved to dress like men. They wore men's clothes, kept their hair very short and acted like men, too. They all liked to date women, not men.

Adults used to say that they're so sweet to their girlfriends. Once you fall in love with them, you're not likely to be attracted to men again. Still, being in a relationship with someone of the same sex gives one a bad reputation in North Korea and, most importantly, parents are opposed to it.

Parents of girls would do anything to keep their daughters from lesbian girlfriends. So, they would call the police or even slap the girls. But even if the parents of a daughter with a girlfriend call the police, they couldn't arrest anyone, since it isn't against the law. You can't punish someone for homosexuality.

All the police could do was make them write a letter in which they promise not to cross-dress, and then let them go. What's important is that lesbians would be an object of ridicule or gossip; however, they weren't shunned or excluded from North Korean society.

Transgender people do exist in North Korea. However, the sex reassignment operation is not done for one's sexual orientation, but for medical reasons. For instance, if a sexless baby is born, the hospital performs the sex-change operation after discussion with the baby's parents.

However, bear in mind that this isn't something that someone I knew experienced, but what I've heard from other people while I was in North Korea. But I can tell you with full confidence that it is impossible to be a transgender in North Korea solely for your sexual orientation. There are two reasons: Firstly, medical technology in North Korea is far behind other countries; secondly, no one could afford the surgery.

Since leaving the North, I have learned more about LGBT issues in the women's studies class I took. When I was in North Korea, I hadn't heard the terms "gay" and "lesbian." All I thought was that they had different sexual preference. As long as they were good people, we didn't have any problem being friends with them, regardless of their sexual preference.

Of course, people would gossip from time to time, because they didn't have anything else to do with their free time. People didn't treat them with contempt and the LGBT people were never shunned or excluded from society.

I believe there's no reason to be opposed to homosexuality, as expressing one's sexual orientation is equivalent to expressing one's preference in a capitalist democratic society.

I'm well aware that some people think gay marriage lowers the birthrate. But there's no guarantee that every straight married couple will have a child. Plus, gay and lesbian couples can adopt kids and give birth to children through sperm donation. Thus, this cannot be an argument against gay people.

I think many people share the same opinions as me, but only when they're not directly involved. But I think they'll have different opinions if they have someone in their family who turns out to be gay.

I personally believe we need to be more understanding of sexual minorities and, in order to be more considerate, we need to pay more attention to them.

Could I marry a North Korean?
DT: In the early 1970s, a Vietnamese man named Pham Ngoc Cane visited North Korea and fell in love with Yi Yong-hui, a local woman.

After lobbying the DPRK authorities for nearly 30 years—and refusing to accept endless excuses ("she's dead;" "she recently got married to someone else")—he was finally given permission to marry her in 2002, leaders of the two countries having discussed the matter at a summit. The answer to this question is therefore, "No, unless you're prepared to be extremely persistent!" The fact is that the DPRK is an extremely ethno-nationalist state.

Je Son Lee:

I'm not too sure about whether an expat—a temporary resident in the DPRK—could marry a North Korean inside the DPRK. But it is possible for *Hwagyo* (descendants of Chinese immigrants) to marry North Koreans. Most *Hwagyo* are men and hold both Chinese and DPRK passports. But when they marry North Korean women, their North Korean spouses aren't allowed to gain Chinese passports. The DPRK doesn't allow its people to take on the nationality of other countries—dual citizenship isn't allowed, nor are you permitted to emigrate. Once you are born in the DPRK, you're forever a North Korean citizen, unless you risk your life to escape from the country.

All of these stories about marrying *Hwagyo* were widespread when I was in North Korea. I've never been married, so I can't be 100 percent certain about the legal procedures of marriage in the DPRK. I've seen many North Koreans who married *Hwagyo* in my old hometown, but I don't know if that's what you'd call an international marriage, because these *Hwagyo* held both Chinese and DPRK passports.

When Libya was a socialist state, a number of North Korean doctors and nurses went to work there. Since the majority of North Korean nurses were female, some of them ended up falling in love with Libyan doctors and marrying them. Of course, I should point out that this is just something I heard while growing up in North Korea; it didn't happen to anyone I knew personally.

One thing I do know, though, is that children of mixed heritage can be found in the DPRK. Most of them are *not* born through so-called international marriages, though. Usually, they are the children of hotel maids or receptionists who met foreigners visiting Pyongyang.

Both white people and black people live in my old neighborhood as well. North Koreans don't get to see people of different races unless they live in Pyongyang. So North Koreans, seeing these people for the first time, used to stare at them. The North Korean government takes great interest in those people, too. They want to hire them as actors or athletes. I heard that the government checks on their aptitude early on, aiming to train them to be successful actors or athletes. Mixed-race children I knew in my neighborhood were taller and better-built than ordinary North Koreans. Some became boxers later in life.

People used to say that mixed-race kids are usually smarter. I don't know if it's always true. But all the mixed kids I knew were smarter and earned good grades at school, too. When a mixed friend of mine found out that he had been adopted, he went all the way to Pyongyang to find his biological mother. But because his mother wasn't living a life that could set a good example for him—she probably had been fired after getting pregnant—his adoptive parents prevented him from meeting his biological mother in person.

The adoptive parents told him, "Honey, we found your biological mother before you. Unfortunately, she has already passed away." He never tried to find his biological mother ever again.

He was good-looking and had a charismatic personality. So, people were attracted to him and he was so popular among his friends. Because he looked so exotic, he drew attention from people. People loved him because they thought he was so caring and diligent.

I think the North Korean government takes good care of mixed-race kids. Most of them are brought up by adoptive parents. Not everyone can adopt a baby in North Korea. Only those with higher social status and income can adopt babies in North Korea. Hence, those mixed children end up being raised in affluent families.

Do North Koreans use condoms?

DT: The simple answer is "no," as Ji-min explains. It is no surprise, then, that venereal disease is a problem. Following the collapse of the economy in the 1990s, many women turned to prostitution for survival. Syphilis and other diseases were rife among such women and the men who paid them. Thankfully, the spread of HIV has been extremely minimal, presumably due to the fact that North Koreans have very little interaction with the outside world.

Ji-min Kang:
While growing up in Pyongyang, I never even heard the word "condom." In the early days after my defection, I didn't even know why condoms existed or how to use one. It was not a matter that I was particularly interested in. I didn't even know where people bought condoms from.

The most shocking thing I saw in South Korea was nationwide sex education in schools. It was inconceivable to me that students could be taught about sex at school. It was so shocking to see female students being taught how to use condoms in the classroom. It was one aspect of a capitalist society I didn't understand in my early days in South Korea.

The sex education one can find in South Korean and American schools doesn't exist in the North. North Koreans aren't taught about safe sex or birth control. Of course, North Korean teenagers become curious about sex during puberty, but there is no way to learn about safe sex. In North Korea, sex is another form of hedonism people aren't allowed to know about or experience.

For the same reason, North Koreans aren't allowed to watch porn, either. If you ever get caught watching porn in North Korea, you're treated as a political prisoner and punished accordingly. Diplomats did bring home pornographic videos, which were then distributed among people in North Korea. But to watch one of those videos you have to be willing to risk your freedom. How many of you are willing to take that kind of risk to watch porn?

Because sex education doesn't exist in the classrooms of North Korea, people are ignorant about safe sex and sexually transmitted diseases. Especially for women, getting a STD is one of the most humiliating things that can happen. Consequently, they suffer from it for a very long time rather than seeking medical help. Since people don't even know about condoms and have almost no information about birth control, illegal and unsafe abortions are common. Due to the country's financial crisis, the birth rate dropped while the death rate was on the rise. For that reason, the North Korean regime banned abortion. Yet, there were still some people who wanted abortions, and out of desperation, they went to illegal practitioners. Many women lost their lives due to these procedures.

I don't know if people in North Korea know about condoms, or if they have access to them now. There's a possibility that things may have changed since my defection. But while I was living in Pyongyang, condoms weren't available for most people. They weren't being produced at local factories or imported from other countries. Vasectomies didn't exist in North Korea, either. The only form of birth control available was the coil (or loop).

A little while ago, I read a newspaper article about condoms being found in the backpacks of high school girls in North Korea. If that article is true—and only if it is true—this means North Korea has experienced a dramatic change in less than 10 years, even if only in Pyongyang. From 1995 onwards, the West provided humanitarian aid, including condoms. The goods ended up on the black market, but the condoms were mostly ignored. Most North Koreans couldn't figure out what they were or how to use them.

During my high school days, one of my classmates had a father working at a hospital. One day, this classmate brought a bag full of condoms to school. Of course, we had no idea what they were. They looked like balloons to us, so we blew them up in the classroom. But, of course, they were slippery and wider than most balloons.

When I lived there, North Korea was a black hole without any information or knowledge about sex. The North Korean regime doesn't allow any form of hedonism or pleasure for its people. The government thinks that its people don't need to know about safe sex. Maybe they thought it would pose a threat to the regime if people enjoyed sex more freely. I can only hope that the people of North Korea will receive education about safe sex sooner rather than later.

Does North Korea have pornography?

DT: As mentioned in the opening essay, things seem to have changed since Yoo-sung left North Korea. These days, there are many young men in Pyongyang who trade Japanese and Chinese porn videos on USB sticks. If caught, they can normally get out of trouble by simply bribing the officer who caught them.

Kim Yoo-sung:

This may sound disappointing to you, but pornographic movies and X-rated magazines are very rare in North Korea. If you ever came across one in North Korea, they're most likely to have been smuggled and distributed on the black market. It's not like in America or South Korea, where you can buy this month's copy of *Playboy* at your nearest bookstore whenever you feel like it. In the North, pornography is illegal. North Korea simply doesn't allow it.

In South Korea, movies and documentary films are rated. In the South, you have to be 19 or over to legally watch porn. It's understandable that people who aren't familiar with North Korean culture might think porn must exist there, too. After all, people are the same everywhere you go, right? But sadly, in North Korea, forget about sex scenes. It's very rare to spot even one kissing scene in North Korean movies.

But that's part of a much larger problem: Sex education doesn't exist at schools in North Korea. When I was a high school student in North Korea, students went on dates but even hugging was inconceivable to us, let alone kissing. The bravest thing we could do was walk together, holding hands in alleys when no one else was watching. If we ran into someone unexpectedly, they would be startled and we'd pretend we hadn't been doing anything as "obscene" as holding hands.

Why would holding hands be considered obscene in North Korea? It's probably all about comparisons: North Korean high schoolers don't have a chance to watch porn, while high schoolers in South Korea or America can easily watch it.

Do you want to know what shocked me the most after arriving in South Korea? It was when I watched the news about a teenage girl who was in critical condition following an abortion. I had almost never heard of news like that in North Korea.

The North Korean government strictly bans pornography. They make sure that X-rated entertainment doesn't circulate among its people. If someone gets caught watching porn or distributing it, they get sent to a correctional camp.

One North Korean guy I met on the way to South Korea said he left the country because he had been caught distributing copies of South Korean porn and he had been interrogated by North Korean police. That's why he had to get away.

If North Korea opens its doors to the outside world or becomes reunified with South Korea, I can only assume that porn movies and X-rated magazines would be introduced into North Korea. But of course, they should be clearly rated "X" and kept away from minors.

Fun and Leisure

[Introduction]

F un certainly isn't the first word that comes to mind when one thinks of North Korea. The grinding poverty that most people have to live with, and the extreme political control of the DPRK state apparatus, must surely make North Korea one of the least enjoyable or carefree places to live in the whole world.

Since Kim Jong Un came to power, there has been a concerted effort by the regime to present a more leisure-friendly image. I myself was taken to one of the manifestations of that policy—the Dolphinarium in Pyongyang, where the dolphins literally dance to the Kim family's propaganda tunes. The development of funfairs and ski resorts has also been the focus of strong government attention.

Such things remain out of reach of the majority, though. Those living in Pyongyang and who have a little free time and money may go to a bowling alley or a water park, but for a poor farmer in Gangwon Province, such things would seem otherworldly. Furthermore, the transport network is so poor that people are largely confined to their hometowns, and certainly wouldn't take difficult, time-consuming trips purely for amusement value.

The average person must make their own fun. As anyone who has visited North Korea will tell you, this often means one thing: alcohol. Just like their estranged brothers and sisters in the South, North Koreans really know how to drink. For the majority this means *soju* and moonshine, and for the rich, imported spirits. Beer is also popular. North Korea actually has an impressive range of beers, since each city has at least one brewery of its own.

Eumjugamu—drinking, singing, and dancing—are part of Korea's heritage, and have been for centuries. So when North Koreans drink, music will never be far away. For young people, this may mean convening in an abandoned building, rigging up some speakers and dancing to (highly illegal) South Korean pop songs. For all ages, a sing-along with a guitar also does the job. As in any country, a man who plays guitar and sings well can be a hit with the ladies in North Korea.

Do North Koreans drink a lot? If so, where do they get alcohol from?
DT: Anyone who has been to South Korea will know that alcohol is a big part of life there. The same is true of North Korea, and maybe even more so. There's a jocular expression in the South that "beer is not alcohol," but according to Je Son Lee, that's hardly even a joke in the North. Korea also has a strong tradition of making moonshine; this was stamped out in the South during the 1960s, but has continued unabated north of the border. Furthermore, North Korea is a tough place to live, and also colder than the South. It's entirely natural therefore to expect North Koreans to enjoy a drink.

Je Son Lee:

There are various ways to purchase liquor in North Korea. The first is by going to the factory (or someone working there), and paying in cash. There were actually several famous beer breweries in my hometown. The second is by going to a local market, where you can buy domestic, imported, and home-brewed alcohol. This is illegal, but the authorities cannot control it. In the past, only domestic booze was allowed at the markets, but imported drinks (including Chinese liquor) also began to emerge. The most common is Kaoliang Liquor from China. As most North Korean booze is strong, Chinese Kaoliang liquor (46–50 percent alcohol) and vodka are popular.

In my hometown, one out of 10 households brewed liquor at home. The most widely used ingredients were potatoes and corn. Liquor produced like this was usually stronger than those of other regions due to the harsh winters. North Koreans have a different name for Korea's famous *soju*. We call it *nongtaegi*. North Korean *soju* usually contains 20–25 percent alcohol in other regions, and 28–30 percent in my hometown. North Koreans are heavy drinkers and they greatly enjoy drinking. Thus, we would occasionally run low on booze, and it was almost inconceivable for us to have any leftover booze in my hometown.

My mom brewed liquor at home to sell. She usually made corn-based liquor. Firstly, she would leave corn powder with yeast on a heated floor and cover it with a blanket for 10 hours. When malt formed at the top of the liquid, she would pour it into a jar and mix it with warm water and wait until it fermented. After that, she poured it in the *gamasot* (cauldron) and boiled it. When the brew starts boiling and the steam comes out, that's the magical moment when the liquid becomes what we call "liquor." The final product was always transparent and had a soft taste.

I still remember when I got drunk after gulping down a mug out of my mom's *gamasot*. While my mom was away, my friend and I began drinking one cup after another. We got drunk and couldn't remember what happened after that. But afterwards my mom told us the house looked as if a big storm had swept through it. We don't remember what exactly we did to trash the house, but we know for sure that we kept giggling and had a good time. That's the magic alcohol does to you, right? I have to admit, my friend and I kept drinking secretly whenever my mom was not home after that.

My dad was another person who greatly enjoyed drinking. There was a beer brewery nearby and my dad and his friends would bring 50–60 liters of beer home. They would drink all night long. They would jokingly say, "We drink beer so we can go to the toilet more often." That's how bad their sense of humor was. Once they started drinking at 9 p.m., all the booze would be gone by the time I woke up the next morning.

People in my hometown considered beer a soft drink. Thus, both adults and children helped themselves to beer. Age didn't matter. As long as you enjoyed the taste of beer, you were free to drink whenever you wanted to.

Bars aren't common in North Korea—at least not in my hometown. People drink at restaurants or kiosks at markets. However, since it is illegal to sell booze in markets, this is done covertly. Until 2000, North Koreans weren't used to dining out. So, they usually drank at home. However, by 2010, North Koreans became familiar with dining out after coming into contact with South Korean and

Chinese cultures. When I was in North Korea, there was only one restaurant in my hometown where they served liquor on the premises and it was run by Chinese people. Such restaurants were popular, at least for those who could afford them.

The legal drinking age in North Korea is 18. But no one seems to care about this: It was normal for North Korean children to buy booze on errands for their parents. It was such a small town, after all. Liquor vendors knew every kid in the neighborhood. Hence, they would hand over liquor to the children on errands without any hesitation because they knew their parents well.

And despite the official legal drinking age being 18 in North Korea, on New Year's and public holidays, adults would recommend a drink or two to boys around the age of 15. In Korean culture, it is rude for younger people to smoke next to adults. However, it is perfectly fine for them to drink along with older people.

Personally, I enjoy drinking alcohol. So, I would always drink with my dad. I became my dad's favorite drinking buddy and he always appreciated my company. I hope I'll be able to drink with him again sooner rather than later.

Do North Koreans like gambling?

DT: There is no formal gambling industry in North Korea, though for Chinese tourists in the special economic zone of Rason, there is always the Emperor, a five-star hotel and casino. Among non-elite North Koreans, gambling is limited to bets between individuals, usually over card games.

Je Son Lee:

Yes, we do gamble in North Korea—at least some people do. Card games such as Go–Stop (which is played in Korea and Japan) and billiards are the most commonly played games. Personally, I've heard of people in my hometown that forfeited their houses or ended up in jail as a consequence of their gambling addiction.

Even when they're not exactly gambling, both grownups and children like to play cards for fun. Playing cards was the most popular form of entertainment in my hometown. Since there aren't many entertainment facilities or amenities in North Korea, playing cards came in handy. It was common for North Koreans to play cards with their relatives on holidays and weekends.

The rules of North Korean card games aren't complicated at all. Anyone can learn to play cards very easily in North Korea. But the competition gets fierce once people start betting. That's what makes the game more intense and attractive, after all. For this reason, both men and women loved to play cards in my hometown. On New Year's, Chuseok and other holiday weekends, grownups play cards during lunch and dinner. The person who wins the most points pays nothing, the one who finishes second pays a little, and the one with the fewest points pays the most towards the meal.

Then, you may wonder, how much money do North Koreans bet on their card games? When people play for fun and entertainment at home, it is usually petty money, such as 100 won per point. But when you're talking about gambling—for real—they bet 1,000–10,000 won per point. While in North Korea, I heard that some people blew all of their money gambling. But I haven't met anyone like that in person.

Students also play card games in North Korea. Schools in North Korea employ janitors, but one janitor cannot watch over the school by himself all day and all night, meaning students have to take turns standing guard from 6 p.m. to 7 a.m. This is not obligatory; only those who volunteer do it. Most students volunteer in order to have a sleepover with their classmates. They play card games together during this "sleepover." Since students don't have enough money to gamble, whichever team loses the game pays for snacks.

I've noticed that South Koreans seem to play Go-Stop [a card game] a lot during family gatherings at New Year's and Chuseok. But some North Koreans don't seem to like the rules of Go-Stop, so there are other kinds of card games as well. In South Korea, people with low incomes often play billiards. But only the rich play billiards in North Korea.

Rumors have reached the North Korean government that people were gambling at billiards. But so long as I know, they haven't come up with any tactics or policies to control it. I guess there are some things even the North Korean government can't control.

What kind of pastimes do people have?

DT: North Koreans have precious little free time, and a lack of options with the free time that they do have. These days though, the uncontrollable influx of foreign media has given young people a new obsession—South Korean *Hallyu*. In the column below, Mina Yoon talks of DVDs of Russian or Chinese movies; however, since she defected, it has become commonplace for North Koreans to get USB sticks loaded with South Korean dramas and K-pop music. People are now daring to consume such forbidden fruits, for two reasons: USBs are smaller and easier to conceal; and, the increasing bribability of officials means that even if caught, you will most likely get out of trouble.

Mina Yoon:

People do not have much in the way of individual pastimes under the totalitarian system in North Korea. For starters, the idea of "free time" is not really common. And even if you do have free time, there aren't many things to enjoy anyway.

The TV we had in our home was an award from Kim Il Sung that my father had received for his outstanding performance at work in 1993. Back then, TV was so rare that only one or two households per town had a set. Our family was the first in our neighborhood. Every evening there was a bunch of kids crowding into my house to watch TV and I had to stand by the foyer like a little gatekeeper. My mother allowed in most of the kids whose feet were clean and who were mature enough not to mess up the house. However, I—as the little autocrat of the house—could be a little bit selective and would invite only kids that I liked. That was why many neighborhood kids tried to impress me. They bribed me with snacks such as corn pancakes, brown rice snack, chestnuts and pine nuts. These days, TV has become more common and the majority of households in North Korea have a set.

But electricity is supplied for only two to three hours per day in North Korea. And even when power is available, the voltage is often too low. When the voltage goes down below 120–130 V, the TV turns itself off. To prevent this, I remember my younger brother always having his hand on the power switch of a voltage transformer. That was our desperate way of watching TV. People who cannot afford a transformer with a capacity large enough to handle this cannot watch TV, even if they have a TV set.

There is only one main channel, the Chosun Central Broadcasting Channel. However, people find it boring because most of the content is focused on Kim Il Sung and Kim Jong Il, or something set up to promote their propaganda. Everyone knows it is all fake. Therefore, people want to watch movies on DVD. People usually watch movies made in North Korea, China or Russia. Only few people dare to watch American or South Korean movies. If anyone is caught watching movies from those countries, there are consequences.

On special occasions, our family split into two teams and played a card game called "Joopae." We put a small bet on the game, and whoever loses has to take over household chores like cooking or cleaning up the backyard. Sometimes on sleepless nights, all of our family members would lie down side by side and play a word relay or sing songs. There are not many houses that have more than one bedroom in North Korea, so it is very common for all family members to sleep in one room together. When my younger sister, a tone-deaf singer, set the mood by singing seriously but with lyrics that were all wrong, we all ended up laughing aloud. Now I am in South Korea my sister and I sometimes go to karaoke. It is funny that my sister's lousy singing sounds way better with the help of the instrumental background of karaoke, but I still miss the old days when we burst out laughing together at her singing in the dark. I remember back then that the game or the singing finished up naturally, and we all went to sleep.

In North Korea, there is a six-day workweek. Even on Sundays, some people have to participate in collective labor, such as road paving, street cleaning or farming. Many in North Korea consider weekends time to work, just like other days, but only on individual tasks such as laundry, cleaning or gardening. Of course, there are some wealthy people who enjoy their pastimes. They might go fishing or watch DVDs.

When I first came to South Korea, a two-day weekend felt too long and boring to me. In hindsight, I think it was only natural to feel that way because I had never learned how to enjoy free time and didn't know what to do with it. Now I have spent a couple of years in South Korea trying to catch up with the rapid pace of life here, the weekend sometimes feels more hectic than a weekday. I go to movies, meet up with friends downtown, grab lunch with them and go shopping. I also spend time with my family and, of course, study. Now I know that even a two-day weekend is actually too short.

Do North Koreans keep pets?

DT: Pets are only for the rich in North Korea. For most people, keeping a pet dog would be an unjustifiable extravagance. Dogs are generally kept for guard work, and even eating. That said though, there is a rising class of *nouveau riche* Pyongyangites who keep animals for companionship.

Je Son Lee:

It is not common for North Koreans to keep pets, because it costs a lot of money to feed them. Still, there are some people who do so.

In Pyongyang, the most commonly found pets include monkeys and dogs. Outside Pyongyang, dogs are the most common. Some keep dogs for their meat and others keep dogs to guard the house when they're not home. But not everyone—few outside of Pyongyang, in fact—can afford to have companion animals because they require a lot of effort and money.

In 2000, I had a Maltese in my house and many people in the neighborhood wanted my dog so badly. It was a cute Maltese my grandfather had sent us all the way from Pyongyang. People always stopped by my house to see him. My not-so-very-thoughtful parents ended up giving away my Maltese to someone else in my neighbor-

hood. I was so sad to see the dog go but it was my parents' decision, and there was nothing I could do about it.

While I've heard monkeys were popular in Pyongyang, they became less popular later on and there is a story that explains why.

First, you need to remember that North Korea is a so-called socialist state. Therefore, when you pay the bills for utilities, everyone pays an equal amount regardless of how much electricity they used. Moreover, you cannot use the electricity whenever you want to. If you end up using electricity without the government's permission, you are subject to a big fine. So it's even illegal to use a microwave or make rice in a rice cooker in the North. This doesn't sound realistic, does it? North Koreans still need microwaves and rice cookers to feed themselves! Public servants randomly search houses and if you get caught using a microwave, you get fined. So people hide their microwaves, and use them secretly.

So let me tell you what happened one time in Pyongyang. One day, a public servant stopped by to inspect a house where they had a monkey. The family took some time trying to hide the microwave above the closet before opening the door for the official. This official was very suspicious, and demanded that they come clean and admit that they had used a microwave. The family didn't back off, but just then their pet monkey, who had been observing the situation, climbed up to the closet, grabbed the microwave, and placed it down in front of the official.

Almost every family has secrets—things they do that are perfectly legal in democratic societies but which are illegal in North Korea. In this case—and others—people began to get into trouble because of their pet monkeys. As a result, people's interest in monkeys declined. Instead, they turned to dogs and piglets as pets.

In regions outside Pyongyang, people keep shepherd dogs for pets instead of small dogs such as Maltese or Shih Tzu. North Koreans feed raw fish or pork to their shepherds, which is easier than buying specialist dog food. Moreover, shepherds are smarter. Other dogs, such as Maltese and Shih Tzu, would eat food given to them by other people. But shepherds only eat the food given by their owners. I always felt that shepherds were like a friend to people, while small dogs like Maltese were little babies that act cutesy to attract attention.

We had a shepherd while living in North Korea. We named him Bun-kae, which means "thunderbolt" in Korean. After my mother got scammed in 2005 my family went through financial difficulties, so my mom sold our shepherd for money. Bun-kae was about 3 years old at that time. Because he was so well-behaved we made a lot of money from selling him. However, three days later, Bun-kae escaped from his new home and found his way back to our house! My mom was so touched that Bun-kae found his way back home that she wanted to take him back. But because there is a saying, "It brings bad luck when an animal which left your house comes back," my family ended up returning Bun-kae to his new home. Later, we brought another dog to our home, but I could never like him as much as I liked Bun-kae.

Are there holidays in North Korea? If so, what do you do on them?
DT: North Korea has rather a lot of public holidays. But when you have a day off, it isn't realistic to imagine you would be able to go to the beach or a resort. Anyone who has traveled around North Korea knows the reason why: the transport network is absolutely dreadful. There are also the inevitable political duties that have to be per-

formed, cutting into precious free time. However, people do enjoy these holidays as a chance to get together with friends and family in their hometowns.

Je Son Lee:
There are numerous national holidays in North Korea, from *Chuseok* (harvest festival, the date of which is set by the lunar calendar) to Independence Day (August 15) to the birthdays of leaders Kim Il Sung, Kim Jong Il and Kim Jong Un. In addition to these government-declared national holidays, North Koreans work six days per week and get their Sundays off. Workers in North Korea are given 15 days of vacation per year and students two months.

On national holidays, every North Korean older than elementary school has to visit the statue of Kim Il Sung at 7 in the morning. Everyone has to get dressed according to the dress code specified by the government. Women have to wear either a dress skirt or *hanbok*. Men have to wear a suit and tie. Everyone has to wear the badge of Kim Il Sung. After this mass event, everyone finally gets free time to themselves. But when there's an important speech by the leader, we have to watch on TV and participate in discussions about it.

The government gives out gifts to children up to the age of 10 on February 16 and April 15. Apart from this, the government also distributes holiday hampers to every family on traditional holidays. These holiday hampers usually consist of a bottle of cooking oil and 500 grams of biscuits, but they're not completely free—we have to pay one third of the price. Since there's a shortage of ingredients, you cannot receive one of those holiday hampers if you happen to arrive too late. You have to wait in the queue from early in the morning. We get nothing else from the government.

After this, most workers have their own parties with food and drinks. You don't have to attend if you don't feel like going; these parties are purely organized and attended by ordinary North Koreans, but you shouldn't say anything to criticize the government in any way while you're at the party. People who are not affiliated with any particular group or working unit throw their own parties with people they're close to. In this case, if you're close enough to share secrets, you would criticize the government a little over drinks. But if anyone in your presence happens to be a spy, you'd be faced with serious consequences.

Most people spend vacations at home. Sometimes people visit their hometown or go on a trip, but this costs a lot of money and only people who can afford it do that. Students are the people who have the most fun on holidays. They gather together to share food and dance together afterwards.

There are no clubs or karaoke rooms in North Korea, so students have to organize everything for themselves. In winter, you usually make your own "club" in an empty house. We have speakers, but when there's no electricity, we can get power by firing a generator with oil. We wanted to play K-pop to dance to, but it's dangerous to do so—if the sound of South Korean music is heard from the house, we could get arrested. Enjoying anything from South Korea is illegal in North Korea. In the case of a sudden police raid, if we failed to hide the tape or CD, it would be used as evidence against us.

Therefore, most of us played guitar at these parties. It's the most popular way of making music, as it doesn't leave hard evidence that could be used by the authorities. Usually, we played K-pop tunes on our guitars and if a stranger or security guard comes by, we can easily switch to North Korean music.

Did you celebrate New Year in North Korea?

DT: New Year—either of the Eastern or Western variety—is more of a day for family in Korea. Even in the much more Westernized South, you don't see many big parties for New Year. It's a time for honoring one's ancestors, and eating homemade food.

Je Son Lee:
I don't remember seeing a New Year's countdown on television while I was growing up in North Korea. However, I remember seeing the sun rising above Mount Baekdu on television on the first day of the year. At Lunar New Year, they would show the "General's Star" on

national television. They talked about whether the new year would be an auspicious one for North Korea depending on the intensity of the starlight. If the star exuded excessive light, it meant that it was going to be an auspicious year, they said.

Now that I think about it, this sounds pretty stupid. But back then, I really believed that it was true and that our General Kim Jong Il was someone that heaven had sent to us. Like all children in North Korea, I'd been brainwashed about the three great figures of North Korea—Kim Il Sung, Kim Jong Il and Kim Jong Suk—since I was very young.

However, not everyone watches the first sunrise or the "General's Star" on television. Due to the shortage of electricity, not everyone can have their TV on. Plus, people are usually busy making *mandu* and *songpyeon* (rice cakes) at that time of the year. Since the Japanese celebrate January 1 rather than Lunar New Year, the North Korean government suddenly decided to urge its people to celebrate Lunar New Year (*Seollal*). But, in the people's hearts, January 1 means a lot to them. It is regarded as the first day of the new year.

On January 1, people pay respects in front of a table full of dishes. This was really for the living rather than the dead, though. For this, participants prepare mackerel, fried tofu, apples, pears, candy, *jijim* (Korean-style pancake), rice, boiled eggs, pork and other side dishes. There should be an odd number of dishes. I'm not sure exactly why, but I was told that it should never be an even number.

When the food is ready, people begin to pay respects. In the past, only men were allowed to offer a glass of liquor to the dead but now both men and women do so. While they pay respects to the dead, they pray that the new year will be a good one and that their dead ancestors will watch over them. People take turns toasting ancestors and, while they do so, they pray their ancestor will help them realize their dreams for the year. When this is over, they add a little portion of every dish to a bowl filled with water. They add a little bit of liquor to this bowl and sprinkle it on the ground outside. They do so because they believe the dead souls are waiting for them outside.

After sprinkling this bowl of food, they turn around and wait between one and five minutes for the dead ancestor to eat the food they've just sprinkled. While they are eating, their living family members shouldn't turn around to look at them. After the ancestor finishes eating, the whole family are able to help themselves to the food. I was told that if we ate before the ancestors we would get upset stomachs. They told me that they'd seen so many people getting upset stomachs because they didn't wait for their dead ancestors to finish eating.

A North Korean proverbs says: "If you sleep somewhere else on January 1, you won't sleep in your own home for the rest of the year." That's why most people try to sleep at their own houses on January 1. Some people would go out to see the first sunrise of the year as well. Before the North Korean government switched to Lunar New Year, January 1–3 were public holidays in North Korea. If Sunday fell on one of those days, we got to take an extra day or two off.

On January 1, the whole family gathers together at 7 a.m. to pay respects with carefully prepared food, as I've already explained. After paying respects and having breakfast, people visit family elders and their work supervisors or teachers at their houses from 10–11 a.m., and bring them presents. People who can't afford to buy big presents will still bring a bottle of *soju* at the very least. We were taught that it is impolite to go to the house of someone older than you without taking any presents. Adults still visit their teachers from kindergarten, elementary and high schools even after they've grown up, on New Year's Day and other important holidays.

On January 2, people are busy hanging out with their friends. People usually drink, sing and dance together at empty houses, from the age of about 15. You need money to do this, right? Mostly, boys pay but sometimes girls do, too. Adults and older people sing along and tap their chopsticks on the table as if they were playing drums. The younger generation usually sing South Korean songs and dance to K-pop. This means they have to find secret places. If you get caught by the security police, you could be in deep trouble (but mostly you bribe your way out).

When the New Year's shenanigans end, people go back to work.

On the first day back at work, people take a pledge to sacrifice their mind and body for the Workers' Party and the Leader. They say it is the first day of combat. The first day of combat begins with people bringing manure from the co-op farm, due to a national shortage of compost. It is not possible for co-op members to deliver all the manure, and so everyone in the country helps deliver manure on that day.

For people like me who lived in an apartment, we had to beat other people to the manure by getting washed and ready in the shared common bathrooms first. But after traders began selling compost at the market, people would simply buy it to complete the first mission of the year. If I was still living in North Korea, I would have been pretty worried about the compost task.

Do North Koreans like telling jokes? What makes people laugh in North Korea?
DT: It should go without saying that human beings anywhere like to laugh and joke around. Unfortunately the standard media portrayal of the North Korean is either that of the helpless victim, or the brainwashed robot—there is little room within the stereotype for someone like you or me, who would like to have a laugh to brighten up their day. That said, there are certainly fewer opportunities to laugh in North Korea than in most other places.

Mina Yoon:
I agree that in tough times laughter is the best cure, but in North Korea people do not make jokes as often as they do in South Korea or other developed countries. I think this is because North Korean people are too tied up with the hardships of life to relax and exchange jokes with other people.

It's not all doom and gloom, though. North Korean people make jokes, too. Despite being struck by poverty and depression, people cannot live their entire life being miserable. And sometimes jokes appear even in the weirdest situations…such as when I recall a goat and a pig that joined the army!

One of my distant relatives was an old man who lived in the countryside raising a goat and a pig. During the daytime, he would stay out cutting the grass to feed his pig and put the goat out to pasture. But one day when I visited his house in the afternoon, I was astonished to find him at home. I asked why he was at home instead of out taking care of his animals as he always did.

"All of a sudden—and at the same time—my goat and pig decided to join the army!!" he said.

Of course, it did not make any sense. But he explained further.

The situation was like this: A few days before, a couple of soldiers sneaked into his barn and stole his animals. Searching for the animals, he found a note saying, "Protecting one's country is the most sacred vocation on earth. Believing what the pig chose to do was a right thing, I am following him.—Sincerely, Your Goat."

When he showed me the note, I didn't know whether I was supposed to laugh or cry. Maybe the soldiers took the pig first and later came back to take the goat, too? They must have felt sorry for the old man and left a note attempting to justify their theft.

I was very upset by the incident. It was understandable that the thieves were starving and needed something to eat, but again, the loss of the pig and the goat would have been heartbreaking to my old relative. I knew how much he had been attached to them. Well, unlike what I would have done in the same situation, he kept the note neatly folded in his pocket. He said he got over that incident by looking at the crime in a way that made him feel he was feeding his own son with good meat. And if anyone asked about his pig or goat, he would answer that they volunteered to go to the army thanks to his scrupulous political education. Well, it was his way of dealing with a huge loss!

North Korean people often try to forget about their misfortune by making fun of it. For example, when I used to work in the market there was a vendor there who used to sell medicine. Although she only carried one kind of medicine—for skin problems—she had the loudest voice in the market. Once, when she was shouting at the top of her voice "Here, here! A marvelous medicine for cracked heels!", another lady responded, "My mouth keeps opening up to ask for more food in these hungry times. Do you happen to have a medicine for that?" The surrounding crowd roared with laughter, empathizing with her sorrow and frustration.

Another notable change after the rations stopped was that the status of men and women was reversed. This was because most of the time, it became the women who took charge of the families' livelihood by making money through market activities. As the men begun to lose their authority in the family, they became known by new nicknames, such as "the daylight bulb," "the almighty lock" or "the bow-wow." Let me explain:

"The daylight bulb" was a joke to describe a man who was useless—like a light bulb during the daytime. "The almighty lock," while sounding a little more useful than the light bulb, drew on the fact that at least a family man could keep thieves away from his home. In North Korea, no matter how sturdy and strong the lock you install on your gate is, you cannot completely protect your home from thieves. Thieves always find a way in. So men are called an "almighty lock" because when they stay home all day, instead of going to work, at least they can protect their homes. A "bow-wow" has a similar meaning, comparing men to the dogs who guard houses. Despite being the brunt of so many jokes, these men could not really complain because they were dependent on the women who went out and earned for them.

There are many more jokes and funny stories that made me cry with laughter. I think you can really enjoy jokes and have a better sense of humor when you're young and don't have too many serious concerns. What I have felt going through all these hard times, though, is that even the best joke can lose its power when people are overwhelmed by constant worry. Sometimes I dream of a day when the people of the North and South finally meet and laugh together at silly jokes, being freed from all these troubles. What happy laughter that will be!

Any Other Questions?

What happens if you have the same name as "the Marshal," Kim Jong Un? Would you have to change it?

DT: There is a well-known photographer in South Korea named Kim Jong-il. And Before Kim Jong Un came to power, there was already a famous actress in South Korea with the same name. Obviously neither of these two had to change their names, though the latter is on record as having been shocked by the sudden appearance of a very unusual namesake. Jong Un (or "Jeong-eun" in South Korean Romanisation) is actually more commonly a girl's name, too.

Je Son Lee:

I think you would have to.

Kim Jong Un rose to prominence after my defection, so I can't talk specifically about him. But what I can tell you is that people with the same names as national founder Kim Il Sung, his wife Kim Jong Suk and his son Kim Jong Il had to change their names. You're allowed to have the same given name as the leader or another important public figure. But you can't share the full name of the Dear Leader.

For example, when you look at the name "Kim Jong Il," "Kim" is the surname and "Jong Il" is his given name. You can be "Park Jong Il" or "Lee Jong Il," but you can't be "Kim Jong Il." Therefore, people who had the same first and last name as the Dear Leader had to change their names after Kim Il Sung or Kim Jong Il rose to power. This didn't affect me, of course; but I heard that the government changes your name immediately after the leader rises to power.

Since the government began deifying the Kim family, parents have taken extra caution to avoid naming their children after the

leaders, even if they had different last names. They would have been too afraid to spell out first names such as "Il Sung" or "Jong Il" on the birth certificates of their children. In the West, I think parents would name their children after former presidents or royalty, hoping that they would grow up to possess their positive and admirable qualities. But in North Korea, you're in deep trouble if you have the same name as the leader. Thus, parents wouldn't dare to give even the first names of the leaders to their children.

One of my friends was named Kim Pyong Il—the exact same full name as one of the sons of Kim Il Sung, a half-brother of Kim Jong Il. As a result, local officials would talk about my friend—just because he shared the same name as Kim Il Sung's son.

And there are still many people who have had to change their names for other reasons, including people with names commonly found in Japan. Such names include "Soon-ja" ("Junko" in Japanese), "Chun-ja" ("Haruko"), "Kyung-ja" ("Keiko") or "Yang-ja" ("Yoko"). Even if they liked their names, they had no choice but to give them up under government order. A considerable number of people around me had these "Japanese-sounding" names and were all obliged to change their names, no exceptions allowed.

South Koreans don't seem bothered about such trivial, petty things, as the wife of former President Chun Doo-hwan kept the name, "Soon-ja" ("Junko" in Japanese, as you'll recall) while in the position of First Lady. Imagine if you were an American named Michael during the Cold War; would the existence of Russians using the name "Mikhail" have bothered you?

It's not easy to change your name if you just wish to do so, though. Of course, if you have enough money to bribe the officials, you can. But if you can't afford to do that, you're stuck with the name you were given at birth.

As *Hallyu* (the Korean Wave of pop culture) flooded into North Korea via China, South Korean names became very popular among North Koreans. In North Korea, almost everyone had names that could be spelled out in Chinese characters. We liked to apply meaning to each syllable. But many South Koreans seemed to have pure Korean names, rather than from Chinese characters. Many North Koreans have recently started to follow this trend, too.

Many babies born after 2000 in North Korea have South Korean-sounding names. I hope the government does not force them to change their names in the future. The North Korean regime has made so much effort to "purify" the Korean language, yet most North Koreans have names that can be spelled using Chinese characters. Isn't it ironic?

I like that more and more babies born in the 2000s have pure Korean names that sound South Korean. I hope this trend continues. I hope North Koreans are given freedom to choose the names they like some day.

Do North Koreans have cellphones?

DT: Especially in Pyongyang, the answer is "yes." When I visited in 2014, I met an Egyptian engineer working for Koryolink, the national mobile network 75 percent owned by Orascom, an Egyptian conglomerate. He said they had 2.5 million subscribers. As of late 2016, there are now 3 million. Koryolink has earned hundreds of millions of dollars in profit on this—but unfortunately for Orascom, they haven't been allowed to collect any dividends yet. Some wonder if they ever will…

Cho Ui-seong:
One of the things that was of the greatest help to me in adapting to this unfamiliar country [South Korea] was my smartphone. Without the help of Naver or Google, I would have settled in much more slowly. But what about cell phone use in North Korea?

Even before I left in 2014, many North Koreans were using cell phones, and a small number had smartphones. The price of phones in North Korean varied from $150 to $700, depending on each phone's design and features. Back then, North Korea's own "Arirang" smartphone was very popular. At that time, the government advertised that such LCD touchscreen phones could offer banking and delivery services through an intranet, but I haven't seen that working in practice.

Cell phones in North Korea began to enter common use in 2009. Prior to that, it was said by many North Koreans that the Guinness Book of Records had named North Korea as the only country in the world without mobile phones. If that was true, the Guinness Book of Records has done a great favor to the people of North Korea.

The introduction of mobile phones dramatically increased access to information for North Koreans. The people most in need of phones are the traders. No one feels the informational backwardness of the country as desperately as them. North Korea already has a fixed-line telephone system, but this is ineffective due to chronic power shortages. Even when the power is on, if it is windy or rainy, lines become crossed and callers are connected to the wrong people. Landline owners have to wait a month for repairs, and there are always many repairs that need making. This is so inconvenient for traders, who need to know what is going on in the market on a daily basis.

As market logic spreads through North Korean society, information becomes money. Prices used to be fixed and economic activity slow, but nowadays the market system (though only tacitly acknowledged) has highly variable prices and a very dynamic economic flow.

If traders can make calls on their cellphones regardless of time, place, or the availability of electricity, they can enjoy great opportunities. The cellphone is a big factor in helping those who are taking advantage of the magic of the "invisible hand" of the market.

Due to the practicality of mobile phones, subscriber numbers have increased massively, in spite of the cost. Over 200,000 people joined in the first year of service, and seven years on, there are 3 million subscribers.

But now the phone is a sort of accessory, going beyond practicality and showcasing the wealth and status of the owner. North Koreans, especially young people, are crazy about cell phones. Among young people who don't have them, there is a common expression—"only dogs and me don't have cell phones." This self-deprecating phrase shows the strength of the desire to own a phone.

University students have a special affection for mobile phones, and even those without much money feel they have to have one. When I was in college, more than half of the students had one, so I think almost all students will by now. Students say that those who have phones are going to be 12 times more successful at dating than those without.

It was funny, but I had friends who seemed to think their phone completed their identity. Think of it as being like those who are so proud of driving BMWs. The funniest thing is that most of them couldn't even use their phones. North Korea's tariff system offers 50 text messages per month, and talk time of 200 minutes. For anything more than that, you'll have to pay extra, and in dollars. Two hundred minutes is shorter than you think, so those who are dating will go through that time in a week. It is quite amusing to talk with friends who whinge about spending lots of money on talking to their girlfriends.

When making a phone call, you tend to keep it short. Even when talking to parents, it is common to cut out basic pleasantries. Sometimes I would let friends who didn't have phones take calls from their parents on my phone, and it really ate up my minutes. When it was someone who kept on talking because they hadn't spoken to their parents in a long time, I would just glance at them with a look urging them to hurry up.

In any case, the cell phone has undoubtedly made a significant contribution to informing the mentality of people in North Korea, the most closed country in the world. It will result in great changes in the future as well. When will the day come when people in the South and the North can talk freely? Let's try and add this to the list of once enormous hopes that have become ordinary daily reality.

Is there anything good about living in North Korea?

DT: This is a provocative question, but having visited myself, I can say that there isn't that much. Or rather, there's nothing much good about how the state or "the system" works. That said, North Korean defectors will usually say that people back home are warmer and kinder. The lack of industrial development also means that the air is clean and you can see the stars at night.

Jae Young Kim:

Although media and news only show the negative side of North Korea, there are positive aspects about life in the DPRK. Of course there are differences between individuals, but compared to my current life in the South, life in the North was mentally rich—even if it was materially insufficient. The reason for this is because of the pure heart and affection of North Koreans. Though there are lots of kind people in South Korea, affection between neighbors is very pure and deep in North Korea, especially in rural areas.

Families and neighbors gather on birthdays and national holidays and share with each other. My mother used to cook a lot for our neighbors. Even though she had to wake up early and cook, she never refused. I used to wake up early and help her. On major holidays, we invited our neighbors (we used to call my mother's friends "aunt") and shared food and stories with them. My mom was really good at making "Jong-Pyun rice cake," and I can still remember my aunts exclaiming how good they tasted. During nights, we gathered together, turned music on and danced. On days when electricity went out, we used to play the accordion, sing, dance and have fun. I used to have so much fun and danced so hard that my socks had holes when I checked them in morning. My father used to be respected as a *gagman* (comedian).

Moreover, North Korea's excellent natural environment is another nice aspect of life. Air in North Korea is very fresh. In spring and fall, my school used to go on field trips. Every year, we went to a cool valley. Water was very fresh and lots of flowers were in bloom. For the whole day, we played scavenger hunt, swam, then ate packed lunch, cooked by my mother. After lunch, we had talent shows.

Although from a material perspective things were often lacking, I sometimes miss the pure heart and sharing culture so common to my life in North Korea.

There is another side to your question... In North Korea, although it isn't common, there are some ordinary people who receive gifts directly from the state. Some people earn the "hero" title and receive televisions and other goods. These people get better gifts than other people on national holidays. But there aren't many of these people—I rarely saw a "hero" in my town. There was one, but he didn't get as many benefits as other "heroes." In truth, the main people who really get benefits from the government are civil servants, such as party officers, police officers, government agents and a few other people. These are the people who live with consistent privileges and have an easy life.

Everything was suffocating and pitiful in North Korea, but it is a country of which I have many positive memories. So if someone asks me "What is North Korea like?" then I say "North Korea is a nice place with plenty of love."

Tell me about student life in North Korea.
DT: Student life is about becoming an adult—making choices for yourself, taking your first strides out into the world, and also experiencing new types of fun. Not so much in North Korea though, where the university is more like a military academy.

Kim Yoo-sung:

I will walk you through what it is like to study at college in North Korea. In order to sit the college entrance exam in North Korea, you must have a reference letter and be endorsed by the National League of Students and your high school. The university makes an admissions decision based on your family background, extracurricular activities and your grades. The Department of Education sends an admissions letter to students who are successful.

One very interesting thing here is that you don't choose a major for yourself. The authorities at your university choose your major for you! Once the university notifies you what you will be studying, you spend the next four years studying that subject. (Just for your information, the major they chose for me was Wood Processing.) It is very rare for a student to take a gap year in North Korea. Most students study for four full years straight until graduation.

Being enrolled at a North Korean college is like being enlisted in the military. Every class has a leader, vice leader and secretaries below them. Each class has a strong, rigid hierarchy with positions held by students along the power pyramid. Those student leaders at the top of the pyramid make sure that students stick to the school rules and code of conduct, and that the students stay disciplined.

Classes begin at 8 a.m. and students must enter the premises by no later than 7:25 a.m. If a student arrives later than 7:25, that student is forced to make a public apology in front of the entire school after the school assembly. School assembly takes place every morning from 7:30 a.m. and lasts for 20 minutes. Assembly at North Korean colleges is held every morning from spring to winter.

There is also a dress code at colleges in North Korea. You must wear a suit and tie and you shouldn't forget to wear a hat that has been especially designed for college students when you go. There's no way around this dress code. A league of college police—not military police—stand at the entrance to enforce the dress code. If you don't comply, you aren't allowed to enter the campus.

Once a week, students take turns to guard the campus. That means you're obliged to stay up from 5 p.m. to 8 a.m. the next morning. In South Korean colleges, guards are hired to watch the buildings and safety of the campus. But in North Korean colleges, it is students that are obliged to perform such duties. Another difference is that cleaners are hired by South Korean colleges to keep the buildings clean and tidy. However, as you can probably guess, it is students at North Korean colleges who have to clean the school buildings themselves.

In addition to taking lectures on the academic discipline chosen for you, you continue to take courses on the three generations of the Kim family and Kim Jong Il's mother, Kim Jong Suk, throughout your four years of college. In other countries, you usually sign up for classes yourself. But North Korean colleges make a timetable and class schedule for you and you don't get to choose. On average, a North Korean college student attends three to four lectures a day. On Saturdays, they attend one or two lectures followed by North Korea's famous self-criticism sessions. You don't get to go home after the self-criticism session; it is followed by a public lecture which is heard by entire school in the auditorium.

There are other activities. Although not necessarily mandatory, you feel pressured to attend, as people can easily notice who is missing. In the second year of college, students must spend six months training with soldiers at their barracks. Therefore, it takes four years and six months for North Korean college students to graduate from college.

In order to graduate with a bachelor's degree, you must write a thesis and pass exams on the subject of Kim Jong Il. A professor is chosen to help you with writing a thesis and, of course, your thesis must pass in order to meet the requirements for graduation.

As I've already graduated from a North Korean university and I'm currently attending a South Korean university, I've found universities in North and South Korea to be very different. In fact, the similarities are few and far between.

What is it like to perform in the Arirang Mass Games?
DT: You've surely seen clips of tens of thousands of North Koreans all moving and holding up cards in unison, making a kind of "human pixel" display at the Workers' Stadium in Pyongyang. Strangely enough, such infamous "card section" performances have also been used in South Korea—in praise of 1980s dictator Chun Doo-hwan, and also by workers at Samsung. Nobody does it anywhere near as scarily perfect as North Korea, though.

Mina Yoon:
In case you haven't heard of it, the Arirang Festival might be the most famous mass performance in the world. It is an absolute masterpiece of performance art, mobilizing about 100,000 people, from kindergarten kids to college students. The Arirang Festival was even listed in the Guinness World Records for its record-breaking scale. However, behind its overwhelming visual spectacle are the painful efforts and hardships of the performers, who must endure repetitive practice and training.

I haven't participated in the Arirang Festival, but I did participate in similar mass gymnastics events in other cities that also used ribbon and card (human pixel) systems. When the performance date was approaching, schools would cancel afternoon classes and train students for the upcoming performance. And when the performance was imminent, schools canceled classes for the whole day. Instead, students gathered in the schoolyard and repeated rehearsals endlessly. The school would not distribute the equipment for the mass games, such as ribbons or cards. The performers were responsible for preparing all those things by themselves.

I still remember how I once made a very special ribbon for the performance. I had to procure fabric to make a ribbon, which was not easy to get. One day, I came home around lunchtime to prepare a ribbon for the mass game I was participating in. There was no one at home. My mom had gone out to work in the farm that belonged to my father's military unit. I had to have a ribbon by the afternoon, but there was no way to reach her. There was no home phone and,

of course, no mobile, so I started to go through my mom's closet; but it looked like there was no decent fabric left.

After a while, I finally found a lovely purple blouse of my mom's. She'd had it for a while. I hadn't seen her in this blouse, and from the many layers of papers that my mom packed it with, I could see it was one of her favorite outfits. I couldn't bear to destroy it, so I put it back in the closet. But then I thought of my teacher, who would scold me if I didn't bring a ribbon. I concluded that I would rather be spanked by my mother than insulted in front of all of the students. There was no way I could stand that much humiliation, so I took the blouse out from the closet. I cut it into 1.5-inch-wide pieces and sewed the pieces together to make a long ribbon. I stuck the purple ribbon on a wooden stick and carried it to training.

What happened when I got back home later? You really don't want to know. Anyway, I think my mom deserved to be angry after seeing her precious blouse torn to pieces.

Usually, the training for the mass games took place in the school-yard. The practice was so grueling that the performers were literally knocked out when it was over. The idea was that a large group of people should be able to move just like a single person, and endless training was therefore a must. Even worse than the very tiring training itself were the dust storms from the ground. The schoolyard was covered with soil, and when large numbers of people made a series of rapid movements on it, a heavy cloud of dust rose up from the ground. Blinded by the thick fog of dust, it was impossible to look ahead in line. When I got home and blew my nose, I could see the black dust coming out. In my mouth, I could feel the grains of sand that had blown into my mouth while we were singing. I think it was a miracle that I did not get pneumonia.

The same went for the card section. It was the performers who had to prepare cards that would be used in the performance. At that time, in North Korea, even toilet paper was hard to find. So I tore up my used notebooks, separated all the pages from them and glued them together to make thick cardboard. I then put them under my bed and slept on them, to make them flat. In the morning, I sewed the flattened cardboard and put the pieces together like a big notebook. Finally, I colored the cardboard.

Let me explain briefly how the card section works. We were trained in the actual stadium of the performance. In the card section, there is a conductor standing in front of the group of performers. The conductor would hold numbered plates and blow a whistle. When the conductor raised up a numbered plate, the performers would unfold the color that matched the number. Even though the conductor would show just one number at a time, there would be different colors assigned to the number according to the performer's groups, so that it would form a huge picture, moving and changing when you watched from a distance.

The performers were divided into many layers of groups, like squadrons, companies and platoons, just like the army. For example, I was number 7 in the 3rd platoon, 3rd company in the 2nd squadron. Squadrons were assigned by school location, companies by schools and platoons by grades. Squads, the smallest units, were divided by classes.

Because the performers were assigned to their spots according to schools and grades, when anyone made a mistake, it was easy to find out who did it. For example, if a performer named Hong Kil Dong accidentally unfolded blue when he was supposed to unfold red, the conductor would call him by name through a loudspeaker, saying something like, "Hong Gil Dong in School A made a mistake. We're repeating this part again." It might feel awful if thousands of students had to start over because of you, so all the performers tried their best not to make a mistake.

As a performer, the most painful thing in the card section was the uncomfortable posture I had to bear for such a long time. We had to crouch and hide under the cards for a better picture. The performers sat down, put the cards on their laps and unfolded them following signals from the conductor, but it would not look very pretty if the audience could see the faces of the performers. Therefore, once we put out the cards, everything beneath our eyes had to be completely hidden under the cards. After curling up like that during day-long rehearsals, my legs felt numb and my neck was practically paralyzed. When I tried to stand up after the rehearsals, I could hear the cracking sound from my joints.

I took part in smaller mass games, but I could imagine how much harder Pyongyang's mass games would be. The most difficult part must be that it has to be accurate and flawless. Just imagine thousands of people moving, but they have to move as one. They have to move simultaneously, depending solely on the sound of music. How would it be even possible? Only endless repetition of exhausting practice and training could increase their accuracy. The burden the Arirang performers felt seemed very heavy. There are thousands of foreign tourists watching them. And they understand that what they are doing is not merely a performance. They know it is an official event to affirm the national status of North Korea in front of the outside world.

I heard of a student who died of appendicitis because he could not leave his spot in the middle of the performance. His appendix burst but he dared not leave his position. Even when the performers are sick, not many of them would think about skipping the performance. They knew they would not be excused. This kind of obedience must be the result of the brainwashing and repressive politics seen in North Korea for so long.

Why have mass games? First, the government believed that, successfully performed, the mass games would elevate the national status of North Korea. North Korean mass games started in the 1970s for honored guests from foreign countries. They disappeared during the era of famine of the mid-1990s, and were then revived in the 2000s to attract foreign tourists. However, there was a far greater purpose than tourism. The mass games in North Korea were designed to highlight the legitimacy and consistency of the regime by showcasing its strong spirit of community for the outside world to see.

Second, these performances were believed to increase the morale and the pride of North Korean people. The government wanted its people to believe that North Korea was the most strongly united country in the world, and the praise earned by the mass games seemed to inspire pride.

And, finally, there might have been some economic boost expected from increased tourism. You may or may not like to watch the mass games, but one thing is very clear: North Korean mass games are the grandest circus that you could ever see in the modern world. They are only possible under a totalitarian ruling system. In societies where individual human rights are respected and freedom of choice is valued, this kind of performance is impossible.

This year, the North Korean government decided to cancel the Arirang Festival. My guess is they canceled it because they could not afford the minimum budget for the performance to replace old costumes and give snacks to the performers. Since North Korea has been isolated due to its nuclear issues and tourism has shrunk, it seems to me like the mass games literally went bankrupt.

I must say I am glad to hear that this year's Arirang Festival has been canceled. At least this year, North Korean students do not have to go through all the tiring training I did. I don't know whether or not the North Korean mass games could be appreciated as meaningful achievements in performance art, but when I think about the price that the North Korean people have had to pay for them, I really hope they will disappear soon. I shall do my share to make it happen sooner.

What is "fashionable" in North Korea?
DT: When researching my book *North Korea Confidential*, I heard that skinny jeans had become popular among young women. They usually wear black jeans rather than blue though, as blue jeans are considered too Western by the authorities. Nowhere are skinny jeans more popular than in Chongjin, a port city that receives big shipments of secondhand clothes from abroad. Chongjin is in fact the fashion capital of the country—even more so than Pyongyang, which is a little more conservative due to increased state control there.

Je Son Lee:
I lived in North Korea for 20 years and while I never paid serious attention to fashion, I can tell you a few things about the different fashions I saw during my time there.

When I was born in 1990, the North Korean economy was experiencing difficulties and wasn't able to produce enough for its people. Despite this, many government officials still had access to products, mainly through a very small black market that existed even back then. As a result of the black market, people in my area began to buy and sell products (including clothes and shoes) obtained from the nearby factories they worked at. This was the start of independent fashion, as I knew it.

Although during the early 1990s, most people wore North Korean-made clothes, Chinese products started to appear in around 1995. Because of those Chinese products I vaguely remember my first day of kindergarten—I wore a dress with frills that was made in China, and shoes with flowers on them. I got a lot of attention from my teachers that day!

You see, in those kindergarten years the government was supposed to provide students with free food and snacks. But when the economy collapsed in the mid 1990s, all the supplies were cut. This meant students from rich families would stand out, wearing nicer

clothes than the other kids. And students from rich families would be looked upon by the kindergarten as a jackpot, their parents being able to help out with supplies and food for the others.

From a fashion perspective, things really started to change during my elementary school years. That's because in North Korea, students from elementary school up to university have to wear school uniforms.

Because of the uniform regulations, a brigade of student guards used to stand at the front gate of my school each day, and students who refused to wear school uniform would be subject to punishment. But many students—including myself—didn't like to wear school uniforms, as we were much more used to wearing pretty clothes made of soft fabric from China. People like me simply didn't like the dark, stiff school uniforms that we were expected to wear.

So, even though students were subject to corporal punishment for ignoring the rules, we often preferred to wear something different to the uniform. Personally, I hated wearing my skirt, so I wore jeans from China and avoided punishment by jumping over the wall to get into class. Fortunately, the brigade of student guards only stood at the front gate in the morning and were given free time in the afternoon. Because other students were doing the same thing, a sort of competition over who had the most expensive, beautiful clothes soon developed.

Unfortunately, when I got to third grade the government imposed an even stricter dress code, so we had to think of new ways to get around it. The best way was to buy clothes of a color and design that looked similar to the school uniform. Many students practically refused to go to school unless they had such clothes. So when white and soft fabrics and frills made their way into North Korea from China, it became a fad to make a blouse with frills to wear to school.

By the year 2000, South Korean dramas were slowly becoming popular. In those early dramas most of the female characters wore bootcut jeans, and soon enough they were not only being worn by North Korean adults, but also by young kids. Of course, many schools tried to stop students from wearing them, but despite their efforts the bootcuts only became more popular.

In the end, the adults who tried to ban all these sorts of clothes at my school gave up. However, by the time 80 percent of students were wearing bootcut jeans, many of us started to lose interest in the style, and soon the trend died out on its own. Bootcut jeans didn't disappear completely, but no one was obsessed with them anymore. Perhaps it was just because the government was no longer trying to prevent people from wearing them so much.

It would take between three to five years for copied versions of South Korean dramas to be smuggled into North Korea via China. As a result of the lag, we did not realize that the fashions we were seeing had often already gone out of style in the South.

Most people I knew made jeans out of colored cloth. Custom-made clothes were always expensive but people paid big money for them, as they were often very competitive about fashion. But nobody had clothes as pretty as my own blue jeans, I used to think. You see, I got hand-me-downs from my mom, who had owned a pair of blue, bootcut jeans—from a designer brand—since she was young.

So what about other designer brands?

While residents of other towns near the border liked to buy Chinese clothes and home appliances, designer brands from European countries became increasingly popular in Pyongyang. Since my grandfather was a high-ranking civil servant in Pyongyang, my parents used to visit the city frequently. Thanks to this, my dad bought designer brands for me, such as Adidas and Lacoste, at the so-called dollar shops (foreign currency shops that couldn't be found outside of Pyongyang). As a result, everyone near Mt. Paektu was jealous of me and my branded clothes.

Of course, not everyone could afford brand new designer clothes in North Korea. Some would buy secondhand clothes from China—which were often much more stylish and of better quality than the *new* clothes being sold in North Korean markets at the time. I was dying to buy those secondhand clothes myself, but I changed my mind when some adults told me that they had probably been worn by dead people. "Why else would they give away such beautiful clothes?" I was told. Since religion isn't permitted in North Korea, people tend to be very superstitious, you see.

Five years before I left North Korea, *Hallyu* (South Korean pop culture) began to dramatically spread across the country. Ever since then, many North Korean conceptions about fashion have truly changed. Lots of the major characters in the dramas and movies were owners of big companies and so they had lots of different clothes. By watching those dramas and movies, we began to realize that the secondhand clothes we were buying from China weren't being given away by the families of the deceased, and that people gave them away simply because they just had too many clothes.

Many people preferred secondhand shoes, too. Because the new shoes available on the markets were often homemade by individual shoemakers and were of poor quality and wouldn't last long, young people often preferred to wear imported secondhand shoes.

As for adult fashion, well, adults aspired to look elegant rather than cool. Among thirty- and forty-somethings, secondhand clothes from Japan were the most popular. They were not only of better quality, but also looked classier than the cheap, tacky clothes being

made in China. The price of Japanese secondhand clothes was therefore double that of the Chinese secondhand clothes.

How about elderly people and fashion? In my opinion, older men in North Korea tend to dress in a classier way than older women. They refuse to wear bright colors or logos, instead preferring to dress in a way that meant they might be mistaken for a high-ranking official. Tailored clothes that look like the ones Kim Jong Il used to wear are expensive, but look so much better than ordinary clothes if they fit the owner well.

Funnily enough, some North Korean clothes were nevertheless popular. A few years before I left North Korea, so-called "general winter clothes" (padded jackets) became popular. Although made in North Korea, they were of a surprisingly good quality and expensive. While a one-kilogram bag of rice would cost 3,000 won, a made-in-North Korea general winter jacket would cost between 100,000 and 150,000 won. Unless you were a high-ranking official or a successful vendor with a big business, you simply couldn't afford one.

I think that North Koreans are even more obsessed with fashion than South Koreans because the clothes they wear indicate their economic status. This notion is still found among North Korean refugees, with some of my refugee friends having bigger wardrobes than my friends who were born and raised in South Korea! That trend is especially prevalent among those who only recently left North Korea.

Funnily enough, some North Korean refugees are still trying to follow trends that have long gone out of fashion in the South, but are still popular back home. I guess old-fashioned trends bring back forgotten memories to us North Koreans in the South.

How do you make yourself pretty in North Korea?

DT: South Korea is a world leader in the production and consumption of cosmetics—for both women and men. In fact, South Korean men spend more on cosmetics than men from anywhere else in the world. This is due to the extremely competitive nature of life south of the border. North Koreans are, like anyone else, interested in looking good, but they have neither the wherewithal or inclination to take it as far as the South Koreans. Often, those who defect to the South feel huge pressure to raise their game…

Jae Young Kim:

In North Korea only people with time and money can really care about beauty. That's why it isn't the serious business it is in South Korea, where I live now. In my opinion, the North Korean standard of beauty isn't therefore on the "outside;" instead, it's on the "inside"—the beauty that allows a woman to take care of both her household and husband.

When I lived in North Korea there was a famous actress named Miran Oh who was extremely beautiful and very feminine. She was popular with girls who all wanted to be like her, and with guys, too (for obvious reasons). I think it's fair to say that Miran Oh must have been the beauty standard for many North Korean women. But as I mentioned, the ability for a woman to be strong and maintain her livelihood is sometimes viewed as a more important form of beauty in North Korea.

When I was young, I wanted to be like my mother—a woman who even many of our neighbors admired. She was really good at housework, calm, and helped my father a lot. For me, she was a proud woman and the type of woman I most wanted to be like. But now I'm in South Korea I have to care more about external beauty, too, since that's such an important part of being a woman here. That's not to say that some of us didn't think in the same way back in North Korea, though.

At one time, double eyelid surgery became very popular among girls in North Korea and even my mother suggested I get it done. But I was really scared about it! You see, there are no professional plastic surgery hospitals in North Korea. Often, you have to get these types of operation done at someone's house. They aren't the most hygienic of places for surgery, but nevertheless many women are on waiting lists to get these kinds of operations. It became so common that the government actually started regulating these types of places.

There are many, many regulations in North Korea on how a woman should look. You're not meant to put your hair down, skinny pants are frowned upon, jeans aren't allowed, and there are definitely no short pants. If you're ever caught breaking these rules you're forced to write a self-criticism report; or if you have long hair, risk having it cut short. Nevertheless, some girls turn a blind eye to these penalties, all in the name of beauty.

While it is a lot poorer than South Korea, just like everywhere in the world women in North Korea want to look pretty. But unlike other countries, there is a lot less foreign influence when it comes to beauty and fashion. Really, China is the only country that really has much influence over us.

Chinese fashions get into North Korea because of the strong trade between the two countries and the fact that we are able to legally watch some Chinese soap operas and movies. So we see what is popular in China through TV shows or through what people crossing the border are saying. The cosmetics and fashion choices of North Korean girls are therefore influenced by Chinese trends.

North Korean women care a lot about cosmetics and usually

Chinese products are more popular than the North Korean ones (I personally always used the Chinese ones). Because my family had a better quality of life than many of our peers, they had the resources to care about my beauty. So from time to time they'd treat me—once, for example, my mother bought me an expensive Chinese cosmetic product for whitening the skin (we don't like to tan like Americans!).

I think it is normal that women in both Koreas make an effort to look pretty, but I guess the main difference between the two countries is economic. That, combined with all that I mentioned above, is why there are such obvious differences in the standard of beauty between North and South.

31901062492592